ANALYSING TWENTY-FIRST CENTURY BRITISH ENGLISH

Conceptual and methodological aspects of the *Voices* project

Edited by Clive Upton and Bethan L. Davies

Routledge
Taylor & Francis Group
LONDON AND NEW YORK

First published 2013
by Routledge
2 Park Square, Milton Park, Abingdon, Oxon OX14 4RN

Simultaneously published in the USA and Canada
by Routledge
711 Third Avenue, New York, NY 10017

Routledge is an imprint of the Taylor & Francis Group, an informa business

British Library Cataloguing in Publication Data
A catalogue record for this book is available from the British Library

Library of Congress Cataloging in Publication Data
Analysing 21st Century British English : Conceptual and Methodological Aspects of BBC Voices / Edited by Clive Upton and Bethan Davies.
pages cm
1. English language – Dialects – Great Britain. 2. English language – Variation – Great Britain. 3. English language – Great Britain – Discourse analysis. 4. English language – Great Britain – Phonology. 5. English language – Social aspects – Great Britain. 6. Great Britain – Languages. 7. English language – Syntax. 8. British Broadcasting Corporation – History – 21st century.
I. Upton, Clive, 1946– editor of compilation. II. Davies, Bethan L., editor of compilation.
PE1736.A523 2013
427′.94109051–dc23 2012044259

ISBN: 978-0-415-69442-1 (hbk)
ISBN: 978-0-415-69443-8 (pbk)
ISBN: 978-0-203-51291-3 (ebk)

Typeset in Bembo
by HWA Text and Data Management, London

Printed and bound in Great Britain by
TJ International Ltd, Padstow, Cornwall

CONTENTS

FIGURES

TABLES

CONTRIBUTORS

David Crystal is Honorary Professor of Linguistics at Bangor University

Bethan L. Davies is Lecturer in Linguistics at the University of Leeds

Susie Dent is a freelance writer and broadcaster on the English language. She works regularly for OUP and the *Oxford English Dictionary*, particularly on new word releases and updates

Simon Elmes is Creative Director of the British Broadcasting Corporation Radio Documentary Unit

Holly Gilbert was Project Worker on the *Voices of the UK* project at the British Library

Jon Herring was Research Assistant on the *Voices of the UK* project at the British Library

John Holliday is Senior Research Manager in the Information School at the University of Sheffield

Alexandra Jaffe is Professor of Linguistics and Anthropology at California State University, Long Beach

Tommaso M. Milani is Associate Professor of Linguistics at the University of the Witwatersrand

Rob Penhallurick is Reader in English Language at Swansea University

Jonathan Robinson is Lead Curator, Sociolinguistics and Education, at the British Library

Mooniq Shaikjee is an MA student at the University of the Western Cape

Ann Thompson is a freelance editor and language teacher, with a particular interest in historical lexicography. She was a researcher on the *Whose Voices?* project at the University of Leeds

Will Turner is a research fellow in the Institute for International Management Practice at Anglia Ruskin University. He was a researcher on the *Whose Voices?* project at the University of Leeds

Clive Upton is Emeritus Professor of Modern English Language at the University of Leeds

Martijn Wieling is a post-doctoral researcher in language at the University of Tübingen

PREFACE

Clive Upton and Bethan L. Davies

Voices was a project conceived in the British Broadcasting Corporation to take a 'snapshot' of the everyday speech and speech-attitudes of its United Kingdom audience at the start of the twenty-first century. It was seen as informing popular understanding of English and other languages, generating programmes for national and local radio and television, and material for the BBC website and publications. It was realised from the start that those concerned with the technical discussion of linguistic issues would benefit from project involvement too. This book makes use of the second of these possibilities.

The contributions to this book are written by a wide range of specialists in both broadcasting and academic language study. The first two chapters set the scene for *Voices* in its historical and immediate contexts, from the points of view of, respectively, a senior BBC producer who has been responsible for many language-focused programmes and series, and an academic with unparalleled broadcasting experience. The chapters that follow these are closely connected to two large research projects making use of *Voices* findings: *Whose Voices?* funded by Arts and Humanities Research Council grant AH/E509002, and *Voices of the UK* funded by Leverhulme Trust grant F/00 122/AP. Four chapters concentrate on issues of language ideology, looking at both the BBC's actions in setting up *Voices* and disseminating its information, and what that information tells us of linguistic matters through public debate. The remaining chapters see their writers taking portions of raw language material generated by the project, processing it to explore a variety of issues and experimenting with it to test its potential.

Voices proved to be a considerable broadcasting success in 2005, with the ripples from it extending through the BBC up to the present time. The intention of this book is threefold: it celebrates an imaginative step by the Corporation; it provides information across a wide range of subjects of linguistic interest and concern; and, as importantly, it suggests just some of the possible ways forward into an existing body of material, some of which is made available through the accompanying website (www.routledge.com/cw/upton).

1

VOICES: A UNIQUE BBC ADVENTURE

Simon Elmes

When an organization – and not only the BBC – announces a 'major new...' anything, we tend these days to become suspicious. The odour of hype, of overselling, and of slight hucksterism hangs round the phrase like cheap perfume. Sometimes, though of course, it is perfectly valid – no-one would complain that the great Radio 4 series *A History of the World in a Hundred Objects* was anything but 'major'. And in many ways the same can be said for *Voices*, a somewhat less trumpeted yet equally ground-breaking initiative on dialect and local language undertaken by a lot of BBC people, but, critically, steered by a small, committed handful, in 2005.

Whatever the precise merits or demerits of the term 'major', the BBC has a long and intimate relationship with language, and with the English language in particular. John Reith and his lieutenants who were, ninety years ago now, in at the very beginning of what was then the British Broadcasting Company, were severe in their precepts about the organization, and from the earliest days 'correctness of speech' was emphasized (though, they insisted, it shouldn't be stilted). 'Correct speech' became a talisman alongside correct dress. BBC announcers were required to wear dinner jackets at the microphone, and in April 1926 the legendary Advisory Committee on Spoken English was set up to regulate and rule on the language used when broadcasting, with luminaries including the then Poet Laureate Robert Bridges, Bernard Shaw, American-born essayist and critic Logan Pearsall-Smith, and later Rudyard Kipling (Briggs 1961: 221). 'Broadcast' itself was one of the first words they debated. How should this new term, or at least a new meaning of an old one, be conjugated? The Great Ones decided it should work on the model of 'cast'; thus they recommended 'we broadcast' not 'we broadcast*ed*'. It is a confusion that still routinely has non-native British English speakers in a muddle.

The formality and seriousness with which the BBC took language from the very beginning belies, however, the nature of broadcasting. Programme-makers and broadcasters are creatures of their times, who love to reflect the spirit of the moment, to catch fashion as it wafts by. It is how we 'connect with our audiences'. So for all its stiff and starchy rule-making and Squeersism about the way people spoke on the wireless, an equal and opposite tug for naturalness has always been felt and enjoyed by audience and programme-maker alike. Indeed, presentation and the 'broadcast voice' were obsessions of early critics and writers on the new medium – the columns of *Radio Times* were often filled with debates on the subject and, in an early instruction to religious broadcasters, pulpit styles were definitely off-limits:

> You are asked to remember … that your vast audience is not a crowd or a congregation but various individuals to whom you are speaking in the intimacy of their homes.… Thousands of them will 'switch off' their sets if the opening is unattractive.
>
> (Briggs 1965: 235)

Today, there is no Advisory Committee on language in the BBC, nor should there be. Long gone is the prescriptivist mentality that would confine language in boxes of so-called perfection. Broadcasters recognize that words and styles evolve (despite what many listeners would wish). Today, the Pronunciation Unit is there to help out on difficult words, and radio producers are routinely encouraged to offer announcers help on how to pronounce names and terms that might present problems. But for the most part, any regulation is limited to the editing of scripts.

When it comes to programmes on language, the BBC, whether on radio or television, has usually (and quite understandably) placed appealing to its audiences ahead of a more academically-driven sense of mission. So while full of real linguistic substance, even Victoria Coren's wonderful television series *Balderdash and Piffle*, in which she attempted to find earlier-than-existing citations for terms in the *Oxford English Dictionary*, was in thrall to entertainment in its format. The choice of the terms under scrutiny was (quite rightly in broadcasting terms) driven by popular appeal rather than by any form of academic need, and the format of the series was given real buzz and excitement by turning the assessment of the 'evidence' for ante-dating of first citations into a sort of Star Chamber of the *OED*'s great and good.

There is absolutely nothing wrong with any of that, but the Reithian mantra of Inform, Educate, and Entertain will always be tripartite, and the entertaining element almost always has a knack of ending up infringing upon the educating part. So with language broadcasting, projects almost always end up being entertainingly unscientific, made for broadcast rather than as definitive research tools. It is apparent that Reith was concerned about this risk to serious broadcasting from the outset:

> Reith's big fear was what he called 'the brute force of monopoly' might disappear and competition would force down standards. He believed in

> public service broadcasting. He did not invent the expression 'entertaining, informing and educating' – that was the American broadcasting pioneer David Sarnoff in 1922 – but he made it so central to the way he ran the BBC that his name became a byword for it: Reithian. Pure entertainment was a prostitution of broadcasting.
>
> (BBC 2012)

Voices, in 2005, is the only exception I know of that offered both true investigative rigour and entertaining broadcasting. But to tell the story of *Voices*, we need to start more than fifty years earlier.

When Harold Orton and Eugen Dieth's great Survey of English Dialects (SED) was begun in 1950 (Orton 1962: 9), it was laid down on formal academic lines. Respondents were selected specifically to reflect a good locational spread in mainly rural locations across England, to offer the richest range of dialectal variants. Their responses to a 1300-item questionnaire were written down phonetically, and conversations were recorded on-site by fieldworkers like the late Stanley Ellis, with whom I had the privilege and great pleasure of working over the years. The recordings are held by the British Library and by the BBC archive, and are wonderful slices of country life from an England half a century and more ago. There are, it is true, aspects of the survey that I personally find unsatisfactory: it is substantially rural, selected to emphasize extremes of dialect use rather than to reflect some sort of median picture, and concentrated on older and often very elderly informants. And of course, as a Survey of *English* Dialects, it does not cover Wales, Scotland, or Northern Ireland (though see Upton, this volume, on this). However, it is a massive and beautifully organized piece of work that allowed for the first time the establishment of a truly accurate linguistic picture of England.

What it was *not*, however, for all its use of audio recording to capture its informants' contributions, was programmes. And so we immediately crunch into the dilemma already mentioned of programme-making set against formalized and rigorous academic enquiry. However, it has not stopped plenty of people over the years making wonderful programmes about the way we speak, scientific or unscientific. I think, in my own lifetime, of Harold Williamson's hugely popular series on radio in the 1950s and 60s called *Children Talking*, which combined the winsome magic of childhood speech and a child's-eye view of the world with big questions of life and death, good and evil. And today, the estimable Stephen Fry has cornered the market, on television as on Radio 4, in programmes about the development of language.

When I first had the opportunity myself to make programmes, Stanley Ellis came up with the idea of revisiting the SED recordings made some 30 years earlier. I, however, was keen to go further and also carry out some new recordings, to spread the net beyond the SED's terrain and locate the voices within the place they reflected. The regional language would be the *vehicle* for the stories of the people and the places they inhabited. We soon discovered that the SED recordings were fairly intractable fare for ordinary programme-making, being rather dense and quite often incomprehensible to the ordinary listener given only one chance to seize the meaning. So *Talk of the Town, Talk of the Country* became altogether new work, with informants (very unscientifically) chosen to reflect a range of ages (we especially wanted to hear from young dialect speakers to chart the changing face of dialect). These were 18 programmes locked into communities, from the Western Isles to Devon, from urban Belfast, Bristol, and Glasgow to DH Lawrence's Nottinghamshire. And they were full of stories told in rich local language. Ellis provided not only a beautiful, lyrical script evoking his own journeys through these places, but also the formal analysis of the consummate linguist spotting nuance and variety and offering expert commentary. They were glorious programmes to make, and I hope, too, to listen to. They were not, however, a survey from which formal data could be extracted.

Likewise, *Word of Mouth*, Radio 4's regular magazine programme about language, which was started by Frank Delaney in 1992 and today continues under the tutelage of Michael Rosen, has for twenty years kept a watchful eye on the way we speak. And Melvyn Bragg's 26-episode *The Routes of English* which I produced devoted one whole series of six documentaries to exploring dialect in the UK. Again, keeping listeners engaged as well as informed was the aim; so while instructive, it could never be exhaustive. Once more the aims of broadcaster and academic researcher diverged rather than coincided.

This is for me precisely why *Voices* was such an exceptional project, a truly 'major' new venture for the BBC. In March 2003, following the widespread interest aroused by *Routes of English*, I was contacted by the BBC Editor of New Media in Cardiff, Mandy Rose, who had come up with a simple and brilliant idea: to 'celebrate the diverse languages, dialects and accents of the UK':

> From black Londoners in Peckham to Loyalists in Portadown, from Treorchy to Taunton, Liverpool to Lanarkshire, the geography of the UK can be mapped in accents and dialects. The diversity of the country can be also reflected in the many languages – both indigenous and immigrant – now spoken here. In an ambitious multi-platform project involving our audience and a range of expert partners BBC Nations and Regions will conduct an audit of the ways we talk across the UK in the early 21st century.
>
> (Rose, personal communication)

It so happened that at the time I was thinking along somewhat similar lines, though Mandy's idea was bigger, better and far more scientifically conceived than mine. Her proposal also had the unbeatable central component of interactive technology, which would make the eventual *Voices* proposition so dynamic and rooted in ordinary listeners' experience. David Crystal, who already had a long track record of BBC Language broadcasting, and Clive Upton, Reader then Professor of Modern English Language at the University of Leeds, were engaged as academic partners, and when family matters overtook Mandy, she passed the baton of leadership to Faith Mowbray. Faith, David, and Clive were superb advocates and advisers for the project, and between them gave it both the organising structure and academic rigour that would both ensure that it happened on time, to schedule and pretty much in the form that Mandy had dreamed.

The other key member of the team was an outstanding radio broadcaster whose recruitment was central to the practical infrastructure of the *Voices* project, without which it would quickly have foundered however much goodwill and energy the rest of us could contribute. He was Mick Ord, who at the time was Managing Editor of the BBC's local radio station in Liverpool, Radio Merseyside. A remarkable journalist and utterly down-to-earth realist, Mick has a marvellous imagination that allows ideas to soar. With Faith providing clear, disciplined leadership and tremendous inventiveness to the essential web proposition – the interactive *Voices* dialect map – and Mick cajoling and demanding and inspiring his colleagues across BBC Local Radio to get out and give their all to this strange project (so different from the normal fare of local council disputes, traffic problems, and crime), *Voices* had the team to make it happen.

The other vital element was money. Pat Loughrey, then Director of Nations and Regions for the BBC, is a lover of words, of poetry, and of people. He had the vision, and the pockets, to be able to see just what a clever piece of work this project was. Not only would it generate hours of stories by and about his listeners to fill airtime in each of the 40 local stations and the national stations in Scotland, Wales, and Northern Ireland, but it would be a marvellously publicizable event, in the middle of sleepy August, that would shout 'BBC local' and 'BBC regional' loud and clear to the country and within the Corporation itself. It also offered an unparalleled academic opportunity to set on record the way the nation was speaking to and about itself in the first decade of the new millennium. For a man who is today Warden of Goldsmiths, University of London, the academic achievement of *Voices* was surely not insignificant.

And so the project was set in motion. Mandy Rose's original ambition in 2003 was:

> a website featuring a multi-layered interactive map [providing] an engaging and educational interface for exploring the subject. Beneath the map the website provides a wealth of background information. Once launched the website will be a growing, live space where users can add their own voices … around a number of themes.
>
> (Rose, personal communication)

To achieve this, the team needed a methodology, a way of gathering material that would provide the data in a sufficiently rigorous manner to satisfy the demands of comparative study within the map. Random collection would simply not do. At the same time, the material gathered by the project needed to satisfy what is – as I have demonstrated – that competing criterion of engaging broadcasting. Enter Clive Upton and his team with a standardized set of questions, based on their existing research (Llamas 1999; Kerswill *et al.* 1999; see Crystal, Upton, this volume) which would, it was hoped, elicit from interviewees interestingly contrasted local terms and constructions. These were focused round six nexuses of ordinary life: 'how you feel'; 'what you do'; 'what they wear'; 'getting personal'; 'what you call them'; and 'inside and outside'. Within these core areas there were a set of very specific questions to be asked – so under 'what they wear' were questions about words for CLOTHES, TROUSERS, and CHILDREN'S SOFT SHOES WORN FOR PE, while under 'getting personal' the terms sought were for RICH, LACKING MONEY, MOODY, LEFT-HANDED, ATTRACTIVE, and so on. Now, these may have seemed somewhat random, but in fact Clive and his team, with their deep knowledge of dialect patterns in the UK, and from the vast resources contained in Orton's SED and previous less methodical dialect surveys and dictionaries, had a pretty fair idea of which terms had in the past demonstrated the greatest diversity and regionality (local terms for LEFT-HANDED for example are as widespread and various as the phenomenon itself). Brilliant too was the way the Leeds method built these research criteria into an attractive and easy-to-reference diagram that looked something like an elongated early sputnik, but which everyone soon came to know as the 'Spidergram' (Figure 1.1).

Thus the enquiry was decently funded, it had a sizeable chunk of academic rigour, and above all it had managerial support within the sprawling BBC. But that was only half the battle, or indeed barely half. Orton's SED took his team well over a decade to capture its 300+ records of how *England* spoke. To achieve what was wanted, it would need to take a tenth of that time. And that meant days, weeks, and months of hard foot-slogging on the part of an army of field-workers. For *Voices*, some 51 'audio-gatherers' as they were rather unattractively termed sallied out from the UK's local and national radio stations to find communities of people with some common thread of interest. And this was where robust methodological structure met the editorially- and entertainment-driven components that are the concern of broadcasters. Amazingly, and uniquely in my experience, the relationship turned out to be a happy and productive one. The fieldworkers were given the task of identifying groups of people in their local or regional radio station area who might be tapped for responses to the survey questionnaire. Groups should represent all layers of society, with as wide an age range as possible, although young children were excluded. There should also be a good geographical spread across the local region in order to contrast urban and rural areas.

The audio-gatherers were given a day's training in questioning and recording technique and issued with precise instructions about how the group discussions were to be conducted. Given the clever range of questions Upton and his team

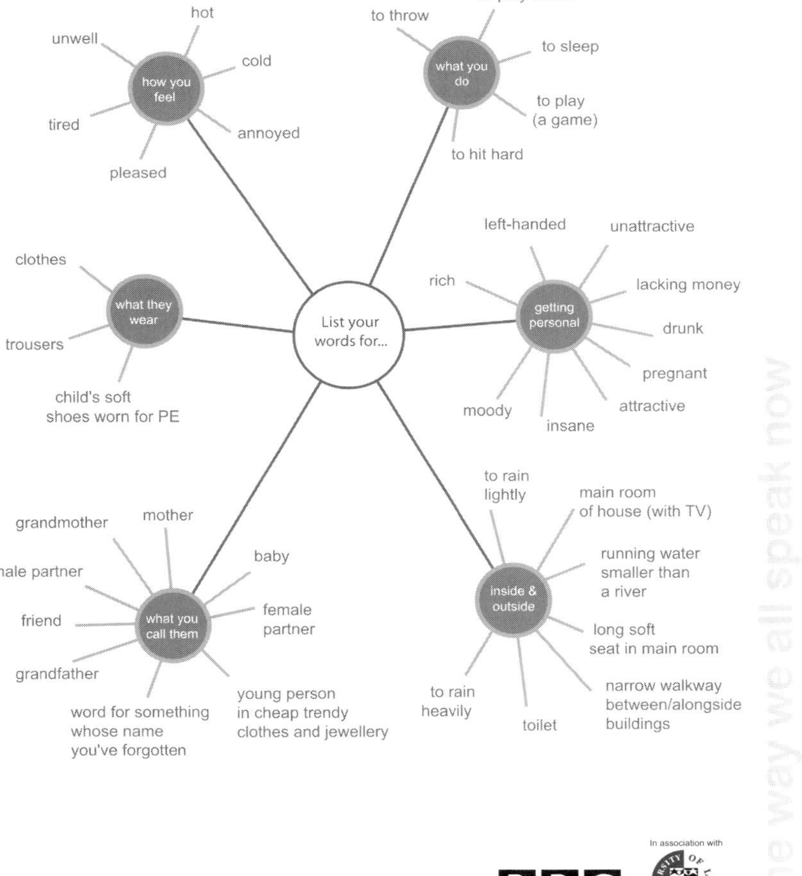

FIGURE 1.1 The BBC *Voices* Spidergram

at Leeds had devised, entertaining and lively discussion was almost guaranteed. But consistency in the methodology was vital in order to allow proper academic comparison to be made. So the audio-gatherers were instructed not to offer answers, while nonetheless guiding the conversation around the topics on the Spidergram. In total, 321 separate interviewing sessions were carried out with 1,200 participants, producing the equivalent of a whole calendar month's worth of continuous recordings (Robinson *et al*., this volume).

Diversity and range was sought at every level, so amongst the groups of local people the audio-gatherers recruited to the cause were hairdressers, barbershop-singers, Young Farmers, grandmothers, historical battle recreationists, teachers, supermarket workers, salad-factory workers, lifeboatmen, aristocrats, gay men, poetry fans, farm-labourers, women golfers, travellers, bowls-club members, agriculture students, A-Level students, members of a fishermen's choir, rugby league fans, garage hands, Tiree islanders, café staff, Welsh hoteliers, Midlands Methodists, parish councillors, Polish immigrants, luxury car salesmen, ex-miners, St Kitts immigrants, Barbadians from Reading, Jamaican Brummies and a group of young actors…

Interviews ranged in length from about 45 minutes to two hours; some were tightly packed with linguistic detail, others meandered delightfully round the intricacies of the speakers' lives, stopping to take in particular dialect terms when the moment arose. And this was where the colour and sharpness of individual experience that makes fascinating broadcasting came in. Not only were the contributors – or as I suppose we should, being suitably academic, call them, 'informants' – recruited from within BBC local and regional radio broadcast areas, the stations themselves made a whole week of programming out of the interviews and the rich seam of stories about local life and history. So in Burnley, Lancashire, I recall with huge fondness the group of elderly men and women who collapsed in fits of laughter as they recalled their experiences of using an outside privy, the Tippler toilet, or 'Lancashire Long-drop' as they knew it:

> An' i' was all very windy as well bicoss it wen' straiught dauwn to the dreain. Saw [so] the win' would coom dauwn the dreain, woon't i'. An' you'd si' there an' you'd bi windeh. You see they din't 'ave lids on – they joost 'ad a saeyt [seat] with an 'ole in, an' my broother use' to frighten me to death becuz 'e use' tuh seay if yuh sit on a long taam, a rat'll coom oop an' bi'e yuh bottom….
>
> [And it was all very windy as well, because it went straight down to the drain. So the wind would come down the drain, wouldn't it. And you'd sit there and you'd be windy. You see they didn't have lids – they just had a seat with a hole in, and my brother used to frighten me to death, because he used to say if you sit on a long time, a rat'll come up and bite your bottom….]

There were 38 specific concepts for which the gatherers sought the speakers' natural vernacular equivalent. Questions on these were put to those interviewed by BBC reporters, were mounted on the BBC's *Voices* website (www.bbc.co.uk/voices), and were printed on cards available at local radio stations, libraries, and elsewhere, in a nationwide call for information on words and attitudes towards them. Some questions were simple – 'what do you call your FATHER, MOTHER, GRANDFATHER, GRANDMOTHER, BABY, MALE/FEMALE PARTNER?' and so on. Others had a more elaborate and looser definition, such as: 'what would you call A YOUNG PERSON IN CHEAP, TRENDY CLOTHES AND JEWELLERY?' or 'what do you call the NARROW WALKWAY BETWEEN BUILDINGS?' From the deep historical knowledge gleaned from dialect dictionaries and the SED, Upton knew well that this last would be likely to elicit terms like *ginnel*, *jitty,* and *twitchel*, but how far across the UK would the more standard *alley* or *alleyway* have spread with its uniforming smoothing-out of difference? As for the trendy young person, the word of the moment in 2004/5 when the survey was carried out was *chav*, and sure enough *chav* turned up routinely right across the country. But there were variants, like the Tyneside *charva*, the more recognizably Liverpudlian *scally,* and the Scottish *ned* from the Central Belt.

Then there were questions about the home ('what's the LONG SOFT SEAT IN THE MAIN ROOM?', 'what do you call the TOILET?' or 'what do you call the MAIN ROOM IN YOUR HOUSE WITH THE TV?'). At first sight, many of these questions appear rather simplistic, yet a seemingly rather obvious question such as 'what do you call someone who's LEFT-HANDED?' can unblock a whole lifetime of changing language and anecdotes to back it up ('I was always called cack-handed at school'... 'I was always told off for using my left hand...'). And the range of language that this particular question untapped was especially striking – most commonly *cack-handed*, but in Scotland *corrie-handed*, *corrie-fisted*, *cloddy handed*, *corrie-dukit,* and *cairy-handy.* As for the LONG, SOFT SEAT, well, clearly that was going to be *sofa* or *settee* surely? And indeed that was the normal rather limited set of options to emerge from the *Voices* survey. I was unprepared, therefore, for the variant that came storming through from the north Midlands, where, for many, this familiar piece of domestic furniture was – uniquely in my experience – a blend, *sofee.*

To the hundreds of hours of recordings collected were added hundreds of thousands of on-line and paper-based responses (Thompson, Upton, this volume) from which to create content for the local stations' output. And for one week in August 2005, *Voices* became a national obsession. On TV there were special programmes reflecting local language, all the BBC's radio networks became involved, and of course in the local stations all over the UK, together with Radio Ulster, Radio Scotland, and Radio Wales, *Voices* week meant special features, buses where listeners could drop in and record contributions, and discussions of all sorts and shapes. On Radio 4 across the whole summer, Dermot Murnaghan hosted a weekly peaktime live programme called

Word4Word, where guests like Lynda Mugglestone of Oxford University, poet Lemn Sissay, and novelist Howard Jacobson joined Upton to discuss various themes about the English language and local speech. Material from the *Voices* tapes was played throughout, and contributions were solicited from listeners by telephone.

One of the most fascinating areas for me within *Voices* was the way we charted the rapidly evolving stock of terms deriving from Britain's vibrant multicultural diversity, such as the transfer of *blud* and *bredren* out of the Afro-Caribbean communities where they were first encountered, via music and fashion, into the whole community, at least amongst younger and often urban speakers. This was territory never touched by Orton and the SED, and it felt very much part of the reality of twenty-first-century Britain. Likewise, in a reverse pollination, young Yorkshire women with roots in Leeds' Asian community spoke with some of the same vowels and used some of the same (though admittedly fewer) local terms as the traditional Tykes whose voices were captured high on the North York Moors.

The evidence that the survey – detailed, nationwide and rigorous – threw up thus provided authoritative contemporary grist to the academic commentary that people like Upton and Mugglestone were able to offer. But at the same time, through the delightful, colourful, and intensely-felt stories and responses of the native speakers interviewed across the country, the evidence was brought vividly to life. These were not laboratory guinea pigs, but a real cross-section of ordinary people *informing Voices* naturally and unforcedly about the lives they led. And in that, it really moved up a gear from the ground-breaking work of the SED fifty years earlier.

And for me, personally, it was as if the spirit that had informed my 1980s foray into dialect broadcasting, *Talk of the Town, Talk of the Country* with Stanley Ellis, had blossomed into something national and all-embracing. I quite remember the sense of exhilaration I felt as I played through the recordings to find material for my own *Voices* book (Elmes 2005), as if in some way I was able to elevate myself above these islands in some panoramic helicopter-shot, and then place a stethoscope against the landscape and listen in to the myriad conversations about ordinary life – living, loving, dying, shopping and working, eating and sleeping.... It was the heartbeat of Britain, a rich medley of vowels and voices telling about lives being lived, now.

And the real legacy of all this devoted and intense work on the part of everyone involved with *Voices* is that you can still hear that heartbeat. The work of Faith Mowbray and her interactive team in Cardiff most definitely endures. Log on to the website or visit the British Library's website (see Robinson *et al.*, this volume) and you can still hear those stories gathered by reporters in parish halls, local clubs, or simply in people's front parlours (or *lounges* or *sitting-rooms* or *back-kitchens*), as fresh as the day they were recorded. Run your mouse over the brilliant interactive map and click on the places as they appear on screen, and you open up a trove of accent and vocabulary offered up by thousands of online contributors that provides a real snapshot of vernacular English from 2004 until data stopped accumulating there in 2007. The 'Language Lab' section allows you to examine every one of the 38 semantic items, grouped under the lifestyle themes, and then to plot graphically where the highest incidence of each term – like *skive*, *bunk off*, *wag,* and so on for TO PLAY TRUANT – lies across the land. It is a fascinating picture, and still seven years on has enough linguistic science about it to match SED's peerless isoglossic maps from fifty years ago (Orton and Wright 1974; Orton *et al.* 1978).

Whether there could ever be another such venture – adventure, too – into the ever-changing way we express ourselves individually and in local groups across Britain, I somehow doubt. *Voices* was a product of its time, when the BBC in its wisdom had the resources and the will to set off on this huge trek. But language never stands still. We hear quite frequently about disappearing languages and places where the last living speakers of whatever tongue are now approaching their final years; yet we do not chart the last users of old British dialect words until we discover to our surprise that no-one knows them anymore.

Or not, as the case may be: Dolly Pentreath, who died in 1777, might have been the last fluent speaker of the Cornish language, but it is likely that it persisted in at least some vestigial form amongst the fishing community for years later. So surveys like *Voices* are always going to throw up new evidence for old words as well as new terms, new coinings that follow social trends and fashion. Thus today in 2013, our 2005 project is already well out of date and the snapshot we made has already been superseded by new usages and acquisitions.

But then, holding back the river of language was always a futile task.

References

BBC (2012) *5: This is the BBC*. Online. Available HTTP: <http://www.bbc.co.uk/historyofthebbc/resources/in-depth/reith_5.shtml> (accessed 25 June 2012).

Briggs, A. (1961) *The History of Broadcasting in the United Kingdom, Volume 1: The Birth of Broadcasting 1896–1927*, London: Oxford University Press.

Briggs, A. (1965) *The History of Broadcasting in the United Kingdom, Volume 2: The Golden Age of Wireless*, London: Oxford University Press.

Elmes, S. (2005) *Talking for Britain: A Journey Through the Nation's Dialects*, London: Penguin.

Kerswill, P., Llamas, C. and Upton, C. (1999) 'The First SuRE Moves: early steps towards a large dialect project', in C. Upton and K. Wales (eds), *Dialect Variation in English: proceedings of the Harold Orton centenary conference 1998*, Leeds Studies in English 30, Leeds: University of Leeds.

Llamas, C. (1999) 'A new methodology: data elicitation for social and regional language variation studies', *Leeds Working Papers in Linguistics*, 7, 95–119.

Orton, H. (1962) *Survey of English Dialects (A): Introduction*, Leeds: E.J. Arnold.

Orton, H. and Wright, N. (1974) *A Word Geography of England*, London: Seminar Press.

Orton, H., Sanderson, S. and Widdowson, J. (1978) *A Linguistic Atlas of England*, London: Croom Helm.

2

VOICES: A CASE STUDY IN THE EVOLUTION OF A LINGUISTIC CLIMATE AT THE BBC

David Crystal

BBC interest about language can be found from the earliest days of its institution, as Simon Elmes (this volume) notes, and regional programmes on local usage were being made as early as the 1930s, but nothing quite matches the flowering of interest in linguistic issues during the 1980s, which helped form the climate for the *Voices* project. This was a decade when the BBC was becoming increasingly concerned about what to do with the volume of correspondence it was receiving from listeners about English usage. Hundreds of letters were being received every week, and there was nowhere for them to go but the Pronunciation Unit. However, many of the topics had nothing to do with pronunciation. Although regional accents, sound changes, and perceived errors (such as intrusive *r*) were common themes, most letters dealt with topics in grammar and vocabulary, which went well beyond the Unit's remit. What should be done with them?

In 1980, a decision was made to address the issue on air. The first I knew about it was when I received a request to write a programme based on this correspondence for Radio 4. Why me? I imagine I must have acquired a limited profile due to a pair of programmes on English usage I had written and presented for Radio 3 in 1976 (*You Said It*), along with sporadic broadcasts I had made since my first foray into the medium in 1965. Whatever the origins of the idea, the outcome was breathtaking. I was sent all the correspondence that was on file – a large postbag full of cards and letters – and asked to make sense of it. The resulting programme, whose title reflected the typically intransigent tone of the letter-writers, was *How Dare You Talk to Me Like That!* (4 July 1981). I analysed the subject-matter and came up with a 'top twenty' list of complaints. The talk was published in *The Listener* (9 July) and the reaction was so great that it was repeated twice over the following six months. The amount of correspondence on usage to the BBC significantly increased, as a consequence. I know, because they kept on sending it to me. I still have most of it, though some of it is archived in the University of Reading library.

This process continued during the 1980s. Radio 4, sensing a new mood, and noting the popular response, tasked a producer (Alan Wilding) to take the usage theme forward, and during the decade I worked with him on several 15-minute programmes: two series called *Speak Out* in 1982, and five series of *English Now* in 1984, 1985, 1986, 1988, and 1990. I had suggested 30-minute programmes, but there was a reluctance at the BBC to devote so much time to the matter. I sensed there was a big psychological difference in-house between a 15-minute and a 30-minute programme. My interpretation was that the former was enough to 'keep listeners happy' on a sensitive subject (such as language), whereas the latter was a serious attempt to engage with the subject. As a new area of broadcasting, the decision-makers felt that 30-minute slots were premature, and I was actually told this by Huw Weldon when I addressed a meeting of department heads at Broadcasting House in 1987 on language policy. But as the decade wore on, and other programmes came to be made (see below), the climate seemed to be changing. Accordingly, I made a fresh proposal in early 1992 for a half-hour series, as a follow-up to *English Now*, to be called *Language Now*, but I was too late. The slot had already been filled by Frank Delaney's new series, *Word of Mouth*, which began later that year, produced by Simon Elmes. Frank had previously created and presented *Bookshelf* for Radio 4, was well aware of the growing popular interest in language, and had lots to say about it. Indeed, he had been a guest on *English Now* at one point. Stimulated by a chance listening to the phrase *word of mouth* heard in song lyrics during a transatlantic plane journey, he came up with what has proved to be the most successful of all radio series on language. He presented it himself for several years, Michael Rosen taking over in 1998. Regional speech has been a recurrent theme.

Accents had never been a dominant theme of *English Now*, because Stanley Ellis was presenting his own series on local speech during the same period: *Talk of the Town, Talk of the Country*. But I couldn't ignore the topic, as it loomed large in the correspondence. And one of the guests I had in my first series was Susan Rae, who had become a presenter on Radio 4, and whose lilting Dundee tones had attracted aggressive mail from listeners accusing the BBC of deteriorating standards of pronunciation. I see her as a personification of the changing linguistic climate within the BBC over the following 25 years. Dropped from her Radio 4 presenting role, her voice remained off-air for some time, but reappeared in the 2000s as part of the reappraisal of the role of regional speech, of which the *Voices* project was a culmination. Her Scottish voice now regularly presents the news on Radio 4 – an analogous development to Huw Edwards' Welsh voice on BBC 1.

The 1980s was a very important decade in fostering this new linguistic climate, and it should not be ignored. In my view, television was the key factor. In 1982, following up the popular interest in the *Speak Out* radio series, in which I had interviewed several TV personalities (such as newsreader Richard Whitmore and sports commentator Frank Bough) about their use of language, I wrote to the Controller of Programmes at the BBC proposing a corresponding series for television. The Head of Continuing Education, Sheila Innes, arranged a meeting with departmental producers, and a great deal of stimulating discussion took place. There was no lack of interest, but no consensus emerged about how to channel it. My impression was that the subject of language fell between the remits of the various departments (such as current affairs, education, and history). Belonging to everyone, it therefore belonged to no-one. The outcome, anyway, was that the proposal never went ahead.

My proposal was for a series on 'language', not just on English, and this is an important distinction. There was an understandable uncertainty about how a supposedly abstract subject, 'language', could be presented visually. (Interestingly, I had had precisely the same reaction to the initial proposal for what would later that decade be *The Cambridge Encyclopedia of Language* (Crystal 1987). This had been turned down by two publishers on the grounds that they could not see how a book 'on language with pictures' could possibly work.) Sheila Innes, noting the point, followed it up with a suggestion that a more focused theme could be a better option. A producer from BBC Education, Bernard Adams, was asked to take this forward, and in 1983 he came up with a series idea, tentatively called 'Your English'. We jointly shaped the proposal, and it was submitted, but again it never went ahead.

However, there was clearly a desire to do something on television, and the next proposal was to resurrect the 'About Language' idea (as it was then being called), offering a blend of 'popular linguistics and language awareness... including elements of Your English, and drawing upon many languages other than English' (letter to me from Sheila Innes, 1 May 1985). Terry Doyle, a senior producer for foreign language output at BBC Continuing Education, took the idea forward, but again, it never went ahead, presumably because plans were already quite advanced for a much bigger project at BBC2, *The Story of English*.

This was a nine-part documentary (495 minutes in all), written by Robert MacNeil, Robert McCrum, and William Cran, and aired worldwide in 1986 (a co-production with the Public Broadcasting Service in the USA). It was widely acclaimed, receiving an Emmy Award and later published as a book. I had very little involvement, other than being used as a consultant for a couple of the programmes. But later I was asked, along with Tom McArthur (the editor of *English Today*), to produce the parallel radio series for the World Service. I thought it would be a straightforward job, as we were being given access to all the television tapes, but soon learned that television does not translate into radio. There were simply too many pictures telling the story! The voices and voiceovers were of secondary importance to the film-makers, and too fragmentary to be directly transferred into a non-pictorial medium. It meant we had to write the scripts from scratch, though having available the same bank of recordings that the television series had used. Once again, regional speech – on a global level, this time – was being given the importance it deserved. Eighteen half-hour programmes were the result, produced by Hamish Norbrook, and broadcast in 1987.

The Story of English, I have no doubt, was a turning-point. It showed that language could be treated televisually, and was not just a topic for radio. Apart from anything else, it presented the *written* language (never a good bet for radio), and it presented the *people* in a way that an audio medium cannot – and there is no language without people. With its global remit, the accents of the world came across beautifully as part of the story, such as the interviews with people on Tangier Island, off the east coast of the USA, where the myth that Elizabethan English was still to be heard there was explored. It also brought a renewed interest in the possibility of a corresponding series on language. If *The Story of English*, then why not *The Story of Language*?

This was in fact a proposal made by Clive Doig, a producer at an independent TV company, Brechin Productions, at around the time *The Story of English* was being made, but postponed for that reason. In 1987 *The Cambridge Encyclopedia of Language* was published, which Clive saw as full of televisual potential, so he resuscitated the idea in 1989, first calling it *The Language Lab*, and then revising it a year later as *The Story of Language*, which he described as 'a tele-encyclopaedia of the languages of the world', and giving dialects a special mention. He sent this in to John Slater, managing editor for history and archaeology at the BBC, and over the next two years the proposal went through various revisions (and titles – *The Tour of Babel*, *The Search for Babel*...) to suit Slater's requirements which, as a historian, he summarized as the need to 'discover history through language'. In early 1991, a meeting was arranged at the Groucho Club in London to take things forward (memorable, as there was a power cut, and we had to discuss language themes by candle-light). But the romantic atmosphere didn't last: the historical angle disappeared when, soon after, there was a hierarchy change, and a new senior manager, interested more in anthropology than history, asked for a fundamental revision. But our energy, after five reworkings, had gone. I had a sense of déjà vu: where, in the vast domain of public broadcasting, would the subject of language ever comfortably fit?

BBC Wales was one place. In Wales, the subject of language had come to the fore as part of the push to obtain official recognition for Welsh, and this was reflected by an increase in programmes on language emanating from that channel. On radio, at various times until 1993, I had a weekly language slot (usually five minutes or so) in the shows hosted by Hywyl Gwynfryn and Mal Pope. It was rare for a week to go by without the topic of accents and dialects being raised, and in 1991 speech variation played a central role (along with song) in a TV documentary called *The Welsh Voice*. But it was the status and future of Welsh which captured broadcasters' imagination. Over the next ten years, I know of ten proposals for programmes or series focusing on the history of Welsh or on the broader topic of language endangerment and death, and one would eventually be made (see below). English accents paled by comparison. But this period of linguistic enthusiasm in Wales was crucial, as one of the leading motivations for the *Voices* project would, ten years later, come from Cardiff.

The 1980s was also the decade in which the repercussions of the 1975 'Bullock Report', *A Language for Life*, were working their way through the schools. This had emphasized the importance of 'language across the curriculum', bringing together mother-tongue and foreign-language learning, and fostering a climate out of which came such expressions as KAL ('Knowledge About Language') and 'language awareness'. One of the consequences was that the BBC was approached by the Schools Broadcasting Council to include a fresh language element in its provision, and this added to the linguistically aware climate which was slowly emerging. Two parallel strands were commissioned. The first was aimed at secondary schools: *Patterns of Language*, a series of ten 15-minute programmes produced by Al Wolff, broadcast in 1986, and focusing on pupils, aged 10 to 13, about to embark on foreign language learning. Wolff had been the producer of a series a few years before, *Web of Language*, scripted mainly by Tony Penman, with Randolph Quirk as consultant. The new initiative, put together by Wolff, Penman, and Tony Adams (Cambridge Department of Education) had diversity as the overriding theme, with four of the programmes specifically focusing on regional variation. I was the consultant for the series and wrote two of the programmes as well as several pieces for the accompanying teachers' brochure. The second strand was aimed at primary schools: *Talk to Me*, a series of six 10-minute programmes produced by Paddy Beechely, broadcast in 1987, and focusing on children aged 6 to 7. The consultancy here involved much more than advising on content: a perspective from child language acquisition was required to ensure that the 'language about language' would be accessible to this age group. The fifth programme in the series, 'Hello! Who are you?', was entirely devoted to different accents, dialects, and languages. A further 10-part series aimed at 14–16-year-olds was aired in 1990, called *Language File*. Accents and dialects were the themes of two of the programmes, 'Whose English?' and 'Talking Proper'.

While all this was going on, a fresh initiative from Terry Doyle led to my submitting, in January 1992, a new version of *The Story of Language*. This time it attracted the interest of Alan Yentob – a promising sign. It was taken up by Peter Riding, executive producer for BBC Continuing Education, and a formal offer was made to BBC2 for five 50-minute programmes to go out mid-evening in Winter 1995 'celebrating the origins, diversity, power and creative potential of languages'. Accents and dialects figured largely in Programme 3. I was actually paid to be a consultant for that proposal – a first! But again, it never went ahead. I never learned why.

Four other factors were important in fostering the climate which led to *Voices*. One was the Open University. As early as 1973, the OU (launched in 1969) was presenting courses on *Language and Learning*, first under Asher Cashdan and later under John Chapman, and included components such as 'Language Variation and English' (Stringer 1973). By 1980, a whole raft of courses on language development, structure, and use was available and proving extremely popular – as they still are. The BBC, of course, was the OU's partner in this enterprise, and several radio and television programmes were the outcome. It is difficult to estimate the impact of these on the evolution of cultural awareness about language (how many non-students watched those late night/early morning OU programmes?), but I don't think it can be understated. Certainly, when I made one of these television programmes myself (*Grammar Rules*, 1980), I was intrigued by the large number of people, none of them OU students, who told me they had seen it. And the constant reinforcement of the theme of language diversity, nationally and internationally, must have helped foster the interest in spoken language, especially in schools, for many of the students taking the English course were teachers – and an enthusiastic and committed cadre at that. (I was the course's external examiner for a few years, and saw at first hand the amazing level of commitment individuals were devoting to their English language study.)

The second major factor was the development of local radio. The vision behind this initiative, as expressed by the pioneer of local radio at the BBC, former war correspondent Frank Gillard, was 'to present on the air, and in many different forms and through a multitude of local voices, the running serial story of local life in all its aspects'.[1] Aware of the success of pirate radio stations around the UK, in 1967–8 the BBC chose eight locations for an initial experiment: Radio Leicester, Sheffield, Merseyside, Nottingham, Brighton, Stoke-on-Trent, Leeds, and Durham. It took a while to build audiences: it was difficult to publicize what was on offer, and the stations were available only on VHF at the time. But the experiment was a success, and in 1969 the BBC made local radio a permanent fixture and created 12 more stations. Then in 1973, the newly-formed Independent Broadcasting Authority (IBA) began licensing a fresh wave of commercial radio stations – over 80 within 15 years. Two years later, Radio Ulster began broadcasting, and three years after that Radio Scotland and Radio Wales. In all cases, the dominant impression the new station conveyed was the 'multitude of local voices', but they had limited resources and airtime, so that in-depth documentaries on such topics as regional dialect were not possible. The budget found for the *Voices* project provided an opportunity to exploit these local interests, at a nationwide level, for the first time. As Pat Loughrey, head of Nations and Regions at the time, has put it (email to me, 29 October 2012):

> the vast Division seemed to me to be defined by their unique voices and experience. Yet in the obsession with daily journalism, chat and disc spinning, those wellsprings had been neglected or ignored in local programmes, in England especially. What they lacked was any shared, non-metropolitan platform for exploration or celebration.

A third element in the decade before *Voices* must not be forgotten: the approaching millennium. From the point of view of English language radio, this was to be marked by a project at first called *A Thousand Years of Spoken English* on Radio 4. In the end it came to be called *The Routes of English*, broadcast as four series of six 30-minute programmes between 1999 and 2001, produced by Simon Elmes, and presented by Melvyn Bragg. I was the series consultant, and contributed to a couple of the programmes. Having such a well-known figure as the presenter gave the subject an unprecedented profile, and the recognition of the importance of regional speech was there from the beginning. In programme 1, Melvyn returned to Wigton, in Cumbria, to explore what had been happening to the local dialect there. The third series was entirely devoted to accents and dialects.

The fourth factor provided the immediate trigger for *Voices*: two projects that in their individual ways acted as trailblazers. The first was the *Video Nation* project for BBC 2, which ran between 1993 and 2000, co-founded and produced by Mandy Rose. The team gave camcorders to a group of people across the UK to record aspects of everyday life. These were broadcast both as short items and as longer programmes on a wide variety of topics. The group was selected 'to reflect the diversity of the UK' (as the programme description put it), so it was a linguistically rich mix of voices. The series didn't make any programmes specifically about language, but it was a theme constantly present in the recordings, and often the speakers would comment on matters relating to cultural and regional identity. Then in spring 2001 Mandy Rose moved from London to BBC Wales to run the newly formed New Media Department, bringing with her two key notions: ideas that would work across the UK, and ideas that lent themselves to public participation.

A bilingual environment is the perfect situation for generating ideas about language. The New Media Department was producing output in both English and Welsh, reflecting life across the whole of Wales, and linguistic issues – along with the associated issues of culture, class, community, and identity – were a regular talking point in the office. There are significant differences between the Welsh and Welsh English of South and North Wales, as well as many regional variations. In addition, the producers had to make decisions about the thorniest question of all: how formal should Welsh be on the BBC? Several relevant programmes were made. I was the consultant and contributor for a six-part television series, called *The Story of Welsh*, presented by Huw Edwards, and aired in 2003. The same year, radio came up with a four-part series called *The Way That You Say It*, on how English is spoken in Wales, written and produced by Steve Groves and presented by Siriol Jenkins.

Other dialect-orientated programmes were being made at the time, and these helped form the climate of language awareness that was growing in broadcasting as a whole in the early 2000s. An important series was *Back to Babel*, made by Michael Blythe, four 1-hour programmes for Infonation Media (at the time, the film-making division of the British Foreign Office) and broadcast on the Discovery Channel and worldwide. I was consultant and continuity contributor for that series, and had the same role two years later in *Blimey*, for BBC 4, three 1-hour documentaries aired in January 2002 on how spoken English has changed since the Second World War. But these were one-offs. It was in Wales that there was an atmosphere of constant language-awareness, and it was perhaps inevitable that Mandy Rose's *Video Nation* experience would prompt her to think about how linguistic variation could be given a pan-UK interactive dimension. She writes (email to me, 19 August 2012): 'I remember on a train trip at that time considering the possibility of moving across an online map and hearing accents change as you travel'.

The second and more immediate trailblazer was an acclaimed Nations and Regions radio project in 2001, *A Sense of Place*, under executive editor Gloria Abramoff, which in effect acted as a testing-ground for the *Voices* project. Forty-three BBC radio stations, including Radios Cymru, Wales, Scotland, Northern Ireland, and Foyle, broadcast a series of documentaries celebrating the distinctive qualities of communities around the UK. Collaboration also came from other channels, such as BBC Education, the *Where I Live* series, and BBC Nations' websites. When Pat Loughrey made the first formal announcement about *Voices*, it was presented as a follow-up project which would 'give people an opportunity to tell their stories' (BBC press release, 31 October 2002).

Mandy Rose had raised her ideas at one of BBC Wales' regular performance review meetings, and found they coalesced well with Pat Loughrey's thinking. Pat was the perfect person to take the project forward. He had a lifelong interest in regional speech, coming from an Irish-speaking background in Donegal. He had taught Irish, done some linguistics during doctoral work in Canada, and made several Radio Ulster programmes and packages on Hiberno English, before becoming Head of Programmes and then Controller in Northern Ireland. Mandy submitted an outline (one-page) proposal. The working title was *The UK Speaks*, with the gloss: 'BBC Nations and Regions celebrate the diverse languages, dialects, and accents of the UK'. The document makes interesting reading, in the light of subsequent events, so I quote its main points here. The operative word is 'audit':

> In an ambitious multi-platform project involving our audience and a range of expert partners, BBC Nations and Regions will conduct an audit of the ways we talk across the UK in the early 21st century.

Potential partners mentioned were the National Sound Archive, the British Library, national and regional museums, the Welsh Language Board and its equivalents in Scotland and Northern Ireland, as well as key university departments. Six project elements were specified:

- Programmes on local and national radio will take a variety of approaches to the accent, dialect and language in their area.
- A website featuring a multi-layered interactive map provides an engaging and educational interface for exploring the subject.

- Beneath the map the website provides a wealth of background information.
- Once launched, the website will be a growing, live space where users can add their own voices by phone around a number of themes.
- Radio phone-ins and Where I Live sites will provide a space for debate, about attitudes to accents, the meaning of particular words and expressions, etc.
- Open Centres, Community Studios, Buses will provide places to gather recordings.

The proposal concluded:

> The ways we speak and the languages we speak in are a precious part of our identity. This project will celebrate the UK's diverse voices and examine some of the issues and tensions that differences of accent and language produce. The project will engage and offer insights across a range of platforms. Additionally, with partnership input, the project will have lasting value as social research; providing a unique audio survey which will capture aspects of regional speech threatened by social change and globalisation.

A period of development research for the proposal was given a green light. The first phase took place during the middle months of 2003, and I became involved at that point. Mandy had brought on board an executive producer in the New Media department, Faith Mowbray (see Elmes, this volume), and in a series of meetings during July and August we discussed how to realize these general ideas into a framework that would be robust from the point of view of sociolinguistics and dialectology. The BBC team was working with a very general notion of 'variation', conceived primarily in geographical terms, and had little sense of the way sociolinguists had identified such other variables as gender, age, occupation, socioeconomic class, and ethnicity, or the kinds of conversational activity that can influence a person's accent. My role at this point was simply to provide a sociolinguistic perspective for the project, identifying the main variables, to summarize the main dialect divisions in the UK, to draw up a bibliography, to identify what was already methodologically 'out there' (such as techniques of word mapping), and to suggest academic and professional contacts. For example, there was a possible point of connection with the UNESCO-supported *Voices of the World* project, based in Copenhagen, which was in development at that time – an ambitious multi-platform initiative that aimed to make recordings of every language in the world, and to make television documentaries on endangered languages.[2] And I felt an early contact with the Leeds Dialect Survey was critical to the success of the enterprise.

For practical reasons, Wales was chosen as a case study.[3] A development producer, Rachel Muntz, was commissioned to explore the shape an online interactive project might take. The Australian Word Map proved to be a fruitful model. A great deal of in-house discussion took place with radio and television colleagues in BBC Wales. There was a meeting with the National

Sound Archive, which was itself undertaking a map-based web project on the accents and dialects of England, part of a plan to digitize selected British Library assets. A think-tank meeting was convened with potential partners, using contacts in Wales to obtain initial reactions, including the curator of audio-visual archives at St Fagans Museum of the National Library of Wales, the chair and head of education of the Welsh Language Board, and linguists from Swansea (Penhallurick, this volume) and Cardiff. The response was enthusiastic, and Mandy recalls the animated character of the discussion, as people talked about their words for things – their 'linguistic biographies', as she put it. It was clear at that meeting that the BBC could do something really valuable if it was able to conduct some fresh research drawing on the network of Nations and Regions.

In the summer of 2003 Mandy and Faith had their first meeting with Clive Upton, who introduced them to the SuRE interview methodology (Elmes, Upton, this volume). This was an important factor in ensuring the acceptance of the project by the BBC. Mandy presented work-in-progress twice to the Nations and Regions management team during 2003, and at the second meeting they were able to describe the SuRE approach, which impressed everyone. The connection with Leeds offered not only expertise, but also legacy (of which this book is an illustration). At that meeting, Pat Loughrey made the critically important decision to commit journalists' time from across the network to conduct the interviews. The next step was to interest other departments. Mandy had not included any proposals for network radio or television involvement in her early proposals, as there was no guarantee that a project which originated in one division of the BBC (Nations and Regions) would appeal to another. However, the promise of high-quality survey recordings, supported by academic expertise, being made available for radio and television programmes proved attractive. In the autumn of 2003, there was a positive response at an initial meeting with Radio 4, and interest from other channels followed.

I had several meetings with the team during 2004, as the project transformed from *The UK Speaks* into *Voices*, and some of the in-house developments during that year are summarized by Elmes, whose primary role was to give a practical realization ('a bespoke BBC version', as he puts it) to the conceptual and methodological apparatus developed by the academics. Interview guidelines were sent out to the local radio journalists, who came together for a 'Big Day' in October 2004, during which ideas were shared and a large number of practical questions dealt with. The project launched in January 2005, with excellent coverage, and a second 'Big Day' was held in Birmingham in February 2005, to assess the impact of the launch and to plan ahead for the major event, the 'Voices Week', scheduled for Week 34, 22–26 August. As Pat Loughrey put it, 'What was really unique in *Voices* was the involvement of all of England' and finding 'a budget big enough to do this work to the highest standards across the whole UK – no exceptions' (email to me, 29 October 2012). Mick Ord, a respected local radio manager, was a critical figure in making all this happen, as was Andy Griffee, the Controller of English Regions at the time.

The Birmingham meeting was a truly impressive occasion, with the entire *Voices* team present as well as representatives from over 40 local radio stations around the country. In a briefing document, Mick Ord and Faith Mowbray outlined the essential differences between the launch material (January 2005) and the output planned for Voices Week. They felt they had only scratched the surface of the linguistic theme in January, and that the later schedule would enable local and national stations to 'dig deeper'. The aim was to include a broader and more diverse range of people in the interview groups, noting that diversity included age, sex, disability, and ethnicity, and not simply regional background. A much wider range of subject-matter was identified, including swearing, young people's language, slang, idioms, the role of standard English, politically incorrect language, the influence of the media upon language, the role of education in fostering language attitudes, body language, community languages other than English, bilingualism, speech disorders, artificial languages (such as Klingon), and sign language of the deaf. Clearly *Voices* was developing into a project 'about language', and not just 'about dialect'. I have never experienced another occasion like this one, where the interaction between so many general concepts of language and the needs and practicalities of daily broadcasting has been explored in such depth. Far more came out of the brainstorming than could ever have been used in a single broadcasting week, but this gave the programme-makers a huge amount of choice in selecting topics that would suit their audiences.

For many of the local journalists, this was the first time they had had an opportunity to discuss linguistic issues 'across the table'. Some of the points were contentious, and it was both informative and reassuring for them to see that the same issues were being encountered throughout the network. For example, there was considerable discussion of how to handle strong language. When local people are recorded in naturalistic situations, talking about everyday topics on which they have real knowledge and often strong opinions, there are risks. They are likely to swear, use abusive names, make racial comments, express extreme views, and generally talk in an unconstrained way which, if broadcast, would offend some listeners or viewers. The BBC of course has criteria which it tries to follow (notions of a 'watershed', for example), but with *Voices*, producers and presenters would be breaking new ground, in that the focus was on the speech itself and only indirectly on the content. They were used to making editorial judgements about allowing the use of swearing in literary contexts, where a usage was justified – for example by a character in a play; but there was uncertainty about what audience reaction would be to conversations in which swear-words might be heard as an apparently indispensable feature. There was a general feeling that great caution would be necessary in selecting material from the recorded interviews.

The meeting, along with the preliminary and follow-up briefing documents, was also extremely informative in drawing attention to the range of content covered by the innocent-sounding terms *dialect* and *accent*. For many of the journalists, there was an expectation that the aim of the interviews was to collect speech samples of a kind that is not normally heard on radio or television – the broader accents and nonstandard dialects of the population. It was thus important to emphasize that the speech varieties normally heard in broadcasting are just as important a part of the mix that constitutes British 'voices' as are working-class accents. Don't forget the 'toff voices', said one of the guidelines. Don't fall into the trap of thinking that there are people who have 'no accent', said another. Expect contradictory results in surveys, said a third. Indeed, some intriguing results had already been raised by the national survey of voices that had been carried out in the first stage of the project. Some results were clear-cut:

> I like hearing a range of accents. (78% agree, 6% disagree, 16% undecided)
>
> I hear a wider variety of accents on BBC television and radio nowadays than I did before. (76% agree, 8% disagree, 17% neither agree nor disagree)
>
> To what extent does your accent change depending on who you are with? (19% never, 81% at least occasionally, 5% all the time)

Some showed opinion evenly divided:

> Regional accents are less distinct than they used to be. (39% agree, 27% disagree, 24% think neither)
>
> Men tend to have stronger accents than women. (28% agree, 38% disagree, 34% neither disagree or agree)

But there were also some puzzling results. In a survey of celebrity voices, Sean Connery came top of the 'most pleasant' poll and Ian Paisley came top of the 'least pleasant' poll; on the other hand, Billy Connolly and the Queen were both in the top ten of each poll! The fact that the Queen's voice generated ambivalence was, to my mind, the most significant result of the entire survey, and one that would have been inconceivable fifty years ago.

Voices Week, in August 2005, did indeed resemble a 'national obsession', as Simon Elmes describes it. For my part, I have never been on so many radio programmes in a single day. During the afternoon of 17 August, for example, interviews with local radio stations were coming in at 10-minute intervals, from all over the country, and I know other members of the *Voices* team were similarly engaged. But the interest both preceded and followed the official Week. I was involved as consultant for two television programmes, both of which impressed me greatly with the originality of their approach. *The Word On The Street* (29 July 2005, BBC2) explored accent change within four generations of a Leicestershire family – the first time I had had the opportunity of observing such a perspective. And *The Way We Say It* (2005, BBC Wales, producer Catrin Mair Thomas) took me, as co-presenter, to parts of Wales I had never visited before, to meet people who seriously broadened my notion of what counted as a Welsh accent. I had known, for example, that there were 'dialect islands' along the North Wales coast reflecting the incomer history of that region. On our recording visit, I met some of these people, including some who had lived all their lives in the area, and, indeed, they had accents that were virtually indistinguishable from those heard in nearby Cheshire and Lancashire. What I was not expecting was to hear them confidently and proudly affirm that they spoke with a 'Welsh accent'. Several of the chapters in this book draw attention to the insights about regional identity, methodology, and ideology brought to light by the *Voices* data, both in the recorded interviews and in the website forum.

The *Voices* project has been repeatedly described using synchronic metaphors – as an audit, or snapshot, or sound-portrait of the language in Britain at a particular point in time – 2005. But it needs a diachronic perspective to really prove its worth. During the project, the point was regularly made that this was a task that only the BBC could carry out to the level of professionalism in interview technique and acoustic quality that such a project requires. The thought that this could be something the BBC might take on board on a regular basis, finances permitting, was mentioned in early discussions; and in a speech at a celebratory retrospective in Broadcasting House in November 2005, having sounded out a few people beforehand as to the ideal distance between audits, I introduced the thought again. The consensus among the senior managers I talked to at the time was that we need such a survey at least once in a generation. However, that is around 30 years, which is a long time for a language that is developing so rapidly. Bearing in mind the way accents, and attitudes to accents, have changed so dramatically since 1980, a shorter time-period suggests itself. There seems to be no risk of a diminution of interest on the part of the listening and viewing public: programmes involving accents and dialects continue to generate huge audience reaction whenever they are aired. And there is a strong argument that *Voices 2*, whenever it might be held, would benefit from being sufficiently close to *Voices 1* to enable listeners and viewers to retain some sense of auditory identity with those who took part in it. My feeling is that 15 years is an ideal gap, which would locate *Voices 2* in 2020 – or perhaps 2022, the hundredth anniversary of daily broadcasting on the BBC.

Notes

1 See the historical summary at <http://www.bbc.co.uk/historyofthebbc/resources/in-depth/local_radio.shtml>.
2 For some of the output of this project, see <http://www.final-cut.dk/films2.php?mit_indhold_id=3&films_id=10>.
3 I am grateful to Mandy Rose and Pat Loughrey for several of the details in the next two paragraphs.

References

Australian Word Map (n.d.) Online. Available HTTP: http://www.abc.net.au/wordmap/.

Crystal, D. (1987) *The Cambridge Encyclopedia of Language*, Cambridge: Cambridge University Press.

Stringer, D. (1973) 'Language Variation and English', in *English, Language and Learning*, E262 Block 1, Bletchley: Open University Press.

3

CONSTRUCTIONS OF EXPERTISE AND AUTHORITY ON A LANGUAGE-THEMED DISCUSSION FORUM

Linguists, linguistics and the public

Bethan L. Davies

Introduction

The focus of this chapter is the open2.net 'Ask an Expert' forum where an academic linguist acted as a resident 'expert', contributing to an open-access discussion board. This is an interesting discursive site to explore the complexities involved in expert–lay communication, in particular the ways in which participants construct claims as authoritative, their perception of different types of expertise and their conception of linguistics as a subject area. Engaging beyond the academy is seen by many linguists as a challenge (e.g. Johnson 2001); the question here is what we can learn from the open2.net experience.

The 'Ask an Expert' forum

The 'Ask an Expert' discussion board under analysis in this chapter was accessed via the *BBC Voices* home page through a link that stated 'Ask an open2.net expert here'; this linked to an Open University (hereafter, OU) site that supported collaborations with BBC programming. Therefore, this forum is somewhat different from the many other discussion boards on the *BBC Voices* website because it was hosted elsewhere and subject to different moderation procedures.[1] In addition, the involvement of both these institutions gave the forum a very strong educational frame (Goffman 1974): the BBC's mission explicitly includes the role of educating as well as informing and entertaining (http://www.bbc.co.uk/info/purpose/), and the OU is recognised as a longstanding provider of tertiary education to a broad social demographic.

The other key difference was the stated presence of a 'language expert' on the site who took part in the discussions by starting threads and also contributing to ongoing threads initiated by members of the public. Diana Honeybone (hereafter DH), an academic at the OU, posted 24 times in 21 different threads over a two-month period. The forum was active from August 2005 to July 2009 – producing 90 threads with over 700 messages – but most activity occurred in its first year. It is important to note that even though this forum was framed as 'Ask an Expert', it was never made clear who this 'expert' was nor the nature of their expertise; DH was only identified by 'Diana Honeybone (OU)' as her forum username.

In terms of engaging with the public, this foray into expert–lay communication seemed to have limited success. DH's precise remit is unknown but her relatively small number of posts and short period of engagement gave her a low profile: the link and the forum existed long after DH had ceased posting. In addition, she did not seem to be very successful in engendering discussion on the site although she personally initiated six different threads and contributed to 15 more. In only one case was her post accepted and positively evaluated by another forum member – and that was when she acted as a dialect informant – though she did manage to seed (Wright and Street 2007) one successful thread. In many cases, her posts were simply passed over or they marked the end of the thread.

While DH was not the only contributor to have a post ignored, such a pattern deserves closer inspection. This chapter will examine the different types of discursive activity in the postings of DH and others to see whether there are differences in the way these are taken up by other participants.

The public's understanding of linguistics

In recent years, there has been much interest within linguistics about the perception of the subject outside the academy (Heller 1999; Johnson 2001; Laforest 1999; Milroy 2001; Rickford 1999). In particular, this has focused on the apparent difficulty experienced in convincing the public that linguistics has something to offer in media debates about language; Laforest (1999: 278) reflects on her own realization that linguists are not perceived as having any special expertise on matters of language:

> Physicists and economists are recognized as having skills most people do not have, requiring special training. But language belongs to everyone and seems transparent to people because they use it daily, something that makes them feel, if they are not absolutely sure, that there is nothing mysterious about it and there is nothing more to understand than what people already know the minute they open their mouth to speak. As a result, the linguist is regarded as someone who complicates matters for the fun of it and whose only goal is to justify his or her own existence: s/he's a specialist of something there's nothing to know about that everyone doesn't know already.

Jean Aitchison experienced a similar rejection of linguistic expertise after delivering a very high profile series of lectures for the BBC that had the express purpose of making current academic knowledge accessible to the public.[2] In the final chapter of the published version (Aitchison 1997), she describes the 'hornets' nest' of both media and individual responses that the first lecture on 'language anxieties' provoked. Again, she found it puzzling that a high-profile professor with many years' experience could be judged (by some) as being ignorant about their specialist field.

Johnson (2001) argues that – although linguistics might have especial difficulties in this area – linguists are not alone in having difficulties in negotiating the expert–lay divide. She makes a connection between the issues experienced here and more generally in public understanding of science, as expressed in Irwin and Wynne (1996). They point out that much expert–lay discourse is based on a deficit model of the public's understanding allied with an absolute hegemony for the authority of the academic subject. In their view, just 'more and better' scientific knowledge is not likely to improve the public's understanding because this project often founders on the rocks of a clash between these dominant discourses and 'local, situated forms of knowledge' (Johnson 2001: 594). Thus, the problem is not the quality of the explanation but rather an ability to engage with the concerns and knowledge of the community: a 'top-down' approach only reinforces the opposition between the two.

From this perspective, the open2.net forum provides an interesting discursive space for expert–lay interaction. It is 'top down' to the extent that the forum is given an explicit educational frame through its association with both the BBC and the OU; this is reinforced by the naming of the forum, which further privileges the notion of expertise (and also brings into being a group of 'non-experts' who can benefit from it). However, this early use of Web 2.0 technologies by a national broadcaster also enabled public participation via a medium that allowed much more autonomy in users' engagement (in comparison to the editorial control exercised in broadcast discussions, for example). *BBC Voices* was always conceived by its originators as '"grassroots", "bottom up" and "all about the audience"' (Ord 2004, in Turner, this volume). Thus, the BBC/OU set up the terms for engagement in this forum but, ultimately, it was the forum's participants who would decide the nature of the engagement that occurred.

Authority, expertise and footings

The analysis offered in this chapter takes a broadly critical discourse analytic approach (e.g. Fairclough 2003) to the participants' linguistic construction of authority and (types of) expertise. This involves issues of turn-taking and turn structure, the evidencing of claims and shifts in what Goffman (1981) terms 'footings'.

These posts constitute an asynchronous 'conversation' between the contributors on individual threads. Therefore, the functions of particular turns and the relationships between them deserve consideration. The exchange structure model (Sinclair and Coulthard 1975) enables an analysis of the roles that a particular person takes within a conversation. In their original data, teachers had the role of initiating exchanges and also giving feedback (evaluation) on the pupils' responses; assuming such a stance of evaluation positions a social actor as taking up an authoritative role. Looking more carefully at relationships *between* turns, the notion of preferred and dispreferred responses from conversation analysis (Pomerantz 1984; Schegloff 1988) also gives an insight into the degree of authority a particular participant is assuming. Specific features of turn construction such as hesitation phenomena, turn-initial discourse markers like *well*, non-minimal turns at talk and accounts indicate a speaker (or writer) is marking their response as dispreferred in some way. Hutchby and Wooffitt (1998: 45) summarize this succinctly: 'preferred actions are characteristically performed straightforwardly and without delay, while dispreferred actions are delayed, qualified and accounted for.' Participants assuming an authoritative stance are unlikely to feel the need to indicate a response as being dispreferred. In addition, first pair parts can be authoritatively structured to heavily predict a specific response.

Where contributors do present an authoritative stance through their linguistic choices, their attempts to evidence this authority should be analysed. Claims to knowledge would be one way of achieving this, for example, invoking knowledge of linguistics in order to support a statement about language issues or giving information about family and location in order to give authority to a post about dialect lexis. In the former case, Matoesian (1999) argues that we are calling on a dominant academic discourse, and making that the principal (Goffman 1981) of our text.

Finally, certain claims to knowledge or choice of discursive moves can also indicate (shifts in) particular types of footings (Goffman 1981). The concept of footing is a tool for investigating the way in which we can manage subtle changes in our presentation of social identities through linguistic cues in ongoing talk. Matoesian (1999: 493) explains footing as 'the metapragmatic processes through which speakers/hearers position themselves relative to one another and to their utterances in the framing of experience; a shift in footing transforms our interpretive frame for the embedded action.' In the analysis to follow, I argue that there are different types of expertise and also different types of social roles (such as teacher, researcher) which interact with them. This interplay can be identified through such macro-level indicators as choices of discursive moves down to micro-level selections of particular lexical items or pronoun choice.

The OU expert's contributions

Across her postings, DH uses several different footings as teacher, dialect speaker and 'expert'. In the first of these roles, she opens several threads, explicitly encouraging contributions from others:

Extract 1[3]

So is it the media?

Some of the speakers in Wednesday's 'word4word' programme were convinced that the media have a big responsibility for changes to today's English language, because we pick up expressions and pronunciations from their example. Other speakers were equally convinced that the media follow existing trends and tendencies that English speakers are already using anyway. So do the media influence the way we speak - has any reader of this forum found evidence on either side?

The key feature that marks this as 'teacher talk' is the non-evaluative opening turn. DH sets out the two sides of the argument using neutral terms of address for each imagined group (*some speakers; other speakers*) and the same impartial reporting verb in the passive (*were convinced*) for both. She also draws on *Word4Word* (BBC Radio 4's series about language aired as part of the *BBC Voices* project) as the basis for her invitation to debate, thus both reinforcing the link between the open2.net forum and the project, and reiterating the educational frame for this discursive space. The post ends with an open question but asks the potential participants to provide evidence for their views: a very teacherly requirement – one cannot just have opinions. It is also a 'delayed knower' question (Berry 1981), typical of teaching exchanges – its intent is not to elicit information unknown to the author but rather to elicit (and evaluate) the knowledge of others. So, while the content of this post is apparently quite neutral, DH is positioning herself as someone with the right to evaluate others' contributions.

DH also takes on this authoritative role of evaluation by producing Feedback moves as well as the Initiate move (Sinclair and Coulthard 1975) in the example above:

Extract 2

Re: Global English

Richard's suggestion is an interesting one. It has been made before - there was, for instance the prize left by the author George Bernard Shaw for the creation of a new alphabet which would represent English phonetically. [...] Anyone interested in reading about earlier attempts at spelling reform in English will find a useful chapter in one of the books on the 'word4word' reading list, 'English: history, diversity and change' edited by Graddol, Leith and Swann, chapter 2. One of the main problems with introducing a new system is the complexity of the symbolic system required; there's also a great deal invested in the use of the present system, both financially and in other senses, so there would be considerable opposition.

> The second message also raises a significant point - which English would be chosen to have its pronunciation phonetically represented: British, American, Australian or that of any of the other countries where English is a first language? There's the further issue of differences in pronunciation within varieties, which I'm sure future 'word4word' programmes will take up. If, for instance, Standard (southern) British English was chosen, it would not represent the speech of a Northern or Scottish child.
>
> Pronunciation also changes over time, so would a phonetic spelling need regular updates to keep in touch with it? What do others think - is it time to make the spelling of English phonetic, and is it feasible?
>
> Diana

There is explicit judgement here, although DH is careful to address negative aspects of her assessment to the idea rather than the person presenting it. She moves from categorising 'Richard's suggestion' as 'an interesting one' to seeing it as having 'problems'. This delicate handling is particularly relevant given DH's use of addressivity (Herring 2001): naming the original contributor and thus 'addressing' the response to them. She also makes a more positive evaluation of another participant's contribution. Thus DH takes on an authoritative stance by taking the role of rapporteur: both summarising and assessing the contributions of others.

There are also other indicators of an educational footing. DH directs 'anyone interested' to an OU textbook, which is on the *Word4Word* reading list (whose existence further substantiates the academic frame for that series). She also lays claim to authoritative knowledge about pronunciation by the use of categorical assertion in her statements about linguistic issues involved in alphabets based on phonetic or phonemic principles. Again, this post finishes with an invitation for further contributions. This too is clearly indexed as a delayed knower question since it follows DH's explicit demonstration of her prior knowledge in this area. Although the thread does continue, no contributors engage with DH's question.

Within her postings, DH does present linguistics as having an authoritative stance on matters of language, although it is questionable how far she explicitly aligns herself with this. It would be clear to other linguists that her posts are steeped in the ideologies of the descriptive linguistics tradition, but it seems doubtful that a non-linguist would necessarily recognize DH's positioning in this way: linguistics itself is rarely mentioned, its implicit role has to be understood by the reader (the example below is atypical in this respect). Thus it is not self-evident that DH's presentation of authoritative knowledge would be seen as a presentation of authoritative *linguistic* knowledge. It also fails to take advantage of the opportunity to raise the profile of linguistics as an area of academic study.

Extract 3

Re: Words

The first aim of speech and writing is, of course, to communicate, so if this can be achieved that's what matters. Modern studies in linguistics tend to concentrate on this, and on appropriateness to context, rather than on 'good/bad' or 'right/wrong' [explanation deleted]. Linguists today would say that local or group dialects don't really have defective grammar if they are different from the standard form - they have equally coherent and full systems e.g. of verb forms, even if they're not the one used in Standard English. For example [example deleted].

DH claims authoritative knowledge of 'Modern studies in linguistics' and 'Linguists today' although it is interesting that in both cases she uses epistemic modality to hedge the *subject's* commitment to these standard tenets of descriptive linguistics. Again, she uses quite extensive explanation (relative to other postings) in making her points. These illustrations mark a shift from invoking the principal (Goffman 1981) of hegemonic linguistic knowledge to herself as the source of these particular examples (and therefore herself as principal). This marks a shift in footing from 'an expert on linguistics' to (linguistics) teacher. To make such a distinction may seem odd to the likely audience of this chapter – most of us are researchers (and thus 'experts' at 'doing' linguistics) as well as teachers. However, it is not so clear that the general public equate these two roles. For example, those who know I teach at a university (including my students, their parents, my neighbours and acquaintances) assume that once teaching is finished, I am then on holiday until the next academic year: there is no sense that I do anything *other* than teaching. In other words, university teaching is likened to (a particular view of) school teaching and this hegemonic view seems resistant to repeated explanations. Wry smiles from colleagues suggest my experience is far from unique. This raises interesting questions about what different types of 'expertise' are recognised and how these are evaluated. The author of the following contribution starts with a number of questions about dialect lexis, but his last paragraph gives an instructive insight into one person's view of the relationship between teaching and expertise.

Extract 4

Raunging

Has anyone heard of the verb "to raunge". I am not sure of the spelling but my gran used the word which meant to "writhe/move around" as in "stop raunging about", or keep still. [further dialect lexis query deleted]

Also, I "studied" A level English Language in the 80's and the view held by our teacher was that language is democratic - whatever the majority

> says, goes - which is an interesting point of view, although a bit confusing at a time when I was studying French and German and the hard and fast rules of language acquisition was a real help. My English teacher's view was that everyone should be able to talk and write the way they want, which to an extent I agree with, however, I think as far as possible people should have the ability to understand what the "correct" version is in terms of grammar, spelling etc, but of course should be able to speak and write as they see fit.

This participant clearly assigns the information taught to him as merely 'the view held by my teacher': at no point is it suggested that this view might be a presentation based on academic expertise. It is assessed as 'interesting' but 'a little confusing' – and we have seen in Extract 2 above how *interesting* can be used to indicate a negative appraisal via a seemingly positive term. The use of scare quotes on 'studied' are also worth noting: is this a reflection on his own approach to learning whilst in this period of his schooling, or is it his assessment of the value in the material he was taught? The apparently negative comments that follow would not rule out the latter interpretation.

This should be put into the context of the well-known adage, 'Those that can, do; those that can't, teach.'[4] Its existence not only reinforces the dichotomy between (university) teaching and researching ('doing') – the two are apparently not compatible – but also positions teachers as not having the authority of 'doers' and therefore not having true expertise. Practice is almost always elevated over theory. Therefore, using discursive constructions that present oneself as a teacher (which is only a claim to outsider knowledge) may conflict with the presentation of oneself as an expert (a claim to insider knowledge).

In the case of this forum, we do not see DH present herself explicitly as having insider knowledge, as being a 'linguistics expert'. She presents authoritative knowledge on linguistics (albeit often rather implicitly), an 'expert on linguistics', but at no point does she identify herself as one of these 'linguists today' either by naming herself as a linguist or by aligning herself with that group by using *we* or other forms of the first person plural pronoun. She employs *we* quite frequently but this is almost always inclusive *we* – to include herself and an 'imagined community' (Anderson 1983) of (British English) speakers – as in Extract 1 above. The only exceptions to this are when she uses exclusive *we* to refer to her community of dialect speakers or her family (see below).

By using inclusive *we* in this way, DH largely aligns herself with the public at large rather than linguistics as a subject or linguistics experts. Certainly, her potential identity as 'expert' is never taken up or ratified by other posters on the forum. It is only as a dialect speaker that she gets such recognition.

Extract 5

Re: Brew

There are about nine different expressions for preparing tea, depending what part of the country you come from. I grew up with 'mashing' tea (Notts/Lincs border) and usually still do; we also said 'leave it to mash' if anyone tried to pour a cup before the tea had stood for a few minutes. [example deleted].

Diana Honeybone (OU)

Re: Brew

Ah, a local (well, near enough!). Ayup, duck!

Shaker

Here, DH evidences her authority to pronounce on a dialect term by invoking lived experience in a particular area. This practical expertise is implicitly accepted by Shaker through the lack of challenge to the suggested term and their use of more regional lexis as an act of identity (Le Page and Tabouret-Keller 1985) to reiterate their own authenticity (and thus authority) to ratify DH's contribution. Here, authenticity can index authority because the authors of these posts have the right to reentextualize and comment on their own usage (Jaffe 2011, this volume; Kelly-Holmes and Milani 2011).

Typical forum contributions

One of the most immediately noticeable contrasts between DH's posts and those of other forum participants is the way in which negative evaluation is handled. Firstly, posters who disagree with each other make no attempt to save each other's faces by focusing criticism on the idea rather than the person. Secondly, disagreements tend to be very direct.

Extract 6

Re: Should we let dialects die?

I just wish that everyone would speak the Queen's English and nothing else, if they are going to speak English. Some of the things that some people speak in the UK should not be called English at all.

Avoura

Re: Should we let dialects die?

Avoura, even the Queen doesn't speak the Queen's English today! If you listen to recordings from the forties or fifties, she -- and the rest of the upper crust -- spoke with a different accent from today's.

Kasper

Kasper's negative evaluation is very direct; Avoura is addressed explicitly, so there is little question of whose ideas are being criticized. There is also no attempt to mark this turn as a dispreferred response (Pomerantz 1984). The post starts with a direct disagreement and it is brief with no use of hedging devices like epistemic modality to act as a softener. Arguably, the use of the exclamation mark acts as an upgrader (Blum-Kulka *et al.* 1989) to emphasize the challenge. This is quite different to DH's post above (Extract 2) where the negative evaluation is downplayed and is also focused on the problematic idea rather than its author. In another post from DH discussed below (Extract 11), no individual posters are picked out and the evaluation from DH concentrates on the explanation of why the issue is problematic rather than focusing on the disagreement *per se*. Indeed, DH sometimes takes the ultimate indirectness option of *opting out* (Brown and Levinson 1987) such as in one thread where her initial posting only gained one very problematic response: here, it would have been all too obvious to whom her evaluations were addressed.

These more direct disagreements are much more common in the open2. net forum than the type of hedged evaluations that DH uses. A more extended instance of this can be seen in the following five consecutive posts from the beginning of a thread. The first post sets out a non-technical description of Welsh pronunciation intended for English speakers trying to pronounce Welsh place names. This debate between (largely) these three posters eventually resulted in more than 40 posts.

Extract 7

How not to sound ridiculous in Wales

Welsh has no dipthongs. So no Y in cake. Which is why a lot of the Clofftafodau[5] mistake the Welsh accent for Geordie.

The other rules are mainly alphabetical.

No V - sub 'f' as in 'Felin' or voice.

F = ff as in Ffairfach or fornicate.

No K, all 'k' sounds are covered by 'c'. S really means s.

You can't pronounce the 'ch' if you are too posh to clear your throat in public. Bwlch-y-Gwynt.

'Y' on its own is generally '..uuh' alongside a 'w' it is an 'i' sound as in wind. Or Gwynt. [further explanation of Welsh pronunciation omitted]

Little Richardjohn[6]

Re: How not to sound ridiculous in Wales

No dipthongs, what about ei?

Weaselbooks

Re: How not to sound ridiculous in Wales

that is two syllables.

Little Richardjohn

Re: How not to sound ridiculous in Wales

Welsh has no dipthongs.
sorry, but simply not true. i think you may be using a non-standard definition of the term diphthong - see here:
http://en.wikipedia.org/wiki/Diphthong
-aw- in iawn, and -oe- in noeth are certainly diphthongs for example. each vowel affects the pronunciation of the other, they cannot be regarded as two entirely separate sounds. [further explanation omitted]

Iestyn

Re: How not to sound ridiculous in Wales

I think if I were to turn 'ei' into two separate syllables, I would sound ridiculous in Wales.

Weaselbooks

The exchanges between Little Richardjohn and Weaselbooks constitute explicit challenges with no hedging whatsoever – the use of *think* and the conditional structure in the last post indexes irony rather than uncertainty. While Iestyn uses the epistemic modals *think* and *may*, the softening effect of this is offset somewhat by the blatant challenge that starts the post and the categorical assertions that follow. These posts set the tone for the remainder of the thread and are indicative of the kinds of challenges that occur throughout the forum.

The second key difference between DH's posts and the forum at large is in the way threads are started. In her six thread-opening posts, DH asks *questions*. These might be delayed knower questions, as in Extract 1 above, but they do not prejudge the answer. In other initial posts, the majority of *questions* that are asked relate to requests for information about dialect words or usage as in Extract 4 above.

If one excludes DH's posts, one from the open2.net moderator (which is similar in construction), the questions about dialect lexis and the four from self-identified students (including a non-native speaker asking about pronunciation), then only about 18 thread openers ask 'real' questions. And a number of these are rather broad or are looking for multiple views rather than the statement of an 'expert':

Extracts 8–9

Irish Influences on Language

Has the Irish 'English' affected the English language?

'bbc' english

when the bbc started the first dialect used was very 'proper', as such this was the marker for 'bbc' english. with the rapid expansion of the bbc, i would be interested to find out what the most popular dialect is on tv. would you rather hear a geordie or scouser reading the news? would a scots accent be preferred when watching the weather? or would a somerset dialect be good for a children's programme? any other dialects that are not represented on the bbc?

The largest category of posts (around 30 out of 90 threads) make opinion-based statements about language mainly in the complaint tradition (Aitchison 1997; Cameron 1995; Johnson 2001). It is evident from the way these posts are structured that their authors are seeking confirmation of their views, not a debate. They heavily predict the preferred response of agreement (Schegloff 1988).

Extract 10

'bought'

I can't get anyone to acknowledge that 'bought' is now almost invariably used when 'brought' is correct. E.g.: 'He was "bought" up in …' During one 'Flog It' programme an expert asked a woman who'd brought some silver items to be auctioned: 'Have you bought (sic) the family silver?' Are we really ready to accept that there's no difference between the past tense of 'to buy' and that of 'to bring'?

Almost as bad is the overuse of 'fantastic'!

This post starts with a presupposition triggered by the factive verb *acknowledge*. By using this kind of construction, not only is the poster discouraging disagreement but also they are making it structurally difficult for a respondent to do so. The yes–no question also draws on a 'common sense' ideology that loss of a linguistic distinction is bad, thus predicting a negative response. This prescriptivist view ignores the frequency with which homonymy occurs in the English language and the ongoing processes of semantic and phonological change that have affected the set of homonymous pairs throughout its history. Of the 11 posts that follow, all but one agree with the hegemonic prescriptive view, some introducing other 'pet hates' such as *could of* instead of *could have*. The last post in the thread – temporally close to the previous ones – goes against this view; it is from DH and presents a more descriptive perspective, as one might expect. It is interesting because of the effect it seems to have on the ongoing debate.

Extract 11

Re: 'bought'

The problem with this expression is that, while both parts of it are verbal: 'could have', no-one pronounces it in this way, with heavy stress on 'have', in normal English speech, whatever their language background. Listen to public speakers, announcers, politicians etc. It is usually pronounced as 'could've'. English is full of verb-contractions like 'we'll' and 'can't', and so it's easy to mistake it for 'could of' as it sounds very similar. In writing, it's normal to spell it 'could have', although if you're writing dialogue in a story or play and want to reproduce your character's manner of speech, writers sometimes use 'could've'.

Like many of DH's other posts, this uses a lot of categorical assertion and it even has a bald on-record order (Brown and Levinson 1987) 'Listen …'; it certainly does not lack linguistic claims to authority. It may be that the lack of questions (even ones asking for confirmation) deter other responses. However, it seems more likely that this is just not what these posters want to hear: they were engaged in the mutual construction of a particular ideological view which DH's post then disrupted. Certainly, there is no engagement with or acceptance of the (authoritative) view presented. Either way, DH's post marks the end of the thread.

A similar pattern of an academic effectively closing the discussion occurs with a thread about the linguistic roots of Basque. In this case, the opening post asks about the validity of the claim that Basque is not related to any known language. This is a *bona fide* question, although there is also a statement of the poster's opinion, too: 'Is this true? If so, how can that be possible? Surely all languages mix with others at some point?' In the discussion that follows, there is broad agreement with the initial claim with some suggestions of how this came about. The following post from Nick P – a prodigious poster across the *Voices* forums – gives a flavour of this discussion:

Extract 12

Re: Basque - unique language?

There are other more widely spoken languages where no definite link has been proved with any other, or is a matter for debate. Japanese and Korean for example.

The bigger and more intriguing question is why there are so many groups of unrelated languages. Or perhaps there is an underlying relationship between them all.

This could account for what linguists call the universal grammar, deep within all languages, and that allows us to translate between them with a fair degree of accuracy. Unless that is the language instinct as proposed by Pinker and others, is so basic to the human psyche that we will spontaneously develop a language if we need to.

This could mean for example that if when groups of early humans spread around the world, and they did so before developing the capacity for speech, then obviously when did language come along it would have happened in isolated and unrelated pockets. Some of these would have developed and spread into major families- Indo-European, Semetic etc etc, while some would have remained isolated and unique such as Basque.

There's really no way of knowing- as they say languages don't leave fossils!

Nick P

It is interesting at this point to compare Nick P's presentation of himself as an expert with that of DH. It is immediately clear that he lays claim to authoritative knowledge about language, as indexed by the categorical assertions in his first paragraph. He goes on to legitimate this stance by rather vague reference to linguistic theory (*universal grammar*, *language instinct*) and the invoking of a 'famous name' (*Pinker*). And on this basis, he is prepared to offer a hypothesis about the origin of language and how different language families came into existence. His last sentence also implies his hypothesis is unchallengeable: it isn't testable because we can never know. Even this is legitimated by invoking *they* – calling into existence a group knowledgeable about language with whom he agrees. In this way, he explicitly both claims linguistic knowledge and aligns himself with linguistics as a subject (unlike DH). He also presents himself as a linguistic expert (not just an expert *on* linguistics) by offering his own analysis: he is 'doing' linguistics not just reporting on others' doing.

Having positioned himself as a linguistics expert (a footing that he repeats in many of his posts), he also avoids using discursive moves associated with more educational footings: summarising others' points, asking readers to engage in learning tasks, asking prompt questions or directing readers to academic texts. All of these are seen in DH's posts (as illustrated in this chapter's examples) as she attempts to engage with readers in the forum. It is interesting to note that Nick P's postings are taken up by other participants far more frequently than DH's.

However, despite Nick P's presentation of himself as an expert, there are issues with the validity of the claims he makes both in this and other posts (in this thread and elsewhere). There are also some similarly dubious assertions made by other contributors to the thread, which prompts a response from another UK academic, Dominic Watt.[7]

Extract 13

Re: Basque - unique language?

A lot of misinformation about Basque flies back and forward - some of the postings here being prime examples - so if you're looking for reliable answers from a properly researched source on the topic take a look at Larry Trask's 'History of Basque' (1997, Routledge). It's mostly pretty technical on the linguistic side, and at 450 pages it's not exactly light reading, but the first 80 pages concentrate on the history of the language and its genetic relationships with neighbouring (and not-so-neighbouring) languages.

Dominic Watt

Like DH's post, there is no discursive space allowed for alternative analyses. Some of the previous postings are categorized as 'misinformation'. The scientific discipline of linguistics is presented as 'reliable' and 'properly researched' through the example of Trask's book and there is an implicit opposition created between this and the forum postings (Jeffries 2010). Although this post displays less hedging than a number of DH's, Dominic Watt is still careful not to pick out the posts of particular people as being 'misinformation' – there are no direct challenges. He also takes up the position of expert on linguistics by directing readers to a particular academic source (and evaluating that, too). He thus positions readers as 'students' who are required to improve their knowledge by acting on the expert's instructions.

Of course, one could argue that this is what 'asking an expert' is all about: experts are expected to know *the* answer – the hegemonic view of science is that such right answers exist. Once this is provided, the possibility of either discussing the merits of other competing 'right' answers (e.g. Basque thread) or continuing to jointly construct a competing language ideology (e.g. bought/brought thread) is removed. This seems to create a conflict at the heart of this forum: if the expert role is accepted by the other forum participants then open discussion/debate is effectively curtailed. And in this forum, it is far from clear that this is what the participants want. The fact that the majority of non-dialect based threads seek validation of the initial poster's opinions (rather than asking a question, for example) suggests that the poster is already satisfied with their own expertise.

If these forum participants are not really seeking answers from a 'linguistic expert', what is their motive for posting on open2.net? Another posting from Nick P may provide some insight:

Extract 14

The Dead and the Barely Living - Cornish and Irish

This posting is to follow up comments on messages I posted on the "Your Voice- Language Ecology" page.

1)- Cornish- you may be perfectly right B Sims, and I may have my facts wrong. [discussion omitted]

2) Paul from Dun Given
The shrinking of the "traditional strongholds"- i.e. where Irish is still used as a first language is exactly my point, because this is what will ensure its survival. People learning Irish in evening classes in America, Australia or Finland will not do this.

Right guys- let's start the debate!!!

Nick P

It is not clear why Nick P attempted to shift an ongoing debate from one of the discussion boards on *BBC Voices* to the open2.net site. Nor was it successful, even though he posted to the original discussion board to signal his intention. However, it is clear that in doing this he was not seeking 'expert' input. Rather, he wanted to be part of a debate. Of course, this is the express view of only one participant but does seem to fit with the two key features of postings focused on here: the lack of a desire to ask questions (other than about dialect lexis) and the willingness to engage in direct challenges. Indeed, it seems that some posters find entertainment value in these types of online confrontations.

Towards the end of the thread on Welsh pronunciation (Extract 7) – a heated debate that led to the explicit involvement of the forum moderator – a spectator to the event posted their evaluation of the thread:

Extract 15

Re: How not to sound ridiculous in Wales

I was looking for the welsh word for 'cake' funnily enough in an attempt to send some sort of funny message in welsh to my friends who live in maesteg in a majorie doors fat fighters style, you know the little britain character?...well anyway i was doing that and came across this absolute bezerk trail.

I've read it both for comedy value at the amazing intelligent bitching that grown men fail to avoid when appearing to have an intellectual debate (it's all about pride:-) - which was brilliant by the way, i personally think the original author of the trail has left with their tail between legs, but was too proud to admit defeat ooh about 5 or 6 messages in and in doing so has made for a brilliant read - GENIUS!

I also read the trail objectively as someone who was genuinely trying to learn a new word in a new language and have to say the original author of the trail's messages were utterly useless and confusing and much better explained by, excuse the spelling 'Iestyn' who looked at the teaching from a learners perspective, not a teacher's, tip of the cap to you my learned friend!

Thank you all though for a brilliant read

It is likely that this anonymous poster came across this 38-post thread when searching for a particular piece of information. However, what kept them reading was largely the spectacle of a verbal sparring match conducted through the medium of an asynchronous computer-mediated 'conversation': it was certainly this that prompted their post. This is a salutary reminder that on the web – as with any kind of media – you are competing not just to gain but also retain the attention of your audience. Laforest's (1999: 278) comment relates to the difficulty in making oneself heard in offline debates about language but I believe the point still holds:

> In the media world, the rules of debate are not the ones we're used to. You are often given very little time to speak, too little to make an argument. If you are not the host's only guest, the struggle to get a word in edgewise can be fierce; this is something unthinkable in a classroom, where the teacher is lord and master. But above all, TV has to entertain. The winner of a TV debate is the one who knows how to be melodramatic, make people laugh or cry; it's a game that academics, with nothing but their theses, arguments and counterarguments to draw upon, are usually not very good at.

open2.net isn't a classroom: the users will reframe its purpose as they see fit, within the constraints of what the host site allows. The moderation on the forum was light, only editing posts that broke explicit rules on courtesy to others, used another language or posted contact details. Beyond that, the shaping of the forum was up to its participants, and they weren't 'asking (academic) experts'.

Discussion

What emerges from this extended analysis is both the difficulties involved in constructing a successful expert identity in this kind of open-access forum and also the tensions around what constitutes expertise. This is particularly delicate for a subject like linguistics, which is little-known outside academia and whose authoritative status is subject to challenge (Johnson 2001; Laforest 1999).

Linguistics as an academic subject has a relatively low profile within the forum, as indicated by the infrequency of tokens like *linguistic(s)* and *linguist* in the corpus (fewer than 10). Concepts and ideas from linguistics are present but they often aren't identified as such: one would already need to know about the subject to recognise its influence on the content. Indeed, explicit reference to *linguists/linguistics* was rare even in DH's posts. So, even though knowledge from linguistics was often constructed as being authoritative, the basis for that authority was not necessarily recognisable. This would seem to be a missed opportunity given that most academic linguists are well aware that such knowledge cannot be taken for granted – top of the FAQs in/about my professional life would certainly be 'What is linguistics?'. It is the lack of recognition of linguistics as an academic subject and the scope of it as a discipline which immediately limits the possibilities for engagement with the community: we have few foundations to build on.

Indeed, the majority of debate topics fall within the two areas of dialect lexis and issues of 'correctness' in writing and speech (particularly in relation to perceived change). While one of the main focuses of the *BBC Voices* project has been regional variation in language across the UK, the *Voices* website itself also contains information and questions about a myriad other linguistic topics. Yet this was not evident in the open2.net forum: these areas largely seemed to mark the legitimate scope for language study for these participants. Milroy (2001: 621) also identifies the same two areas as being the main focus of non-linguists' interests in language:

> ... the popular view is that only the standard language ... has regular structure. Variant forms don't have regular structure, and they don't count anyway, even though they may be quaint and interesting.

This illustrates the dual focus across most of the open2.net language debates: ideologies of correctness alongside a huge interest in regional variation. And while I do not wish to categorize linguistic variation as merely 'quaint and interesting', Milroy's phrasing usefully indicates that engagement in such topics is considered 'safe' – in comparison to the discursive struggle surrounding ideologies of correctness. One could also add that dialect lexis is an area that is open to claims of authority, given appropriate evidence of location and/or upbringing.

There were also a large number of contributors who were sufficiently confident of their own expertise on language to post authoritative statements on the rights and wrongs of linguistic issues: they saw no elevated role for an academic discipline about language. These forum participants were seeking to have their language ideologies confirmed by others, not to be challenged on what they viewed as self-evident truths. Such contributors drew on their lived experience of language: what they were taught, changes in pronunciation or lexis they have experienced, empirical conclusions they have drawn and so forth. Their claim to authoritative knowledge is based on lived experience within a culture and its rationalisation (Barton 1996; Laforest 1999). Johnson (2001) and Milroy (2001) both point out that such actions are hardly surprising – the difficulty of separating language as an object of scientific study from the cultural, social and emotional values with which it is imbued cannot be overstated. Indeed, how many of 'us linguists' would admit (not so) secretly to, say, prescriptivist ideologies about the use of the semi-colon, people writing *could of* rather than *could've*, Americanized spellings, emotional attachments to or dislikes of particular languages, linguistic varieties or accents, etc. It is probably not surprising, therefore, that such contributors on open2.net did not welcome challenges to their own expertise and were likely to reject or just ignore the conflicting claims to expertise made by others.

This brings us to the notion of expertise and its subtypes. I have argued above that when participants construct themselves as 'experts' in an academic subject, they have to contend with indexing expertise in particular *roles* as well as in *subject knowledge,* and with the fact that these two aspects interact. So, an individual can present themselves as having authoritative knowledge about linguistics, being an 'expert *on*' the subject ('knowing'), which can be distinguished from someone who constructs themself as a 'linguistics expert': a person who is apparently engaged in the *production* of linguistics knowledge ('doing'). While being accepted as a 'linguistic expert' also guarantees the assumption of authoritative subject knowledge, the reverse does not apply. This is further complicated by the way in which the cultural role of 'teacher' seems to interact with this relationship between *knowing* and *doing*. Being identified as a 'teacher' seems to block the possibility that one is also involved in 'doing' as well as 'knowing'; this persistent belief seems to apply as much to those involved in tertiary education as to those employed in the school sector. There are also questions raised about the validity of teachers' claims to authoritative knowledge and their ability to convey this effectively to their students (Extracts 4 and 15, above).

Johnson (2001) also comments on this generally negative evaluation of those who work within education: it is another field where potentially 'everyone is an expert' (particularly with respect to teaching methodologies). This cultural perspective on teaching and teachers may explain why discursive moves that apparently index an educational footing do not gain much response. Presenting an expert identity of 'teacher' does not seem to construct an authoritative identity that is acceptable within this discursive space. Education does not appear to be the motivation for these forum participants.

This seems to be somewhat of a paradox given the location and the way in which the open2.net forum is framed. The partner institutions involved both have an explicit educational remit and the forum itself is accessed by the hyperlink 'Ask an expert'.

However, that is probably the lesson of web 2.0 content: it has opened up exciting new possibilities in terms of user-to-document interactivity (McMillan 2002), and thus more opportunities for engagement with the public, but this does not guarantee that potential participants will take up the frame that is offered: you can invoke a particular kind of 'public' (Gal and Woolard 2001) but you can't make it contribute to your forum. It has to be remembered that this type of open-access forum is not the same as a discussion board within the context of a virtual learning environment associated with a particular course. In the latter, the educational frame has been explicitly accepted by the students and the role of teacher has undisputed authoritative status; in the former, this is determined by all the participants.

We cannot know these individuals' motivations for browsing and/or contributing to the open2.net forum but, for most, some form of 'infotainment' is likely to have been the goal: it is a leisure activity. We have seen in extracts above some people's desire to share information and also evidence of others' activity in searching for information. There has also been the desire to contribute to debates or to watch the verbal sparring of others. What was not in evidence was an explicit desire to be *taught*.

In conclusion, then, what lessons does this have for linguists trying to navigate the expert–lay divide? The first is that there are no easy answers to this issue: Diana Honeybone had an unenviable task in what was a relatively new technology in 2005 but there are equally no magic bullets in 2013, either. What we can infer is that trying to engage with the public within a teacher–student frame is unlikely to be successful. Both Johnson (2001) and Milroy (2001) argue that we need to work *with* the community more and show more awareness and understanding of the reasons for the language ideologies that they hold rather than trying to impose 'linguistic truths'. However, this does not solve the problem of the generally low profile that linguistics has in the community, and that is perhaps our first challenge. In Irwin and Wynne's (1996) discussion of the public understanding of science, they seemed to be able to take for granted that the existence and scope of the disciplines under question were recognised by the public, even if their authority was not. Maybe we need to start with 'This is what linguists do' rather than 'This is what linguists say'.

Notes

1 The key difference was the lack of delay in postings becoming visible as moderation occurred *after* material went on site rather than as a precursor to its appearance.
2 The Reith lectures, 1996. Later published as Aitchison (1997).
3 Examples are reproduced exactly with any spelling errors intact. Contributors do not always sign off with a name because this is already indicated in the post's automatic header. All forum threads are available at: http://www.open.edu/openlearn/history-the-arts/culture/english-language/words-language-points-debate.
4 Often seen as a misquotation of 'He who can, does. He who cannot, teaches.' George Bernard Shaw in *Man and Superman (1903) 'Maxims for Revolutionists', maxim 36.*
5 *Clofftafodau* literally translates as 'cripple-tongued' but seems to be used here as a particularly derogatory way of referring to those non-Welsh speakers who are seen as clueless about Welsh pronunciation.
6 This may be the well-known tabloid columnist Richard Littlejohn but this is impossible to verify.
7 Dominic Watt was not identified as a linguistics expert either by affiliation (DH is clearly associated with the OU) or by himself. However, he does clearly position himself as an academic expert here.

References

Aitchison, J. (1997) *The Language Web: The power and problem of words*, Cambridge: Cambridge University Press.
Anderson, B. (1983) *Imagined Communities: Reflections on the origin and spread of nationalism*. London: Verso.
Barton, E. (1996) 'Negotiating expertise in discourses of disability', *Text*, 16(3): 299–322.

Berry, M. (1981) 'Systemic linguistics and discourse analysis: A multi-layered approach to exchange structure', in M. Coulthard and M. Montgomery (eds) *Studies in Discourse Analysis*, London: Routledge and Kegan Paul.

Blum-Kulka, S., House, J. and Kasper, G. (eds) (1989) *Cross-cultural Pragmatics: Requests and apologies,* Norwood, NJ: Ablex.

Brown, P. and Levinson, S. (1987) *Politeness: Some universals in language usage*, Cambridge, Cambridge University Press.

Cameron, D. (1995) *Verbal Hygiene*, London: Routledge.

Fairclough, N. (2003) *Analyzing Discourse: Textual analysis for social research*, London: Routledge.

Gal, S. and Woolard, K. (2001) 'Constructing languages and publics: authority and representation', in S. Gal and K. Woolard (eds) *Languages and Publics: The making of authority*, Manchester: St. Jerome Press.

Goffman, E. (1974) *Frame Analysis: An essay on the organization of experience*, New York: Harper and Row.

Goffman, E. (1981) *Forms of Talk*, Oxford: Blackwell.

Heller, M. (1999) 'Ebonics, language revival, la qualité de la langue and more: what do we have to say about the language debates of our time?', *Journal of Sociolinguistics*, 3(2): 260–266.

Herring, S. (2001) 'Computer-mediated discourse', in D. Schiffrin, D. Tannen and H.E. Hamilton (eds) *The Handbook of Discourse Analysis*, Oxford: Blackwell.

Hutchby, I. and Wooffitt, R. (1998) *Conversation Analysis: Principles, practices and applications*, Cambridge: Polity Press.

Irwin, A. and Wynne, B. (eds) (1996) *Misunderstanding Science? The public reconstruction of science and technology*, Cambridge: Cambridge University Press.

Jaffe, A. (2011) 'Sociolinguistic diversity in mainstream media: Authenticity, authority and processes of mediation and mediatization', *Journal of Language and Politics* 10(4): 562–586.

Jeffries, L. (2010) *Opposition in Discourse: The construction of oppositional meaning*, London: Continuum.

Johnson, Sally (2001) 'Who's misunderstanding whom? Sociolinguistics, public debate and the media', *Journal of Sociolinguistics* 5(4): 591–610.

Kelly-Holmes, H. and Milani, T.M. (2011) 'Introduction: thematising multilingualism in the media', *Journal of Language and Politics* 10(4): 467–489.

Laforest, M. (1999) 'Can a sociolinguist venture outside the university?' *Journal of Sociolinguistics* 3(2): 276–281.

Le Page, R.B. and Tabouret-Keller, A. (1985) *Acts of Identity: Creole-based approaches to language and ethnicity*, Cambridge: Cambridge University Press.

Matoesian, G.M. (1999) 'The grammaticalization of participant roles in the constitution of expert identity', *Language in Society*, 28(4): 491–521.

McMillan, S.J. (2002) 'Exploring models of interactivity from multiple research traditions: users, documents, and systems', in L. Lievrouw and S. Livingston (eds) *Handbook of New Media*, London: Sage.

Milroy, J. (2001) 'Response to Sally Johnson: misunderstanding language?', *Journal of Sociolinguistics*, 5(4): 620–625.

Pomerantz, A. (1984) 'Agreeing and disagreeing with assessments: some features of preferred/dispreferred turn-shapes', in J.M. Atkinson and J. Heritage (eds) *Structures of Social Action: Studies in conversation analysis*, Cambridge: Cambridge University Press.

Rickford, J.R. (1999) 'The Ebonics controversy in my backyard: a sociolinguist's experiences and reflections', *Journal of Sociolinguistics*, 3(2): 267–275.

Schegloff, E.A. (1988) 'On an actual virtual servo-mechanism for guessing bad news: a single case conjecture', *Social Problems*, 32: 442–457.

Sinclair, J. McH. and Coulthard, M. (1975) *Towards an Analysis of Discourse: The English used by teachers and pupils*, London: Oxford University Press.

Wright, S. and Street, J. (2007) 'The European Union in cyberspace: multilingual democratic participation in a virtual public sphere', *Journal of Language and Politics*, 5(2): 251–275.

4

DIVERSE VOICES, PUBLIC BROADCASTS

Sociolinguistic representations in mainstream programming

Alexandra Jaffe

Introduction

In this chapter, I explore language ideologies and the construction and attribution of expertise related to linguistic diversity in the BBC *Voices* website and, in less detail, on the companion website to the PBS programme 'Do You Speak American?' (henceforth, DYSA). As several recent publications on language and the media have shown, representations of language and speakers in the media are inherently ideological. They both reflect and shape foundational ideas related to the nature of language, the indexical relations between forms of language and categories of speakers or other cultural or sociopolitical entities (ethnic group; nation) and the evaluation/ranking of codes and speakers (Coupland 2003; Gal and Woolard 2001; Gieve and Norton 2007; Jaffe 2000, 2007; Jaworski 2007; Jaworski *et al.* 2003; Johnson and Ensslin 2007; Kelly-Holmes and Milani 2011; Lippi-Green 1997; Milani and Johnson 2010).

The issue of expertise is central, as Milani and Johnson point out, to the functioning of language ideological processes in the media, which 'lies to a considerable extent in their practices as gatekeepers in the regimentation of "expert systems" on language-related issues'. They go on to emphasize the role media representations about language play in 'opening up discursive spaces … thereby giving a public voice to a variety of social actors who compete with each other in staking various claims regarding what counts as legitimate knowledge in the domain of language' (2010: 5). In this perspective, the multimodal documentation, narration, staging, analysis and evaluation of sociolinguistic diversity found on these websites is fundamentally heteroglossic. It is also a terrain of discursive contestation and competition: whose voice, what perspective will prevail?

The following analysis of how different participants (speakers of named accents or dialects; linguists; media professionals and website participants/ audiences) are positioned in these websites is informed by a framework I developed for the analysis of representations of different categories of speakers in the DYSA broadcast (Jaffe 2011). This framework couples a focus on the representational strategies used to construct sociolinguistic *authenticities* (Coupland 2003; see also Bucholtz 2003) vs. sociolinguistic *authorities* (Jaffe 2011) with an attention to the role of semiotic *mediation* in the *mediatization* of linguistic difference. These elements will be described in more detail below; here, I want to introduce two general principles that emerge from this analysis. The first is that authority/expertise and authenticity are often co-constructed in opposition to one another. This means that one cannot study one without studying the other; another consequence is that the representation of speakers as 'authentic' is often at the expense of their authority (Jaffe 2009a, 2011). This is because the tropes of 'spontaneity' and 'naturalness' associated with authenticity preclude those speakers' portrayal as exercising control over the mediation (interpretation/framing) of their speech. In contrast, authoritative speakers/writers take or are given agency as mediators/interpreters of their own and others' speech.

Sociolinguistic authenticities and authorities are also centrally implicated in the agendas and structure of the two programmes and their websites. One set of goals can be understood within the institutional framework and mission of PBS and the BBC, which are both non-profit, public service corporations. This implies certain relationships and commitments to the public being served. The overt agenda of both programmes is to project a (unified) national public, characterized by regional, social and linguistic diversity (see Milani *et al.* 2011). The public being served is thus the public being described. Both programmes are also oriented towards giving voice to, and legitimating speakers of the diverse dialects, accents and languages depicted in the programmes and doing the same thing with respect to their audiences and their sociolinguistic questions and attitudes. At the same time, the public service mission of the two programmes and websites is a pedagogical one that constitutes their publics as targets of ideological transformation. That is, both *Voices* and DYSA aim to *transform* circulating negative attitudes towards and characterizations of sociolinguistic diversity. This pedagogical work is accomplished by the work of experts: linguists and journalists who discursively frame how the audience is to interpret the diversity they see, hear or read. It is also accomplished by media producers, in their selection, editing and juxtaposition of both diverse 'subjects' of the programmes and the expert commentaries. Thus at some basic level, we can understand these programmes as crucially engaged in the semiotic management of authority/expertise and authenticity.

Stance

This management can be productively examined through the lens of *stance*. Stancetaking is embedded in all communicative acts in the sense that speakers/writers are obliged to take up a position with respect to a variety of stance objects. These necessarily include the form/content/truth value of speakers' own utterances, but can also include others' utterances, circulating discourses, sociolinguistic stereotypes and so forth (see Dubois 2007 and Jaffe 2009b). Stancetaking is also socially and interactionally constituted: the notion of the stance triangle (Dubois 2007) shows that all acts of positioning vis-à-vis a stance object are simultaneously acts of stance towards other subjects. Another corollary of the dialogic, social and interactional dimension of stance is that, in addition to being taken up voluntarily by speakers/writers, stances can also be offered or attributed to them.

Tension: expert alignment/disalignment with the public voice

Because stance is a position taken vis-à-vis a stance object (or objects), stancetaking and stance attribution automatically involve deixis: the *emplacement* of speakers and their interlocutors and audiences. In this light, the BBC *Voices* and DYSA projects do not just address their national publics, but also offer them *positions* from which to take up a progressive stance of appreciation of linguistic diversity. One of these positions is the everyday experience, practice or knowledge of distinct dialects or accents: a position of personal authenticity and also, authority. With respect to the pedagogical/transformational agenda mentioned above, this emplacement is the source of tension, because those everyday perspectives are at the nexus of contrasting 'takes' on diversity. On the one hand, tapping into lay knowledge connects the public with a discursive history of dialect appreciation. This is the entry point for 'expert' commentary by linguists that aligns with and builds upon non-expert knowledge and perspectives, usually in the form of 'factual' or technical elaboration related to word origins (historical linguistics), phonetics/phonology or dialectology (the encyclopaedic enumeration of data on variation). Here, the linguists' expertise is both distinct from and complementary to the lay public's, because it is centred around language as a formal system rather than language as a social, cultural and political practice. At the same time, the position offered to the public is one that is entrenched in discourses that have, as Milani *et al.* (2011) point out, 'centripetal' tendencies – the fragmentation of the nation into opposed, incommensurate, local, closed sociolinguistic enclaves. These discursive positions are also embedded in dominant language ideologies that include 'misinformation', stereotypes and attributions of stigma related to accent and dialect that the two programmes and websites are attempting to counter. The expert linguistic voice involves stance disalignment with the public; it has a corrective rather than a complementary function.

The management of this tension is thus one of the central challenges for these projects, since it has a direct bearing on both the persuasive and entertainment value of the programming and websites, which can only succeed in transforming public opinion about linguistic diversity if that public cooperates in being moved from one position to another. Thus the analysis below focuses on the stances (of authority and authenticity) that are taken up and mutually attributed to the following categories of participants on the websites: speaking subjects (sources of data), linguistic experts, people contributing to online discussion forums and the audience/public of web visitors/consumers of this assemblage of voices and representations.

The programmes

Voices was a BBC project that involved over a year of data collection. Local BBC journalists went out into their communities and recorded over 1200 people talking about themselves and talking about their language. These data were incorporated into six 45-minute radio programmes called *Word4Word* that were broadcast in 2004, as well as into programming at all of the participating BBC local radio stations. The *Voices* website was launched simultaneously with the programming, and includes links to archived *Word4Word* broadcasts, interactive features, teaching materials and links to the Open University where there is another open discussion forum and a host of additional resources (texts by linguists on various topics, detailed instructions about how to collect and interpret sociolinguistic data and suggestions for further study or reading).

'Do You Speak American?' (DYSA) was a television programme produced by PBS and first aired in three one-hour segments in 2004. It differs from the *Voices* project in the sense that it does not take on some of the crossover academic or archiving functions that *Voices* does – either in the data collection methods used, or in the archiving of the sound recordings. Like the *Voices* website, the DYSA website has robust academic content: texts on a host of topics, full transcripts of all the programmes and detailed curriculum packets. The website also includes sample clips from the broadcasts to illustrate specific themes, video interviews with featured sociolinguists and dialectologists and interactive features (online quizzes, a language map exercise and an email-based 'ask an expert' function).

In both cases, then, there is a corpus of tightly-scripted media representations of linguistic diversity that includes the voices of media professionals, linguistic experts and 'everyday people' whose speech is the object of interest. At the same time the websites offer visitors links to additional data and interactive discussion boards that are linked to, but autonomous from, the programmes.

Authority, authenticity, mediation, mediatization[1]

Sociolinguistic authenticities, in Coupland's (2003: 421) formulation, are ideological formations: assumptions about the sources of authenticity that are embedded in discourses about language. He organizes them into the following taxonomy of sources/types: (1) attested and attestable language; (2) naturally occurring language; (3) language encoding fact and truth; (4) fully owned, unmediated language; (5) language indexing personal authenticity; and (6) language indexing authentic cultural membership (see also Bucholtz 2003; Montgomery 2001; Thornborrow 2001; Van Leeuwen 2001). My companion list of *sociolinguistic authorities* (Jaffe 2009a, 2011) includes the following sources: language that (1) is indexically linked to standard or 'pure' language (in speech or writing); (2) indexes high-status genres, registers, modes and identities; (3) displays metalinguistic control (authorship, entextualization, recontextualization, etc.); (4) is represented as 'unmarked'; (5) does the work of framing and evaluation in discourse/interaction/writing; and (6) is implicated in the production of knowledge.

In the analysis below, we will consider how sociolinguistic authorities and authenticities appear, interact and are mediated semiotically in written forums available on the websites in which there is a mixture of public and academic/journalistic voices.

Here, *mediation* refers to the dialogic process of meaning making. This movement – and the semiotic work that is involved in accomplishing it – can be more or less foregrounded. When mediation is backgrounded, texts and utterances are naturalized; communication is represented as transparent and 'spontaneous'. Thus, low mediation has a conventional connection with strategies of sociolinguistic authentication. High mediation, on the other hand, draws attention to the mediator's agency; it thus has a connection to the representational construction of sociolinguistic authorities. *Mediatization* involves all the representational strategies and choices involved in the production and editing of text, image and talk in the creation of media products about language. These include processes of selection, placement, sequencing, perspective-taking, stylistic choices, choices and combinations of various semiotic modes and foregrounding and backgrounding as they relate to the depiction of speakers and their language varieties.

Discussion forums: analysis

These forums take slightly different formats in the two websites. The DYSA 'Ask an Expert' forum consists of a selection of private emails responded to by an academic, with a different academic featured each month (until September 2006). The *Voices* website has a number of forums. The main forum to be discussed below is accessed through a link from the *Voices* front page to the Open University (OU) and is entitled, 'Ask an Expert'. In this forum, the public can initiate discussion threads, and there is very limited editing or censorship. This forum has one expert (an OU faculty member) who posts threads herself and responds selectively to public postings. The public voice is also present in a much more mediated fashion in two other contexts on the site. In the first, a selection of reader comments is posted on the first page of each topic in a section of the website titled, *Your Voice*. These tend to be short individual comments rather than discussion. Secondly, some academic/journalistic texts accessible on the website embed or incorporate reader comments.

Voices *'Ask an Expert'*

On the home page of the Open University's *Word4Word* forums, the OpenLearn team endorses a particular form of reader/poster engagement in the written texts that frame these pages. The topmost rubric asks web readers, 'Have you ever wondered how and why people from around the British Isles have different ways of saying the same thing? *Word4Word* on BBC Radio 4 talks in tongues as part of a nationwide language project'. The ensuing text goes on to evoke shared experiences of 'impassioned' conversations about lexical variation and gives examples of prompts: 'What, for example', it asks readers, 'did you call those soft shoes with laces that you wore for school sports: was it pumps or plimsolls or perhaps daps or tackies? Would you be more likely to say "Have you any bairns?" or "Do you have any children?" And how would you describe "a young person in cheap, trendy clothes and jewellery?" The answer will probably depend a lot on your age and gender, as well as the place where you grew up!' These differences and similarities (presumably between speakers who share a dialect) are represented as 'defining and revealing our backgrounds and allegiances'; their discussion is 'how we say who we are'. This discussion, while presented as essentially harmonious (Milani *et al.* 2011), is also presented as requiring mediation. One mediator is the journalist Dermot Murnaghan, who is credentialed by being 'born in Ulster and raised in Yorkshire' and being 'more than familiar with two of the nation's most distinctive local variants of the language'. The other mediators are 'a panel of experts in the nuances of the English language' (http://www.open.edu/openlearn/body-mind/ou-on-the-bbc-word4word-word-about-the-series).

From August 2005 to November 2006, there were 76 topics posted in this forum, with over 700 messages. Approximately a third of the topics respond directly to the call for participation described above with dialect lexicon postings, where participants share their regional lexical particularities with the implicit goals of confirming them with other speakers as well as discovering other dialectal terms used for the same things. A sample of words and expressions included in these postings includes: *monkey's blood*, *stepmother-jag*, *bunking off*, *mythered*, *twittens and alleys*, *smitlish*, *knackered*, *raunging* and *brew*. The following post reflects the general tenor of the category:

> I have never come across anyone outside the Blackburn area of Lancashire that knows or uses this term for those annoying shards that grow down the side of the fingernail and inflame the finger. I've got umpteen books on Lancashire dialect and it is never listed.

> Does anyone else in the country (or even county) use it? If not it is surely one of the most localised words in the British dialect.
>
> (http://www.open.edu/openlearn/history-the-arts/culture/english-language/debate-stepmother-jag)

Another third of the topics evoke standard language ideologies, as noted by Davies (this volume). Approximately one third of this subset does so by asking for advice about correct pronunciation ('either' as /iːðə/ vs /ʌiðə/, 'scones' as /skɒnz/ vs. /skəunz/, spelling (<practise> vs. <practice>) or usage ('Is it a lounge, living room, sitting room: what is the "right" term for this room?'). The majority of the standard language ideology postings, however, are ones that censure 'incorrect' usage. For example, GH Jones posts the following:

> I can't get anyone to acknowledge that 'bought' is now almost invariably used when 'brought' is correct. E.g.: 'He was "bought" up in …'
>
> During one 'Flog It' programme an expert asked a woman who'd brought some silver items to be auctioned: 'Have you bought (sic) the family silver?' Are we really to accept that there's no difference between the past tense of 'to buy' and that of 'to bring'?
>
> Almost as bad is the overuse of 'fantastic'!
>
> (http://www.open.edu/openlearn/history-the-arts/culture/english-language/debate-bought-and-brought)

Other examples targeted for censure include 'could of' in place of 'could have'; 'using plural verbs for singular nouns'; incorrect use of apostrophes; lack of grammar instruction in schools, negative effects of text messaging on literacy and 'a pacific new topic' (targeting mispronunciation and/or spelling of 'specific').

It is important to note that several of these topics had very large numbers of responses, representing more than a third of the total message count. The very longest of these threads, with 284 messages, was titled 'metres and yards'. On the surface, the linguistic elements under discussion are not really about language, and the variation in usage is not dialectal. However, in this discussion (and a subsequent one on 'Celsius' vs. 'centigrade') people's willingness to use the metric system acts as a surrogate or parallel stance object for the forms of language variation commented on in most of the other forums on the site. Most participants write from a shared discursive and ideological position that presumes a single 'best' form of measurement that is indexically linked with social stances that go beyond the linguistic and include orientations towards modernity vs. backwardness ('metric' choices being construed positively as more modern by their proponents), as well as orientations to meanings that accrue to linguistic items through embodied experience (used by proponents of Imperial measures) as opposed to formal, abstract systems of signs (construed as artificial and alienating). In short, the robust debate and large numbers of posts on these topics by web visitors ostensibly engaged with a site about language diversity can be explained by its resonance with second order indexicalities (and their ideological underpinnings) present in debates over dialect diversity. These include the relationship to a 'more dialectal' past (the present being conditioned by some dialect levelling) that can be positively construed as 'tradition' or negatively construed as 'backward'. They also include competing language ideological orientations towards dialectal diversity as embodied *practice* vs. as a formal linguistic reality. Finally, there is the issue of linguistic hierarchies. As we have seen, the unmoderated debate presumes the existence of a single best usage and/or a single best stance on variation, which we have noted as the predominant perspective in the 'language ideology' category.

The remaining third of the postings has an academic flavour. There are four threads that raise philosophical/social issues related to language variation, three initiated by the Open University linguist on the forum, Diana Honeybone. There are another five posts that I have labelled 'commentaries', in which the posters reflect and take a position on some sort of linguistic issue. The majority of this category, however (16 total), are genuine queries for which academic knowledge is relevant (such as, 'is Basque a unique language? Are dialects becoming homogenized?'). Three are from students seeking help with research projects in linguistics.

The role of the linguist expert

In this forum, Diana Honeybone (DH) is identified as Open University staff, but is not introduced formally to participants with a description of her academic credentials. With respect to the role that she plays, we can note first of all that her presence is quite modest: in a corpus of 76 threads and over 700 messages, DH only posts 24 times. This is far fewer than some of the big users of the site. In nine of those 24 posts, DH responds as a dialect speaker herself. In five of these posts, she makes no reference to her status or knowledge as a linguist. For example, in response to a dialectological post on the term *stepmother-jag* for bits of nail, she writes, 'I hadn't met that interesting word for them before; perhaps it is a local one in the Blackburn area? We called them "idle-backs" on the Notts-Lincs border' (http://www.open.edu/openlearn/history-the-arts/culture/english-language/debate-stepmother-jag). If we look at her stance in terms of Coupland's criteria of sociolinguistic authenticities, we can see her aligning with other 'lay' posters by evoking her own 'ownership' of 'naturally occurring', 'attested' language that indexes her own personal authenticity and shared cultural membership with other regional speakers.

In the other four postings in which DH responds as a dialect speaker, this form of self-reference accompanies more academic content. In one of these instances, she describes the number of variants across the country for 'brew' (brewing tea) and then reveals how she says this in her region of origin. With reference to the criteria of sociolinguistic authorities, then, she takes a stance that indexes a high-status identity (academic) and genre of discourse and implicates her in the production of knowledge. It also displays metalinguistic control: she mediates (frames) her authenticity as a dialect speaker in reference to a wider knowledge base of linguistic diversity in the UK. While DH's stance is thus a blend of authenticity and authority, it is the authenticity dimension that is taken up/ratified by another poster, who aligns with her *as a Yorkshire speaker* in the following comment: 'Ah, a local (well near enough). Ayup duck!'.

In the remaining 13 posts, DH either initiates a discussion topic (four instances) or responds to discussion threads from a linguistic or sociolinguistic perspective. In seven of these 13 academic posts, she is either the first or one of the first responders to her own query. This is much more pronounced in the earliest threads in the bulletin board (August 2005); in 2006, she intervenes only once with a sociolinguistic perspective on change/standards in a thread started as a critique of 'Using plural verbs for singular nouns', intervening mostly to offer her own contributions to lexical dialect items.

A mitigated academic voice

I think that we can interpret DH's mixed stances (academic/dialect speaker) as a strategy of mitigation of her academic voice. This relates to the way that the discussion board is framed: as a public forum where the interests of that public are primary. And of course the topic area in which she does this mitigation – dialect lexical items – is the very domain in which the public can simultaneously experience authority and authenticity with respect to matters linguistic. This is reinforced by the main interactive element on the website, where visitors can submit terminology associated with the lexical Spider diagram (Elmes, this volume), which are entered into the database. The lexical diagram also constitutes the core of the research methodology used to collect speech samples, and is recommended to website readers who want to do their own interviews. This mitigated stance is also reflected in the way that DH frames her academic responses and commentaries. For example, when she weighs in on the thread 'using plural verbs for singular nouns', where participants noted (and in some cases decried) this practice in British English, she writes:

> the rules of grammar are generalizations based on observation of current usage of the language. A living language is always in a state of change [mentions some historical examples]. That's one of the fascinations of watching language in use; we can not only compare today's English with past forms, but also see new changes taking place. So the more examples that people can collect and communicate, the better - it's one of the great values of a forum like this.
>
> (http://www.open.edu/openlearn/history-the-arts/culture/english-language/debate-plural-and-singular)

The other participants' discussion of contexts of use of singular verbs for plural nouns is thus authenticated as a form of linguistic data collection. This also reframes the nature of the thread, which actually had a strong purist dimension. Other posts follow a similar pattern – by ending with references to readers' roles or ideas, or introducing a light-hearted topic.

The interactive and discursive construction of DH's academic authority

As Carr emphasises in her review of research on expertise, expert status has to be continually reaffirmed and enacted by would-be experts (2010: 23). Similarly in an interactive forum, we have to view authority as an interactional product. Expert claims on authority may or may not be ratified by other participants. It is interesting to note that on this discussion board, few participants interact directly with DH, although they frequently do so with each other. In several cases, her thread initiations are not picked up by anyone; the most dramatic case being one titled 'Dialects and when we speak them', where she uses personal examples in an effort to get people to discuss contextual influences on the use of dialect. Only one person responded – a very frequent poster going by the username Little Richardjohn.[2] In his response, he reiterated a theme he had pursued in other threads somewhat erroneously (and in the face of many challenges) that 'it's all about imitation'. DH did not challenge this point of view. In other cases, her commentary is simply passed over without comment as other participants continue the debates they have been having with each other. She is never explicitly asked to intervene on a matter of debate, and her comments on the discussion board are never invoked as authoritative sources of data in subsequent discourse. Overall, despite the fact that the link to this board is entitled 'Ask an Expert', both DH's own presentation of self and the way that lay participants interact with her do not represent her (or perhaps linguists in general) as having the final word about language. This is another way in which the discussion board symbolically locates discursive authority – the right to talk about language – with 'ordinary' speakers.

In this light, it is interesting to compare and contrast DH's discourse with that of the handful of (male) heavy participants in this forum, who tend to post long texts in which, in contrast to DH, they make bald on-record claims to authoritative knowledge. For example, in a thread on the influence of the media (http://www.open.edu/openlearn/history-the-arts/culture/english-language/debate-are-the-media-blame), Nick P writes a long post in which he discusses the varied fates of all words and forms, no matter how they enter a language, and sums it up with the following comment: 'As I've said again and again, languages are like that – only a plonker wouldn't give us ultimate respect for saying that!' In another thread, Nick P asserts that 'Anybody with any knowledge of language and linguistics would know that there's really no such thing as "correct English"'. Poster Akfarrar responds to another person's query about the pronunciation of 'scones' with the statement that 'both are right'. Dominic Watt (a linguist who would be known to academic readers of the board, but who isn't formally identified as an expert here – by himself or by the OU) notes that:

> a lot of misinformation about Basque flies back and forward - some of the postings here being prime examples - so if you're looking for reliable answers from a properly researched source on the topic, take a look at Larry Trask's *History of Basque*.

In contrast to these postings, DH never makes reference to 'misinformation' or in any way directly criticizes the accuracy of anyone's assertions; nor does she ever make overt reference to 'knowledge of language and linguistics' or make bald judgements of 'correctness', even when it is to endorse multiple standards (as Akfarrar does). That is, she goes out of her way to respect (or at least not directly challenge) the sociolinguistic attitudes of the public participants in the forum.

In short, the stances taken by DH give participants the opportunity to take up an authoritative stance with respect to language and linguistic diversity. This is not to say that all participants' bids for authority were ratified by others; in fact, this very issue was at the heart of the struggles in a significant number of threads where posters accused others of elitism, pedantry, ignorance, bias, etc. But both the structure of the forum and the silences and mitigated authority of DH left those participants free to bid for that authority. The dynamic at play in these forums reflect the way in which 'realizing one's self as an expert can hinge on casting other people as less aware, knowing, or knowledgeable' (Carr 2010: 22). Attributing expertise to the public requires, in this frame, relinquishing one's own claims to it.

Reentextualized debates: archived titles/blurbs

These patterns are also reflected in the reentextualization of the *Voices* discussion boards in the one-line blurbs thematizing the topic under the title of each archived debate on the Open University website (http://www.open.edu/openlearn/history-the-arts/culture/english-language/words-language-points-debate). Each one of these blurbs summarizes the contribution of an individual poster and his or her position as a way of thematizing each topic. These participant roles are indexed in large part by the choices of verbs used to characterize the posters' contributions (italicized in Table 4.1 in the second column). By far the largest participant role category is that of information-seeker: this is in keeping with the preferred mode of interaction with the forums (and with the topic of dialect diversity) that we saw in the OpenLearn introduction to the archives. In the other participant categories, we can see that verb choices depict many forum 'guests' and 'members' as active agents: they are attributed high-authority stances as evaluators, advisors, providers of information, 'noticers' of linguistic phenomena and discussion/topic initiators. In terms of sociolinguistic

TABLE 4.1 Examples of participant roles in the representation of speakers in archived blurbs

Participant Role	*Descriptor*
Evaluator	**Negative (Overt)** Forum guest Marilyn *locked horns* with her local newspaper over punctuation Forum guest GH Jones *railed against* the collapse of a distinction **Neutral/Covert Negative** Diana Honeybone of The Open University *suggested* that sometimes the heat of debate can reveal secrets about our upbringing
Advisor	Forum member Little Richardjohn *offered advice* for making yourself understood in the Principality
Information-seeker	Forum guest Sara W *wondered* if there was any reason for a separate word for men with eating disorders How do kids missing school describe their behaviour, *wondered* The Open University's Diana Honeybone;
Reporter	The Open University's Diana Honeybone *recalls* a meeting with a word she'd assumed was local Forum guest Denise *recalls* a childhood treat
Topic or discussion initiator	Community member 'Little Richardjohn' *asked the forum a question* about the names used for places. Diana Honeybone of The Open University posed a provocative question [about letting dialects die] The Open University's Diana Honeybone *raised a question* about what influences
Knowledge seeker or producer	Keith Hodgkin was a guest in the forums who had *made a discovery* about what we call the scales we measure heat in Forum member Rob Owen was *on the trail of* the words borrowed from Indian languages

authorities, they display metalinguistic control, do the work of framing and evaluation and, by participating in the construction of knowledge, are aligned with high-status registers and identities. DH (underlined in Table 4.1) has a very modest presence in these authoritative representations, the strongest of which are two instances where she is described as a topic initiator. At the same time, in the Evaluation section, she is depicted with verbs that mitigate the force of that authority: she 'suggests' instead of 'railing' or 'hating' verbs used by other evaluators. She is not among the few posters who offer explicit advice or who are cited as producing knowledge, but she is present among the much more stance-neutral 'reporters'. She is also present twice in the 'information-seeker' category, where participants are portrayed as 'asking' and 'wondering'. DH, like others in this category, is positioned as taking up an interactional stance of equality rather than authority with respect to others in the forums.

Voices *Comment Boards*

The question of the reentextualized blurbs discussed above is an example of the mediation by website producers of discourses about language produced by the public and by the resident linguist. We turn here to another part of the *Voices* website where this mediation also takes place rather overtly: the *Voices* Comment Boards. Here, reader comments are selected for display on the front page of topic areas that feature web articles written by an academic or media professional. The following analysis considers the propositional content of reader comments, their relationship to the article theme and content and if and how they are incorporated into the academic/journalist text.

No reader comments included in web articles

There are three article topics in which no reader comments are included: 'Nonsense Talk'; 'Classroom Talk'; and 'Language and Place' (http://www.bbc.co.uk/voices/yourvoice/nonsense3.shtml; .../classroom_talk3.shtml; .../feature1.shtml/). The 'Classroom Talk' article is followed, however, by two comments that both contest some of the claims about gender inequality made in the article, and also disagree with one another. Below the article on 'Language and Place' (written by Peter Trudgill) there are two posts by people who align with the academic tone and author by listing their academic credentials ('Haran Rasalingam, BA Hons Linguistics from London' and 'David Andrews BA-status, PgCertSpEd, in Finland') and another who disaligns/parodies these academic stances by not giving his full name and listing his 'place' in nonstandard (authentic) spelling ('Chris H from Hull ('Ull)').

The lack of incorporated reader comments in these articles has several implications. It indirectly buttresses the authority of the web author by representing that author as not needing to be in dialogue with the public, a dialogue that is present elsewhere on the site and in the majority of the web articles. At the same time, by failing to mediate public comments (which are mediatized by virtue of being included on the page), the authority of those comments stands unchallenged.

In the following categories, reader comments are included in the text. As with all forms of reentextualization (see among others Bauman and Briggs 1990; Hill and Irvine 1993; Lucy 1993; Matoesian 2000; Urban 1996), the authors mediate others' voices: evaluating them and aligning/disaligning with them.

Reader comments embedded in the text with clear editorial judgement

An example of this first category of entextualizations can be found in a section of a longer article on language change dealing with americanisms (http://www.

bbc.co.uk/voices/yourvoice/language_change.shtml). The author Philippa Law writes that 'Patsy from Cornwall deplores Americanisms', cites Patsy directly and makes an unequivocal authoritative assessment:

> *She's right* [3] that English originated in England, but *it's not right* to imply that other varieties of English are versions of 'our' language. Americans don't speak a different version of British English; English speakers in the UK and the USA speak modern dialects which have both evolved from 16th century English...

Another article by Law on 'Swearing' (http://www.bbc.co.uk/voices/yourvoice/swearing2.shtml) uses the following unattributed citation from a reader as a section heading: 'Swearing demonstrates a poor command of English. Can't they think of anything else to say?' and asserts:

> *If truth be told*, everyone uses swear words – or their euphemistic equivalents – on occasion. If nobody used today's swear words, they wouldn't remain in the language – but you can be sure that other words would take their place [...] *Most linguists would maintain* that swearing does not show a poor command of a language, but rather demonstrates that you know the language very well.

In both of these articles, Law uses rhetorical strategies that lay direct claim to authoritative knowledge, constituted in opposition to public ignorance/misconceptions.

Reader comments embedded and reframed

In another category of reentextualizations, reader comments are embedded in the text, but the writer's original stance is reframed. One example occurs in the previously mentioned article by Law on 'Language Change'. In a section titled 'Change in Pronunciation', the subheading reads, 'A rogue "r" demonstrates how rules of pronunciation can change'. This is followed by a quotation of the following reader comment: 'Why do reporters and news readers say "lore" for "law" and "sore" for "saw" etc? It never used to happen.' The author (Law) comments that:

> Web-reader Jean O'Rourke has spotted a bit of language change in action. Where words like saw and idea come before a vowel, there's an increasing tendency among speakers of British English to insert an 'r' sound, so that law and order becomes law-r and order and china animals becomes china-r animals. Linguists call this 'intrusive r' because the 'r' was never historically part of the word [...].

Here, the author reframes what is actually a complaint as a (neutral) observation of a 'subtle' change-in-progress. This incorporation of the public into the expert voice is an indirect way of forging discursive consensus where it may not have initially existed. The author simultaneously shores up the authority of her position by citing an academic text under the 'further reading' rubric.

Selective embedding in support of the article's stance

This form of reentextualization is illustrated in an article on 'Language Ecology' (http://www.bbc.co.uk/voices/yourvoice/language_ecology.shtml). Two very similar reader comments are featured at the very top of the article, with the reader names listed below. One of them reads:

> Language is a part of how we are, and to suggest that the world would be better if we all spoke one language is as absurd as to suggest that we should all have the same colour eyes.
>
> Myfanwy Alexander, Cymru

The rest of the article contains abundant citations of readers who emphasize the language–culture–identity link. They include the following, under the subheading of 'Identity':

> Many speakers of minority languages are fiercely proud and defensive of their language. Language forms an important part of anyone's identity. Nerys Jenkins in Belfast says, 'Telling me not to speak Welsh would be like telling me not to breathe: I just couldn't do it.' To let someone's language die out is to let part of their identity die too.

Note here that the author paraphrases Jenkins' words *without editorial comment*. This strategy of withholding rhetorical mediation construes Jenkins as an authority with whom the author aligns. A similar strategy is used in a section on the link between language and culture, where the author supports her position that 'if a nation loses a language, it may also lose its links with a tradition of jokes, music and literature' with a citation from another named reader who is a speaker of Scottish Gaelic and identifies it as 'the most important part of an ancient culture'.

This position is not actually a unanimous one on the Comment Board for this topic: one contributor claims that the multiplicity of languages in the world is 'irrational' and another that language death, while regrettable, is an inevitable and logical process. In short, public dissent on the perspective presented by the journalist on this topic is passed over in silence.

Reader comments embedded as illustration with no overt evaluation or reframing

This final category of entextualization is illustrated in an article entitled 'Received Pronunciation and BBC English' (http://www.bbc.co.uk/voices/yourvoice/rpandbbc.shtml). Written by Dr. Catherine Sangster, it includes abundant citations of Comment Board participants, often in the question–answer format illustrated below:

> But should the BBC really be championing one particular accent of English? Does the BBC have a particular responsibility to hold back the tide of language change?
>
> Patsy from Cornwall thinks that the BBC does have such a responsibility, and that it sometimes falls short: 'BBC presenters, newsreaders and journalists, who are role models for children, are guilty of misusing the language.' Other contributors agree – Phil Rogers from Bournemouth argues that 'Estuary English is flooding the country, and the BBC is to blame', while Peter thinks that 'the BBC has helped with the Americanisation of the way we pronounce Iraq'.

This text is the very last section of the web page on the first of the three topics. When readers click 'next', they are taken to the next topic in a new web page where the author discusses the circularity of BBC English and RP, but does not directly take on any of the opinions expressed in public comments cited on the previous page. These public comments, then, are left as illustrations of diverse opinions. Since the goal of the article is to get people to question some of the taken-for-granted assumptions they have about RP/BBC English, this lack of overt commentary frames the public comments as 'data' that are open for examination. The lack of closure thus suspends – and perhaps precludes – acts of alignment with the sentiments they express. This contrasts sharply with the article on 'Language Ecology', where there is direct alignment of the authorial voice with reader comments, and their shared positions are *not* represented as ideological, or open for critique or examination.

In the *Your Voice* section, then, the public voice is given front page status. At the same time, compared to the OU Discussion, that voice is channelled in a number of ways. First, public participants do not select the topics, so they are positioned as responders rather than initiators. As we have seen, journalists/academics both control the topics of the discourse and exercise direct or indirect control over the framing of public commentary. Through processes of mediation and mediatization, journalists and academics sometimes represent public voices as naïve and as 'data' that they can analyze and judge – and in so doing, occupy an expert or authoritative stance. In other instances, carefully selected fragments of the public voice are cast as an 'authentic' expression of self-evident truths (as in the 'Language Ecology' topic).

In contrast, in the OU Discussion Forum, there is little academic mediation of the public voice and lay participants are free to bid among themselves for both authenticity and authority with respect to language diversity. This results, as Milani *et al.* (2011) point out, in a 'tip' in favour of dominant language hierarchies and ideologies.

The Voices *Recordings*

The final section of the *Voices* website where we find the co-location of public voices and expert commentary is one of the three main rubrics featured on the *Voices* homepage: the *Voices* Recordings (http://www.bbc.co.uk/voices/recordings/). This section features a map of the United Kingdom: each clickable point on the map opens a page that includes the speaker/s' name and photo, a linguistic self-description and a brief transcript. Many pages have voice clips and longer transcripts. Some of these include a rubric titled 'Find out more about the speech in this clip', and written by a linguistic expert introduced by name and title: 'Jonnie Robinson, Curator, English accents and dialects, British Library Sound Archive'.

An analysis of 12 speaker transcripts in the 'Under 18' and '18–25' age groups which include Robinson's expert commentary reveals several interesting patterns. First, the expert commentary focuses primarily on 'speech' as a set of formal, dialectal features: the recorded speakers become 'data points' on the map. Thus, Robinson draws attention to the Welsh features of James' and Peter's English; Sajia's blend of vowel sounds; Gemma's and Ayeshah's Yorkshire accent features (including GOAT-fronting); Barry's Norfolk glottal stop and East Anglian vowels; David's codeswitching; Kieran's use of 'like'; Jamie's glottalization of /t/ and Grant's lexicon and rhoticization. In some cases, the speakers themselves topicalized formal or sociolinguistic features of their own or others' speech and Robinson's commentary serves as an authoritative academic *expansion* on their chosen topic. Liam, for example, talks about the 'blend' of accents in Milton Keynes. In response, Robinson writes about speech and its importance for identity, and names 'dialect levelling' as a contact phenomenon, ratifying and expanding on Liam's perspective. Similarly, following Jason's remarks that people change how they speak to 'move up' socially, Robinson discusses audience design, accommodation and forms of prestige. In five out of 12 instances, while Robinson clearly adopts a stance of authority, producing knowledge and mediating the readers' interpretation of the voice clips and transcripts, he aligns with these speakers, taking up a complementary stance towards a shared stance object: the speakers' recorded utterances.

But in other cases this alignment is not present. This can be explained in two cases by the fact that speakers topicalize aspects of their experiences that have limited linguistic or communicative content (clothing, television). However, Victoria complains about other people's terminology for cows, presenting herself as an expert and as someone who can play with language; Sajia talks about how she makes people laugh; Kieran discovers to his surprise and embarrassment that a shopkeeper in India understands the English that he thought would be a 'secret language' and Gemma discusses a personal sociolinguistic experience: being upbraided by her mother for her pronunciation. None of this *talk about language* is taken up by the expert dialectologist, who focuses instead on dialect features in their speech. This erasure short-circuits the sociolinguistic authority that accrues to speakers who display metalinguistic control and take up roles as agents in framing/ evaluation and the production of knowledge.

Do You Speak American? 'Ask an Expert'

Let us turn now to the parallel section of the DYSA website, also labelled 'Ask an Expert'. This features a different expert each month and does not provide archives of all of the experts who have participated. The expert for October 2006 (the last one accessible on the website) was Edward Finegan. He launched the discussion with a lengthy posting, which began as follows:

> Do you object to "gonna," "snuck," and "like" (in, like, "I'm like I don't care")? Are you one of those who from a mile away can spot a split infinitive ("to swiftly resolve") and take offense? Or are such points of linguistic usage unimportant in the overall scheme of effective communication? [...].
>
> (http://www.pbs.org/speak/ask/)

In the remainder of this text, Finegan does not conceal his own views and is clear about not subscribing to a purist position. Viewers were invited to respond through a web-based email interface, which let them know that only some emails would be selected for a response. The web page presents that selection. This contrasts with the *Voices* website, where public contributors and web readers alike were given access to the process of selection – that is, because they can see all the postings, they can see the ones that the experts have *not* chosen to respond to. From this perspective, the DYSA format allows both the expert linguist and media professionals to exercise significant control over the shape of a final, web-published product without displaying how they do so. The format and procedure also reinforce Finegan's expert status, as he both launches/frames the topic and has the last and authoritative word.

At the same time, Finegan also relinquishes a form of textual authority that we saw the writers of the texts in the *Your Voices* section of the *Voices* website use: the embedding of selected voices of the public inside a longer text. That is, Finegan directly addresses each contributor of a question or comment (often by name), and makes his opinion about his or her comments relatively explicit. We see this in the following extract:

Nitin from North Carolina writes:

> [...] Furthermore, there is the issue of misspelling. I feel that the Internet is responsible for the growing 'alternate' spelling movement that is based upon phonetics. Here is a list 'you're vs your', 'to vs too', 'very vs vary', 'there vs their', 'here vs hear' and the list goes on. Over time the Internet English becomes ingrained into all forms of communication [...]

Dr. Edward Finegan responds:

> *As you know, Nitin*, English is in flux and always has been. It's just like every other living language in that regard. Pronunciations, words, grammatical constructions, meanings – they all evolve [...] Confusions like your for you're and there for their are prompted not by the Internet itself, of course, but by the speed at which we compose e-mail and text messages. From such merged spellings, *we can infer* that the writers pronounce them alike. For venues more formal than e-mail, many such mergers would be caught [...] By the way, *if you examine* the letters submitted to me here, *a sharp eye like yours* will spot similar misspellings [...]

Finegan's language is inclusive ('as you know' and 'we can infer') and in that sense, holds out the promise that Nitin could align with his knowledgeable voice. It is also, as we saw in the *Your Voices* texts, an example of *reframing* that turns Nitin's adherence to a standard-language ideology into 'a sharp eye' that 'examines' and 'infers.' But he also openly contradicts her. In this sense, Finegan's expertise is rather openly displayed. By responding directly and by name to all the emails he selected, he also indexes conversation, despite the fact that there is no actual interaction in this web feature: Nitin cannot answer him back. In doing so, he allows both the original writers of emails, and subsequent readers of the page, to assess his answers both for their content and for their interactional qualities – in this case, how he has handled his expertise. In contrast, when public comments are embedded in longer texts (as in the *Your Voice* articles) the reader of those texts is *not* invited to evaluate how the writer responded to the original poster of a comment.

Comparison and contrast: expert voices

If we consider the contexts in which experts intervene on these two websites, we see that they take up more or less mitigated stances of expertise, and do so more or less overtly. Some forms of embedding/revoicing of public comments discursively include the public in an expert community of sociolinguistic practice; others reinforce the boundaries between expert and popular knowledge. These strategies, along with the way public participation is structured, have consequences for the stances available to public commentators, as well as for the extent to which dominant language ideologies are represented. The forum with the greatest public freedom, and the most mitigated academic voice, is the one where those dominant language ideologies have the greatest presence.

Conclusions

In the analysis above, we have seen a variety of factors that shape the kinds of authorities and authenticities that accrue to both public/lay and expert/linguists' voices on these two websites. First, different parts of the sites are organized around different participation structures that affect the degree to which the voices of commenters/posters and depicted speakers (in the 'Voices Recordings' section) are *mediated*. On one end of the continuum, there are the very lightly moderated *Voices* Discussion Forums. In them, the manager exercises little to no censorship; and the forum expert linguist, Diana Honeybone, both limits her interventions and adopts discursive and participation strategies that constitute what I have called a mitigated academic stance: one that does not have immediate or overwhelming authority compared to other participants. This relatively equal footing is also a function of the way that those other participants position themselves and interact with her. That is, Honeybone's comments and discussion starters are not given any special status and are sometimes ignored; at the same time, forum members and guests take up highly authoritative stances regarding language. As a consequence, these forums are democratic places in which the voice of the public is dominant.

Public comments and speech in some other parts of the *Voices* website are more heavily mediated. First, they are mediated by being filtered/selected. Second, they are mediated through various forms of reentextualization in which they are discursively recruited in the service of the (expert) author's stance. In some cases, this involves the erasure of debate and contention among commenters or the ideologically motivated recasting of public comments: for example, complaints about diversity glossed as more neutral 'noticings' of that diversity. In still other cases, mediation involves overt evaluation (sometimes negative) of the lay voices in the recordings and in the comments. Public voices are also mediated in more indirect ways when they are treated as data rather than engaged with as propositional content. In all these cases, experts (producers, linguists, journalists, academics) display, exercise and accrue authority. In fact, we could argue that the mediation of others' voices is an essential component of the exercise of professional authority and legitimacy for these kinds of professionals.

The analysis of the DYSA 'Ask an Expert' forum reveals that the exercise of power through mediation of others' voices can be at least partly offset by the explicit *mediatization* of that process. In other words, Finegan exercises authority overtly, using rhetorical devices that index direct interaction and debate with members of the public who have written with their questions. In many instances, his evaluations of public perspectives/commentaries and the sociolinguistic ideologies underpinning them are very similar to those made by experts on the *Voices* site. He too recruits his public readers to a preferred stance as noticers/appreciators of linguistic diversity. However, to a greater degree than in these parallel *Voices* forums, Finegan addresses his interlocutors as legitimate participants in a debate where he is nevertheless willing to assert his authority. Thus Finegan's strategy is interactionally democratic, but this democracy comes at the price of a highly limited exercise of a public, lay voice of the kind we see in the *Word4Word* Discussion Forums.

An analysis of the interaction between linguists and the public in these various forums helps us to notice and understand the ambivalent status of the expert linguistic voice in both websites, where it is sometimes boldly asserted and sometimes mitigated by academics and media professionals alike. On the one hand, the appeal to scientific authority is an attractive tool, and linguists and producers alike may want to construct linguists as having equivalent claims to exclusive knowledge as other recognized public 'experts'. On the other hand, as sociolinguists and linguistic anthropologists, we also know that these kinds of authority claims have a variety of consequences that may conflict with our interests in engaging the public without alienating them on matters linguistic. We may also be cautious about promoting new, simplified orthodox discourses about language as antidotes to old, reductive language ideological discourses. The representational tensions we see in these programmes do not, therefore, reflect media problems that we can solve, but rather, dilemmas of representation of non-dominant languages and codes that we continue to struggle with.

Finally, I want to touch on the ways in which these programmes – and linguists' interventions in them – are shaped by, embedded in and reproduce prior discourses that are permeated by dominant language ideologies and hierarchies. We see this in the *Voices* Discussion forum, which is dominated by a very traditional (and apolitical) discourse about lexical diversity in regional dialects coupled with a strong standard language ideological discourse. This reflects prevailing 'folk sociolinguistics'. Diana Honeybone's case shows that, put in the position of respondent to these discourses, it is clearly difficult *not* to validate the appreciation for lexical diversity and to do so every time it comes up. At the same time, this practice ratifies speakers' locations ('emplacement') as members of distinct 'speech communities' whose very identities and legitimacy is constructed in opposition to other, similarly construed groups of speakers. Thus the acts of mutual recognition and appreciation that are targeted by the BBC and PBS projects and websites are fundamentally fragile: susceptible to the fragmentation evoked by Milani *et al.* (2011) if left unmanaged. Second, given the programmes' and websites' persuasive, pedagogical and entertainment intent, it is difficult for linguists to *invalidate* dominant discourses every time they come up in reader comments, because doing so pits the linguist against the public. This motivates diplomatic attempts to recast and reshape the public voice, and to mitigate the academic's authority, attempts which have the unintended consequences of leaving prior (dominant) discourses and hierarchies more or less intact.

We can also see the presence of those prior discourses dramatically represented in journalistic framings of both linguistic expertise and public opinions. If we go back to Finegan's expert page on the DYSA website, we find that it was introduced by the following heading:

> **State of American**
>
> Is American English in trouble? Is it falling apart as some would suggest, or merely changing with the times?
>
> (http://www.pbs.org/speak/speech/correct/prescriptivism/)

Similarly, in the *Your Voices* section, the section of the article (cited above) on American influences on English written by the journalist Philippa Law begins like this:

> **Language Change by Philippa Law**
>
> Americanisation – Don't worry, it's not as bad as you might think.
>
> (http://www.bbc.co.uk/voices/yourvoice/language_change.shtml)

In both of these cases, the 'linguistic' perspective ('changing with the times', 'not as bad as you might think') is introduced in second position as a *potential* antidote to the prevailing discourse. From a journalistic perspective, it is the contrast or conflict between the popular and the academic that gives the topic its appeal: it is a strategy for audience engagement. This dovetails with academic or pedagogical perspectives and strategies (acknowledging people's attitudes; exploring their origins). What is less certain is the extent to which this voicing of prior/dominant discourses about language is reproduced vs. transformed in the forms of media we have examined.

Notes

1 See Jaffe 2011 for a fuller discussion.
2 This user name closely resembles Richard Littlejohn, a tabloid columnist. We cannot know if it is the columnist or someone appropriating his name; in any case, the user name indexes someone with a public voice.
3 Italics here and in following excerpts are included to highlight key points and were not in the original texts.

References

Bauman, R. and Briggs, C. (1990) 'Poetics and performance as critical perspectives on language and social life', *Annual Review of Anthropology,* 19: 59–88.

Bucholtz, M. (2003) 'Sociolinguistic nostalgia and the authentication of identity', *Journal of Sociolinguistics*, 7: 399–416.

Carr, E.S. (2010) 'Enactments of expertise', *Annual Review of Anthropology*, 39: 17–32.

Coupland, N. (2003) 'Sociolinguistic authenticities', *Journal of Sociolinguistics*, 7: 417–31.

Dubois, J. (2007) 'The Stance triangle', in R. Englebretson (ed.) *Stancetaking in Discourse*, Amsterdam: John Benjamins.

Gal, S. and Woolard, K. (2001) 'Constructing languages and publics: Authority and representation', in S. Gal and K. Woolard (eds) *Languages and Publics: The Making of Authority*, Manchester: St. Jerome Press.

Gieve, S. and Norton, J. (2007) 'Dealing with linguistic difference in encounters with Others on British television', in S. Johnson and A. Ensslin (eds) *Language in the Media*, London: Continuum.

Hill, J. and Irvine, J. (eds) (1993) *Responsibility and Evidence in Oral Discourse*, Cambridge: Cambridge University Press.

Jaffe, A. (2000) 'Introduction: Non-standard orthography and non-standard speech', *Journal of Sociolinguistics,* 4(4): 497–513.

Jaffe, A. (2007) 'Corsican on the airwaves: Media discourse, practice and audience in a context of minority language shift and revitalization', in S. Johnson and A. Ensslin (eds) *Language in the Media*, London: Continuum.

Jaffe, A. (2009a) 'Entextualization, mediatization, and authentication: Orthographic choice in media transcripts', *Text and Talk*, 29(5): 571–94.

Jaffe, A. (2009b) 'Introduction: The Sociolinguistics of stance', in A. Jaffe (ed.) *Stance: Sociolinguistic Perspectives*, Oxford: Oxford University Press.

Jaffe, A. (2011) 'Sociolinguistic diversity in mainstream media: Authenticity, authority and processes of mediation and mediatization', *Journal of Language and Politics*, 10(4): 562–86.

Jaworski, A. (2007) 'Language in the media: Authenticity and othering', in S. Johnson and A. Ensslin (eds) *Language in the Media*, London: Continuum.

Jaworski, A., Lawson, S. and Ylänne-McEwan, V. (2003) 'The uses and representations of local languages in tourist destinations: A view from British holiday programmes', *Language Awareness*, 12(1): 5–29.

Johnson, S. and Ensslin, A. (2007) 'Language in the media: Theory and practice', in S. Johnson and A. Ensslin (eds) *Language in the Media*, pp. 3–24, London: Continuum.

Kelly-Holmes, H. and Milani, T. (2011) 'Thematising multilingualism in the media', *Journal of Language and Politics*, 10(4): 467–89.

Lippi-Green, R. (1997) *English with an Accent: Language, Ideology and Discrimination in the United States*, New York: Routledge.

Lucy, J. (1993) *Reflexive Language: Reported Speech and Metapragmatics*, Cambridge: Cambridge University Press.

Matoesian, G. (2000) 'Intertextual authority in reported speech: Production media in the Kennedy Smith rape trial', *Journal of Pragmatics*, 32(7): 879–914.

Milani, T.M. and Johnson, S. (2010) 'Critical intersections: Language ideologies and media discourses', in S. Johnson and T. Milani (eds) *Language Ideologies and Media Discourse*, London: Continuum.

Milani, T.M., Davies, B.L. and Turner, W. (2011) 'Unity in disunity: Centripetal and centrifugal tensions on the BBC Voices website', *Journal of Language and Politics*, 10(4): 587–614.

Montgomery, M. (2001) 'Defining "authentic talk"', *Discourse Studies*, 3/4: 397–405.

Thornborrow, J. (2001) 'Authenticity, talk and mediated experience: Introduction', *Discourse Studies*, 3/4: 391–2.

Urban, G. (1996) 'Entextualization, replication and power', in M. Silverstein and G. Urban (eds) *Natural Histories of Discourse*, Chicago: Chicago University Press.

Van Leeuwen, T. (2001) 'What is authenticity?', *Discourse Studies*, 3/4: 392–7.

5

AFRIKAANS IS BOBAAS

Linguistic citizenship on the BBC *Voices* website

Tommaso M. Milani and Mooniq Shaikjee

Introduction

It is a sociolinguistic truism that people have strong opinions about language(s). Around the world, language is often a central motive for struggle. That language also matters to people in apparently more 'trivial' and less cruel everyday circumstances emerges from a quick review of articles in the daily press. For example, it is not uncommon to witness in British and American newspapers the bemoaning of allegedly incorrect language, which is seen as ultimately leading to the 'degradation' of Standard English (see e.g. Cameron 1995; Ensslin and Johnson 2007; Thurlow 2007). By the same token, the rather mundane – albeit no less heated – investment in language issues is evidenced by the 8,500 postings submitted to the different virtual discussion platforms on the BBC *Voices* website.

What is key here is that, whether articulated in spoken interactions or included in print or new media discourse, pronouncements about language(s) are never 'about language alone' (Woolard 1998: 3) but are rather the outer manifestation of deeper social concerns about ethnicity, race, nationality, gender, sexuality and so forth, a point that has been reiterated in the vast literature on language ideologies (see Milani and Johnson 2008, 2010, for an overview).

The reproduction and contestation of specific links between language and broader socio-cultural issues will be brought under investigation in the present chapter. To this end, we will analyse the discussion board dedicated to Afrikaans which is part of the broader discussion section of the BBC *Voices* website called *Multilingual Nation*. The reason for the choice of this specific data set is manifold. Not only is Afrikaans one of the eleven official languages and the third most spoken 'home-language' in South Africa (after isiZulu and isiXhosa),[1] but it is also one of the most emotionally fraught topics within the 'national conversation'

(Ord 2005) of post-apartheid South Africa, an issue which constantly fuels a variety of local media debates about aesthetic qualities and the allegedly endangered status of Afrikaans. Because of its transnational character, what the virtual discussion board on BBC *Voices* will offer us is a very different vantage point from those presented in the literature thus far (e.g. Milton 2008; Orman 2008; Painter 2009), a body of scholarship which consists nearly exclusively of broader 'macro' sociological and social-psychological analyses of media and political discourse within South Africa.

In contrast, *Multilingual Nation* will provide us with a useful 'micro' context in which to conduct detailed critical discourses analysis, shedding light on *alternative* discourses about the value and function of Afrikaans *outside* South Africa. In order to do this, we will draw and expand on Stroud's (2001, 2003) idea of *linguistic citizenship*, an important but, we believe, somewhat neglected theoretical concept through which to grasp the everyday life of language politics (see also Williams and Stroud 2013) in a world of accelerated human mobility, cultural contacts and exponentially intensified virtual connections.

Before delving into detailed textual analysis of relevant excerpts, however, we want first to offer a concise overview of the history of Afrikaans, followed by a few reflections on theoretical developments in the academic field of language politics.

Afrikaans: a brief historical overview

Under the rule of the Dutch East India Company (1652–1750), the area of the Cape Peninsula developed into a culturally heterogeneous area populated by Dutch and other European settlers, the last survivors of the autochthonous Khoikhoi and Khoesan inhabitants, as well as a large population of slaves brought from India, the Indonesian archipelago, the Malaysian peninsula and other parts of Africa. At the time, *lingua francas* like Portuguese Creole, Malay and Dutch facilitated intercultural communication. However, a local, Dutch-based pidgin developed as well. Drawing upon the different resources from the various languages spoken in the area, this 'hybrid' linguistic variety – later called Cape Dutch or *Kaaps Hollands* – became increasingly used in Dutch households between the settlers, their slaves and Khoikhoi and Khoesan domestic servants. It also soon became the L1 of locally-born slaves in the area, as well as the L2 of the settlers' offspring who became exposed to it during their formative years. Since the Dutch East India Company was not involved in developing any formal schooling, there was little or no 'official' promotion of standard Dutch in the Cape. This in turn proved to be a fertile ground for the spread of Cape Dutch/ *Kaap Hollands*, which would be later standardized as Afrikaans (Roberge 2006: 16ff).

As the Cape Peninsula area came under British rule in the early nineteenth century, the antagonism between the Dutch settlers and the British grew, especially as a consequence of the increased Anglicization campaigns. The tensions culminated in the 1830s and 1840s in a northward migration – the so-called *Great Trek* – of the Dutch farmers or *Boers* towards the areas occupied by today's Free State and Johannesburg. What is most notable is that British supremacy had an extraordinary catalytic effect on the *white* Dutch population in terms of ethnic identity and linguistic consciousness. As Roberge notes,

> [a]wareness of a common language, homeland, history, and origin fostered not only group solidarity against British hegemony but [also] an inchoate sense of ethnic identity, whereby the term *Afrikaner* came to acquire a political meaning.
>
> (Roberge 2006: 24–25).

To this, it could be added that the *taalliefde* – or deep attachment that Afrikaners developed towards Afrikaans – is seen by them as an essential component of their ethnic/national identity and culture, as is evidenced 'by the titles … of two of the most notable books written on the relationship between the Afrikaners and Afrikaans' (Orman 2008: 110): *Die taal is gans die volk* ('The language is the entire people') (Zietsman 1992, cited in Orman 2008: 110) and *Tuiste in eie taal* ('At home in one's own language') (Steyn 1980, cited in Orman 2008: 110).

In sum, the end of the nineteenth century set in motion the creation of an indexical link between Afrikaans, race and ethnicity, so that Afrikaans became conflated – equated even – with whiteness and Afrikaner ethnic identity. Related to this is the erasure of non-white speakers – the descendants of the slaves in the Cape – and their exclusion from the Afrikaans 'imagined community' (Anderson 1983). As Orman (2008: 112) points out, the inextricable connection between Afrikaans, whiteness and Afrikaner ethnicity, together with the concomitant exclusion of non-white speakers, is most patent in the *Verklarende Handwoordeboek van die Afrikaanse Taal* ('Explanatory Dictionary of the Afrikaans Language') where the entry *Boeretaal* ('Boer language') is defined as synonymous with Afrikaans. This definition is not an innocent 'slippage', but is rather a conscious attempt to claim that 'the Afrikaans spoken by the Boers is the only normatively valid variety of the language' (Orman 2008: 212).

Afrikaans did not remain a linguistic marker of an 'insubordinate' ethnic minority speaking against British dominance, instead it acquired increasingly nationalistic overtones during the twentieth century. Elevated to official status in 1925 and brought on a par with English, Afrikaans became a key element in the 'syntax of hegemony' (Billig 1995) of Afrikaner nationalism after World War II. By 'syntax of hegemony', we refer to the symbolic processes through which one part of a totality, in this case the minority group of Afrikaners and their language, aspires to become the metonymic representation *par excellence* of the whole: South Africa and 'South Africanness'. The most patent manifestation of this linguistic aspect of nationalism can be found in the role played by Afrikaans as the main language through which the state political apparatus of separation – *apartheid* – was implemented and made (in)famous world-wide. The linguistic component of this nationalistic enterprise can also be found in the decision to legislate Afrikaans as one of the languages of instruction in the so-called 'Bantu Education' for Black people, a political choice that ignited the Soweto uprisings in 1976.

In post-apartheid South Africa, Afrikaans has retained its status as official language (albeit now on a par with other 10 languages). Moreover, in 2007, Afrikaans was the second most common language of instruction (after English) in primary and secondary schools, with 12 per cent of learners studying through the medium of Afrikaans. At a symbolic level, however, Afrikaans continues to be viewed in much of the public imaginary as the 'language of the oppressor' (see Roberge 2006: 33). That said, one should be wary of 'master discourses' in historical reconstructions because they erase a more complex reality, one in which uncomfortable feelings and truths are brushed away because they could disturb the neat fabric from which narratives of domination and resistance gain their force and political appeal. As Dlamini (2009) points out, Afrikaans occupies a liminal position amongst many Black speakers in post-apartheid South Africa, one in which negative connotations linked to shared memories of separation and injustice co-exist with more 'nostalgic' feelings of personal events. Indeed, this duality is what emerges in many of the postings on the BBC *Voices* website.

Theoretical scaffolding: the everyday life of language politics

In line with current scholarship (see Blommaert 1999b; Shohamy 2006), we view language politics as a complex nexus of practices which is not reducible to the decisions made by politicians with regard to status and value of language in a particular society. Rather, language politics encompasses a multiplicity of acts of linguistic negotiations in everyday life, not least in different media spaces. However, as Johnson and Ensslin caution, the media are not necessarily conduits of dominant discourses but can 'also enable marginal agencies to surface, and potentially alter, previous hierarchical relations' (Johnson and Ensslin 2007: 13).

It is these 'marginal agencies' that the notion of *linguistic citizenship* (Stroud 2001, 2003) aims to capture. Stroud explains that linguistic citizenship denotes:

> the situation where speakers themselves exercise control over their language, deciding *what* languages are, and what they may *mean*, and where language issues … are discursively tied to a range of social issues – policy issues and questions of equity.
>
> (Stroud 2001: 353, italics in original)

As an example, Stroud offers the case of Northern SiNdebele, which, unlike Southern SiNdebele, was not recognized as one of the official languages of post-apartheid South Africa. The speakers of Northern SiNdebele constitute a clear manifestation of linguistic citizenship in the sense that they found themselves in the position of 'having to argue that Northern SiNdebele was a language, which meant a grassroots investment in developing orthography, grammar and glossaries for school' (Stroud 2001: 349). This, in turn, led to the development of 'grassroots strategies to demand the use of SiNdebele as a medium of instruction in primary education' (Stroud 2001: 349).

In comparison, the examples from the BBC *Voices* website which we will analyze in the present chapter may appear to be of a more trivial and personal nature. That said, we would like to propose that the notion of linguistic citizenship should not be restricted solely to describing public 'macro-events' of political mobilization but also can be usefully employed in order to understand the many ephemeral and apparently banal 'micro-occurrences' of agency *on grounds of language* that unfold in daily interactions – whether private or public.

More specifically, it is our contention that contexts of migration as well as online spaces are particularly rich 'epistemological sites' (Sunderland 2004) in which to analyze the ordinary acts of linguistic citizenship, contesting commonsensical linkages between language, territory and ethnic/national categories. This is insofar as migration brings with it dislocation: a particular experience of being 'out of place', of unsettled 'rootedness' and ultimately of identity troubles. This is *not* to say that migration necessarily entails a rethinking of fixed categories of belonging and 'the celebration of *happy hybridity*' (Otsuji and Pennycook 2010: 244, italics in original). The blurring of identity boundaries may indeed occur (see e.g. Blackledge and Creese 2010; Milani and Jonsson 2012; Rampton 1995), but those who have 'moved there' and those who are 'already there' may end up reproducing strict boundaries along lines of ethnicity, nationality and religious affiliation, for example.

Similarly, the inherently *trans*-national nature of the Internet has brought about the unsettling of individuals' traditional sense of space. Once again, one should be careful in drawing too easy conclusions about the demise of categories of (spatial) belonging as a result of virtual connections (Hine 2000; Kelly-Holmes and Milani 2011). For example, in a study of the discussion board on Welsh on the BBC *Voices* website, Milani *et al.* (2011) show that the 'nation' still remains a key category framing both the BBC's ideological agenda as well as internet users' comments. Either way, we believe that the Internet:

> has brought with it a super-heteroglossia of voices, whether hegemonic or non-hegemonic; the 'cacophony of voices' (Stroud 1999) which is typical of any text has been exponentially amplified through new digital technologies.
>
> (Kelly-Holmes and Milani 2011: 482)

All in all, human mobility and virtual connections, together with the cultural and linguistic encounters that accompany them, have magnified – exacerbated even – the discursive processes of *negotiation* of the status and value of different languages (see Blackledge and Creese 2010; Pavlenko and Blackledge 2004). And most crucial for an understanding of such negotiations is the co-existence of both subversive and conformist discursive acts (see also Milani and Jonsson 2012).

Afrikaans on *Multilingual Nation*

Multilingual Nation is a complex forum which encompasses 37 discussion boards, each of which is dedicated to a specific language, the only exceptions being Urdu/Hindi and Croatian/Serbian which share one discussion board, respectively. As Davies *et al.* (2012) have described in detail elsewhere, two main types of layout have been employed by the BBC to *frame* the introductory page presenting each discussion board. In Format 1, a rather short essay on the language of the discussion board, usually written by an academic expert, is preceded by a list of quotations from the speakers of that language collected by BBC radio journalists. In contrast, Format 2 does not include any authentic quotes from speakers of the language, but contains a much longer academic essay.

The Afrikaans discussion board is framed following Format 1 and has a total of 42 postings, excluding the five quotations from Afrikaans speakers that are used to frame the page. Posters are required to include their name as well as their present location along with their comments although, of course, we cannot be sure whether this information corresponds to their 'real' identities and locations. The majority of commentators (23) seem to be based in the UK, whereas the rest are from locations such as the US, Canada, New Zealand, Namibia, the Emirates, Saudi and elsewhere in Europe. Only four participants claim to post from a location in South Africa. Judging from the content of the comments, 19 posters in total appear to be South African-born living overseas, eight are non-South Africans and the nationality of the rest is unclear. A more in-depth examination of the content of the postings reveals clear patterns in the discussion, particularly in the emergence of discourses around education, language endangerment, identity and belonging, to which we will now turn.

Afrikaans, playfulness and foreign language acquisition

There is little doubt that the BBC *Voices* project had an overt social purpose in that it aimed 'to celebrate and explore the diverse languages, dialects and accents of the UK … at the start of the 21st century' (Rose and Mowbray, n.d.). Much of the discourse around Afrikaans on this discussion board is indeed celebratory, and comments about the aesthetic appeal of the language are heavily present such as in the cases of *Afrikaans is bobaas* or *Afrikaans is die baas* [Afrikaans is tops] (see also conclusions below). However, the discussion board appears to have a further function: it has been used as a space for non-L1 speakers of Afrikaans to playfully practise and display their command of the language, as we can see in Extracts 1, 2 and 3.

Extract 1[2]

Donald from Michigan, USA

Ek leer myself die taal praat. [*I am teaching myself to speak the language*] I am learning Afrikaans as part of my education in South African literature. My hope is to be accepted at Universiteit Stellenbosch so it's a tough road! Not many resources exist to learn die taal [*the language*] here in the US so a lot of my knowledge comes from a handful of books and newspapers online like Rapport and Beeld.

Extract 2

Steve, London

Ek wil ook die mooi taal leer!! [*I also want to learn this beautiful language*] Studied German at university and love languages. Started learning bits from the Internet. Find it pretty easy to pick up having learnt German. My thoughts are echoed by Aidan's comment above - Afrikaans developed in a unique setting, and in a very short space of time became quite distinct from its Dutch (inter alia) roots. The language has only been written for just over 100 years - let's not let another language, beautiful like any - die out for the wrong reasons.

Extract 3

Jenny Harris from Worcester, England

Ek ook probeer om die taal te leer! [*I am also trying to learn the language*] As for influenced by French, there's not that much French influence on the Afrikaans language itself, as the Huguenots mostly learned Dutch right away, so most French in Afrikaans, like 'meubels' for furniture from 'meubles', comes through Dutch. [...] As far as I can make out, Afrikaans is in no danger of dying out - more people speak it than Danish (I think).

Donald, Steve and Jenny are three of the eight non-South Africans on this discussion board who express an interest in learning Afrikaans; they also begin their posts with a brief attempt at writing in this language. Perhaps unsurprisingly, the usage of languages other than English is not uncommon on the different boards of *Multilingual Nation*. For example, Milani *et al.* (2011: 22) argue that several posters employ Welsh as a semiotic resource through which to position themselves as 'authentic' mother-tongue *speakers* of the language, and thus validate their Welshness. Needless to say, Donald, Steve and Jenny do not make any claim of 'native competence', but the reason for choosing to begin their comments with a statement in Afrikaans is, in our view, not unlike the one underpinning the usage of Welsh studied by Milani *et al.* (2011): it is a metapragmatic cue through which these three posters discursively construct a 'community of practice' (Lave and Wenger 1991) of Afrikaans learners and *authenticate* such a subject position (see also Bucholtz 2003).

Observe in particular how this 'synthetic' (Fairclough 2001) community of 'authentic' learners is initiated by Donald – the first one to state in Afrikaans to be learning this language – and is continued by Steve, and later Jenny, through *implicit* forms of addressivity (Herring 2001). As Davies *et al.* (2012) point out, posts on *Multilingual Nation* appear in reverse chronological order; they are unthreaded and asynchronous. Moreover, there is no comment function allowing one to reply directly to another poster, and users are unable to see the time comments were posted. This makes it necessary for posters to employ explicit forms of addressivity (e.g. referring to one another by name) when replying to comments in the discussion (Davies *et al.* 2012: 209). Despite not overtly referring to Donald's comment, we would argue that Steve and Jenny subtly indicate whom they are addressing through the similar structure of their postings. Furthermore, the adverb *ook* [also] overtly marks their aspirations not to be left out from this 'imagined community' (Anderson 1983) of peers.

Whilst the usage of Welsh was 'serious business', leading to a heated debate about who counts as 'Welsh', the deployment of Afrikaans seems to be of a different nature. In this context, it is worth reiterating that the BBC *Voices* project did not only have a strong social commitment but also aimed to be entertaining (Rose and Mowbray n.d.); in our view, it is only through such *pleasurable* 'keying' (Coupland 2007) that one can make sense of the usage of Afrikaans here. In other words, the discussion board can be understood as a playful platform where some posters have fun trying out their knowledge of the language.

Other participants, mostly South African-born like Liebrecht below, join the discussion on language learning by stating that they know of or are acquainted with other non-South Africans who are attempting to learn Afrikaans, displaying much excitement that so many people are interested in the language.

Extract 4

Liebrecht from Caledon, South Africa

I love my language and I can't see why ANYONE would want to be ashemed of and their own language culture! I always get the feeling that English-speaking South Africans really want to speak Afrikaans, but most are too self-conscious and lack confidence to do so... shame! I would NEVER laugh at someone trying to speak Afrikaans, but respect and admire them instead! And I've come across especially Germans learning Afrikaans!!! Incredible!!! Afrikaans is also offered at universities in Poland, Russia and a few others. Afrikaans will never become extinct, even if it tried... :-D

Three other posts also make reference to various universities in South Africa and around the world that offer Afrikaans as part of their curricula. What emerges from the content of these commentaries is that the sheer fact that someone might be interested in learning Afrikaans is interpreted by the participants in this discussion as a positive enterprise, something to be proud of and celebrate.

Interestingly, unlike similar ideological debates about the study of 'small' or 'less spoken' languages, there seems to be a rather unusual consensus about the positive worth of learning Afrikaans. No mention is made of, say, the overall number of speakers of the language or its purchase on local or global markets (see Milani *et al.* (2011) for a discussion of these issues in the Welsh context). In other words, posters seem to go 'against the grain' of what has usually emerged in analogous metalinguistic discussions. And this is most likely because commentators are outside the national territory where arguments about cost vs. utility tend to dominate.

Instead, the comments by Donald, Steve and Jenny, together with the support of Liebrecht and other posters, can be seen as acts of linguistic citizenship through which non-native speakers take ownership of Afrikaans, albeit momentarily, highlighting that the worth of this language should be seen as proportional to the real, purported or intended investment that people are willing to make in order to *learn* it. But even within such an idyllic picture where both 'foreigners' and South Africans strongly support Afrikaans, there lurks an element of disorder and disturbance – the fear that this language might be under some form of 'threat' – as emerges in the last lines of both Steve's and Jenny's comments.

Afrikaans and language loss: a question of life or death

Debates about Afrikaans being in danger of extinction are common in the South African media landscape. To take but two examples, the well-known South African writer Breyten Breytenbach has recently bemoaned that 'Afrikaans is going to die within the next ten years', giving rise to a public debate on a popular programme on the South African broadcaster, Radio 702 (see Fourie 2010). Other, less known South African citizens take a very different stance. One of these is Clive Simpkins, a member of the public who, in an online blog debate about the place of Afrikaans in South African schools,[3] went as far as calling for the euthanasia of the Afrikaans language. In a blog entry, Simpkins accused the government of attempting to preserve the language by keeping it 'alive' on the 'life-support system' of education. By suggesting that Afrikaans is being kept artificially alive, Simpkins constructs it as a fading language of no use to anyone, which needs to be actively 'put out of its misery' rather than being allowed to continue a painful existence.

In comparison, the discourses of language endangerment on the Afrikaans board of the BBC *Voices* website are far less stark. In this context, the fear that Afrikaans might die out was not triggered by the short expert article opening the discussion board, nor by an inflammatory post. Rather, the first implicit reference to the possibility of language loss is by Lynette from Ripley, who states that:

> *Extract 5*
>
> [...]
> If you have the benefit of learning more than one language, take that second or third language and never stop developing your use of it. Do whatever you can to maintain and improve it. Then use it to promote understanding between different cultures.

This commentator is speaking in very general terms, underscoring the value of language learning in order to foster *individual* multilingualism as the base through which to improve cross-cultural communication. The implicature is that if one does not 'maintain and improve' L2 and L3, one loses them. In contrast, Steve in Extract 2 above is the first to dramatically focus the issue of language loss and relate it to the specific case of Afrikaans, bemoaning the possibility that this language might be on the verge of extinction ('die out'). As the only possible explanation for the potential forthcoming death of Afrikaans, this commentator alludes to the responsibility of some 'wrong reasons'. What these might be remain unsaid, but can be inferred if we read these words as an intertextual reference to a previous comment (see Extract below).

> *Extract 6*
>
> **Johan from London**
>
> I love the Afrikaans language. I mainly communicate in my social circles in Afrikaans, as I have soooo may Afrikaans speaking friends here. It is very sad that (after going through some of the letters) that so may people associate the 'taal' [*'language'*] with Apartheid. I've moved to London because of these wrongs in the South African past. These wrongs were done by people and not by a language. I am proud to be a South African, and proud to be Afrikaans.

Commenting on the emergence of discourses of language endangerment throughout the world, Heller and Duchêne (2007: 4) maintain that these discourses are nothing but the manifestation of broader preoccupations about 'threats' to the social order. As already noted in the historical overview above, the emotion that surrounds debates about Afrikaans is caused by deeply entrenched feelings ensuing from the associations between this language and South Africa's overtly racist past. *Afrikaans* as a language has become so inextricably intertwined with *the Afrikaner* as a person, who in turn is seen as the main or only figure responsible for the wrongdoings of apartheid (see also Orman 2008). Accordingly, any attempts to overcome this past and build a post-apartheid sense of 'South Africanness' appears to entail the erasure of both Afrikaans and Afrikaners.

It is these controversial linkages that are questioned by Johan in Extract 6 above. Building on his personal experience of migration, this commentator distances himself from South Africa's violent and intolerant past. Whether true or not, his statements allow him to discursively frame himself as liberal and in opposition to (racial) discrimination. But what is most important is that Johan engages in a local act of linguistic citizenship in the sense that he is seeking, albeit momentarily, to reconceptualize the meaning of Afrikaans. This is realized with a discursive move through which Johan seeks to *de-couple* the connection between language, its speakers and the responsibility for the apartheid past. In doing so, he is also accomplishing important identity work, forcefully maintaining that being a liberal South African and being Afrikaans are not necessarily incompatible. In his view, these are not only two identity positions which can comfortably co-exist but can also be reasons for personal pride.

Whilst Steve and Johan refer to the *symbolic* reasons for the devaluing of Afrikaans in post-apartheid South Africa, other commentators take a more 'rational', instrumental view of the factors underpinning the endangerment of this language. From such a 'pragmatic' perspective, the survival of a language can only depend on its speakers. Or, put differently, as long as a language has a large numbers of speakers who use it continually, it is in no danger of dying out, as the next example illustrates.

Extract 7

Werner from Dubai

Our language is definately under pressure. In South Africa some people are trying to boycott the language. Attendants all over refuse to react to requests in Afrikaans. Despite it being near impossible for them to be oblivious of the meaning of your words. Outside South Africa Afrikaans will probably not carry over into the next generation in any significant way. It's just not necessary. That is why I was surprised. I never knew that Afrikaans is offered in Abu Dhabi, a mere hour's drive from where I live in Dubai! Peculiar. In my department we are only two who speak Afrikaans. When we find the time we just babble away in 'Die Taal' [*'The Language'*]. It's delightful! I am amazed however that so many people are trying to learn Afrikaans. It certainly is not something you need on a regular basis. Even in a relationship with an Afrikaner. The greater majority of us speak English fluently. It's great that you are trying. It's my first language and I enjoy the way it feels on my voice. Lank lewe Afrikaans! [*Long live Afrikaans!*]

In discussing the pressure that he believes Afrikaans faces today, Werner looks at the position of the language both within South Africa and abroad. At a national level, he mentions the 'boycott' of the language on the part of 'attendants all over' thus alluding to the fraught feelings about Afrikaans especially among many non-white speakers. Admittedly, there is nothing in the text which could be taken as an explicit reference to race but the word 'attendants' (as a synonym of 'waitron' or 'helper') not only has social class connotations but also carries subtle racial undertones in South Africa, a context where the majority of service personnel still remains non-white.

With regard to the future of Afrikaans outside of South Africa, Werner takes a more ambiguous position. On the one hand, he is not reticent in expressing his satisfaction in enjoying the sound of this language, a form of personal pride which reaches its climax in the slogan 'Long live Afrikaans'. Nearly paradoxically, however, he shows surprise at the number of non-South Africans who are interested in learning this language. He also states that Afrikaans will not be transmitted to the next generation as this language is not needed, due to most of its speakers being bilingual (Afrikaans/English). In this way, Werner subscribes to a view according to which languages disappear if they are not necessary for communication, thus downplaying the fact that many people, like the posters in the previous section, might choose to learn languages for enjoyment or personal enrichment.

The issue of the intergenerational transmission of a language, and its interconnected problems, is reiterated in a slightly different way in Mariselle's comment below.

Extract 8

Mariselle Stolz Germany

> […] In Germany there's a few SA Clubs. Afrikaans could also be taken as subjekt at the Frankfurt Univ. and one of the biggest language schools in the country. A few family's teach there children Afrikaans as home language, also so they can comunicate with Ouma [Grandma] and Oupa [Grandpa] in South Africa…Germans learn Afrikaans in a short time and the same the other way around although after a few years you realize just how many differences you have coming from your culture only. A language is far more than that what you say. I do hope my kids would keep up speaking Afrikaans… it's not alwys easy to keep your Afrikaans as pure and good as it should be and I do hope to have DSL one of these days so we could listen to SA radio and also not just stagnate but grow with this beautifull 'still baby' TAAL [*LANGUAGE*]. […]

Unlike Werner, who underscored the instrumental function of a language as a tool for communication, Mariselle draws upon another common trope in debates about language endangerment, namely that a language is 'far more than what you say'. What this means can be inferred through the preceding sentence about cultural differences between Germans and Afrikaans speakers. Here this commentator seems to espouse a rather essentialist understanding of the language/culture link, a view which materializes in other postings stating that 'language [...] is a way of life'. From this perspective, there is a univocal relationship between a language and a culture, in such a way that every language is seen to express a specific conceptualization of the world. From this it follows that Mariselle's worry about her children not maintaining Afrikaans might be the manifestation of a deeper concern that she, as a migrant parent, feels about the loss of the Afrikaans culture and the total assimilation of her offspring into German society.

In a migrant context of language/culture loss, it might not be unexpected then that the poster also expresses fear for the alleged 'degradation' of Afrikaans. As Heller and Duchêne (2007) have pointed out, preoccupations around the imagined purity of a language and its boundaries are among the most common concerns that are at the core of discourses of language endangerment. Other languages are viewed as 'threats' or 'virus-like attacks on the essence of the languages in question which necessarily undermine their health and potentially lead to their demise' (Heller and Duchêne 2007: 4). In the specific case of the comment above, the threat to 'purity' is represented by speaking a language in a foreign, 'non-authentic' context which is far removed from the country of origin. Hence, one could suggest that Mariselle's longing for a faster internet connection so that she can listen to South African radio (more specifically, *Afrikaans* radio) via audio streaming is ultimately an expression of desire for linguistic 'authenticity'.

Whilst symbolic reasons for the preservation of a language (e.g. the beauty of a language, the death of a culture) are more difficult to oppose, rational and instrumental arguments (e.g. the number of speakers, communication needs) can be easily countered, as can be seen in the examples below, which are sections of postings already reproduced above in their entirety (Extracts 3 and 4).

Jenny Harris from Worcester, England

[...] As far as I can make out, Afrikaans is in no danger of dying out - more people speak it than Danish (I think).

Liebrecht from Caledon, South Africa

Afrikaans is also offered at universities in Poland, Russia and a few others. Afrikaans will never become extinct, even if it tried... :-D

Both commentators employ statements of fact to convey their nearly complete certainty that Afrikaans is not in danger of extinction. Admittedly, both Jenny and Liebrecht employ mitigating discursive resources to tone down the forcefulness of their utterances. Note in particular the smiley face which is indicative of a jokey, humorous tone, as well as the hedges of epistemic modality ('As far as I can make out' and 'I think') which soften the writer's degree of commitment to truth. In contrast to Werner's argument of lack of utility, these two commentators refer to number of speakers and the fact that Afrikaans is offered as a subject at foreign universities as sufficient reasons for Afrikaans not to disappear any time soon.

In conclusion, the discussion about the endangerment of Afrikaans on the discussion board of *Multilingual Nation* simultaneously resembles and differs from similar discussions in 'national' (i.e. South African) media. The similarity lies in the types of argumentation strategies employed in order to support the idea that Afrikaans is on the verge of extinction (or not). The main difference lies in the lower degree of 'heatedness' and the general atmosphere of respect in which the pronouncements have been made on the BBC website (cf. Orman 2008; Shaikjee 2011). The examples above allow us to get a glimpse of the 'superdiverse heteroglossia of voices' (Kelly-Holmes and Milani 2011: 482) from the general public which the Internet allows to be 'heard'. The main trait of these voices is that conformist stances drawing upon essentialist discourses of language and culture go in tandem with more subversive acts of linguistic citizenship which aim at rethinking well-established links between language and identity. The reformulation of the ties between language, ethnicity, national identity and space will be explored in more detail in the next section.

Afrikaans, identity and the time/space connection

Gal (2010) has highlighted the semiotic processes through which nationalism operates, superimposing language, speakers and territory in such a way that they are joined together to form an inextricable nexus (see also Milani *et al.* 2011; Stroud 1999). In the case of Afrikaans, we have already discussed that this language has become over time an *icon* (Irvine and Gal 2000) of white, racist, Afrikaner nationalism in South Africa. As a further token of empirical evidence, one can take the following excerpt, which is positioned at the very top of the Afrikaans discussion board, and is part of the framing of the introductory page (see above).

> *Extract 9*
>
> **How you feel about speaking Afrikaans:**
>
> I feel proud to speak Afrikaans but I do feel it is increasingly used as a tool of identity by the far-right back in S.A., so it does tend to be safer to just speak in English among everybody outside the family, whether they are white, black, coloured or Indian. **Hendrik** (bold typeface in original)

This comment encapsulates most vividly the duality of feelings that many Afrikaans speakers embody in the post-apartheid context. Hendrik, like many other participants on the discussion board (see Extracts 6, 7 and 8), is not shy to overtly express his personal pride in the language. On the other hand, however, Hendrik also manifests a particular political and racial sensitivity to using

Afrikaans in the public sphere. It is as if the very act of speaking this language, irrespective of the actual content of the utterance, could potentially associate him with white supremacist political discourse.

One could go as far as suggesting that Afrikaans has reached the status of a *chronotope*, that is, a specific nexus of time and space. As Bakhtin puts it, chronotopes are:

> points in the geography of a community where time and space intersect and fuse. Time takes on flesh and becomes visible for human contemplation; likewise, space becomes charged and responsive to the movements of time and history and the enduring character of a people … Chronotopes thus stand as monuments to the community itself, as symbol of it, as forces operating to shape its members' images of themselves.
>
> (Bakhtin, 1981: 7)

As a chronotope, Afrikaans is not just a material relic of the apartheid past of South Africa, but is also a ghostly lens through which many speakers (including Afrikaans speakers themselves) interpret the present and project the future. Such a view, however, seems to be fairly marginal if one takes into account the totality of postings on the discussion board. Indeed, a few other commentators suggest that speaking Afrikaans in public is discriminatory, but referred mainly to those circumstances abroad in which other speakers might not understand the language spoken in that context. Rather, most commentators did not buy into the facile normative overlapping of language, ethnicity, nation, people and discrimination but actually questioned such links, as the examples below will illustrate.

> *Extract 10*
>
> **Breyton Van De Hojdenbojden from Leicestershire, England**
>
> I speak Afrikaans with my friends at my local South African social club. I see it more as a sign of S.A's horriffic past back home, but not in England. In England I just see it as a way not to have to stress to speak English!

> *Extract 11*
>
> **Brian Sperryn from Kent**
>
> As with all South Africans, I speak at least 2 languages - English first, Afrikaans second… it wasnt until recently that I actually started speaking it again and I think its great to be bilingual. I do think its very rude for afrikaans speakers to speak afrikaans among people who dont understand it though as many people cant join in the conversation, even if I can. I'm still very proud of afrikaans, it makes me feel like I belong to something rather than being just an English colony.

Extract 12

cynthia from dublin Ireland

> I love speaking Afrikaans eventhough I am living miles away from my home country. My husband is an english born South African and I find that he is now speaking more Afrikaans than when we actually lived in Cape Town! I don't think we will ever forget the fact that we are true south africans no matter where we live in the world or how hard we try to be different.

Needless to say, these three comments were written from very different points of view. One could guess from the name given by the first poster that he identifies as an Afrikaans speaker. In contrast, Brian and Cynthia's husband are bilingual speakers with English as their main language of choice or upbringing. These differences notwithstanding, what emerges in the extracts above is how the experience of migration has allowed the speakers to perform a clear break with, and reconceptualization of, Afrikaans as a chronotope of past/apartheid South Africa.

It is at this juncture that Deleuze and Guattari's (2004) notions of *deterritorialization* and *reterritorialization* can help us to better explain this point. As Patton explains it, deterritorialization is the process through which 'something departs from a given territory, where a territory can be a system of any kind: conceptual, linguistic, social, or affective' (Patton 2010: 143). Reterritorialization instead 'refers to the ways in which deterritorialized elements recombine and enter into new relations in the constitution of a new assemblage or the modification of the old' (Patton 2010: 143).

How deterritorialization and reterritorialization operate in re-texturing the chronotopic fabric of Afrikaans is perhaps most vividly captured in Breyton's comment. South Africa is still viewed by him as 'home', despite the fact that he has 'departed' from it and now has settled down in the UK. But it is precisely the physical/geographical rupture with South Africa that allows him to be able to resignify Afrikaans and invest it with a new meaning. Notably, dislocation from one context to the other does not entail historical amnesia: Breyton indeed subscribes to a similar view to Hendrik's, according to whom Afrikaans in South Africa is a living testimony of the apartheid past. In Breyton's description, however, Afrikaans in the UK presents the characteristics of a deterritorialized element which recombines in a new, and to a certain extent, subversive assemblage: it is a way of countering the hegemonic presence of English in the UK, a style of being positively different.

If choosing to speak Afrikaans in a local South African social club in the UK might sound like a relatively 'unmarked' choice for an Afrikaans speaker, it is in our view a rather poignant statement for those who would usually identify as English language speakers, such as Brian or Cynthia's husband.

For Brian in particular, the spatial break with South Africa allows him to perform a temporal rupture with the historical past of South Africa as a British colony. We saw earlier that Breyton's move enabled him to enter a parallel time/space in which Afrikaans is saturated with positive meanings in his personal life of a migrant in the UK, very different from the ones still present 'back home'. Similarly, Brian's positive feelings for Afrikaans enable him to express a proud feeling of belonging to South Africa, and simultaneously to achieve a sense of distinctiveness from the English-speaking majority in the UK, something that could also account for Cynthia's husband's increased usage of Afrikaans in Ireland.

All in all, through deterritorialization and reterritorialization, Breyton, Brian, Cynthia and her husband have been able to disentangle themselves from the chronotopic lamination of Afrikaans/past/apartheid, and inaugurate a new spatial/temporal nexus, one in which Afrikaans is proudly mobilized in the creation of a present South African migrant space.

Conclusion

It has been pointed out recently that the field of language politics has concentrated too much on top-down political decisions about languages performed by the state (see in particularly Shohamy 2006). Reasoning along similar lines, it could be argued that the literature on language debates has given priority to 'real historical' actors (Blommaert 1999b) (e.g. politicians, journalists, cultural figures, activists, translators, etc.) in the (re)production, circulation and contestation of language ideologies in mainstream media (see the contributors to Blommaert 1999a; Johnson and Ensslin 2007; Johnson and Milani 2010). Less attention has been paid to how such ideas and beliefs are being taken up by no less real 'men and women on the street'. It is these grassroots views that this chapter has aimed to bring into the spotlight, in order to illustrate the everyday life of language politics – a form of 'politics from below' (see Alexander 1992) or a 'politics as usual' (Wodak 2009), in which ideas and beliefs about languages are reproduced and contested by everyday people in apparently mundane contexts such as the Afrikaans discussion board on the BBC *Voices* website.

Of course, we will never know whether these grassroots voices will have an impact on broader discourses in South Africa. But this is ultimately irrelevant. What is more significant is that the discussion board on *Multilingual Nation* opened up a discursive space which has enabled the emergence of *alternative* discourses to the ones usually circulating in South African media and society.

The main point that we want to make in this chapter is that stating that *Afrikaans is bobaas* [Afrikaans is tops], as Graeme from Abu Dhabi wrote on the BBC *Voices* website, is most unlikely to be a chauvinist manifestation of ethnic nationalism. Rather, it is a linguistic performance geared to creating and authenticating a South African migrant identity. As such, it can be viewed as an act of linguistic citizenship through which a member of the public actively participates in the reinterpretation of the meanings of Afrikaans in trans-national spaces of migration with the help of the tools provided by a platform for online communication.

These apparently banal forms of linguistic participation in an online environment remind us that politics '"happens" when one may be led to least expect it – in the nooks and crannies of everyday life, outside of institutionalized contexts that one ordinarily associates with politics' (Besnier 2009: 11; see also Butler 1990). As students of the social life of languages, not only should we be aware of the everyday acts of linguistic citizenship through which speakers agentively oppose dominant language ideologies; we also shouldn't downplay their destabilizing force, which manifests itself by disrupting – albeit locally and momentarily – well-established ideas about languages, identity and culture.

Notes

1 South African statistics about language usage only tell us one side of the story. These data rely mainly on speakers' self-report of language usage, and the focus on home language (in the singular) fails to account for the multilingual repertoire of the South African population, the majority of which has at least some knowledge of Afrikaans.
2 All examples have been reproduced here as originally posted on the discussion board, retaining any typographical errors.
3 http://clivesimpkins.blogs.com/clive_simpkins/2006/06/its_time_for_ak.html

References

Alexander, N. (1992) 'Language planning from below', in R.K. Herbert (ed.) *Language and Society in Africa: The Theory and Practice of Sociolinguistics*, Johannesburg: Wits University Press.

Anderson, B. (1983) *Imagined Communities: Reflections on the Origin and Spread of Nationalism*, London: Verso.

Bakhtin, M.M. (1981) *The Dialogic Imagination: Four Essays*, Austin, TX: University of Texas Press.

Besnier, N. (2009) *Gossip and the Everyday Production of Politics*, Hawaii: University of Hawaii Press.

Billig, M. (1995) *Banal Nationalism*, London: Sage.

Blackledge, A. and Creese, A. (2010) *Multilingualism: A Critical Approach*, London: Continuum.

Blommaert, J. (1999a) *Language Ideological Debates*, Berlin: Mouton de Gruyter.

Blommaert, J. (1999b) 'The debate is open', in J. Blommaert (ed.) *Language Ideological Debates*, Berlin: Mouton de Gruyter.

Bucholtz, M. (2003) 'Sociolinguistic nostalgia and the authentication of identity', *Journal of Sociolinguistics*, 7(3): 398–416.

Butler, J. (1990) *Gender Trouble: Feminism and the Subversion of Identity*, New York: Routledge.

Cameron, D. (1995) *Verbal Hygiene*, London: Routledge.

Coupland, N. (2007) *Style: Language Variation and Identity*, Cambridge, UK: Cambridge University Press.

Davies, B.L., Milani, T. M. and Turner, W. (2012) 'Multilingual nation online? Possibilities and constraints on the BBC Voices website', in S. Gardner and M. Martin-Jones (eds) *Multilingualism, Discourse and Ethnography: Approaches to Mixed-Language Written Discourse*, London: Routledge.

Deleuze, G. and Guattari, F. (2004) *A Thousand Plateaus: Capitalism and Schizophrenia*, London: Continuum.

Dlamini, J. (2009) *Native Nostalgia*, Auckland Park, South Africa: Jacana.

Ensslin, A. and Johnson, S. (2007) 'Language in the news: Investigating representations of "Englishness" using WordSmith Tools', *Corpora*, 1(2): 153–85.

Fairclough, N. (2001) *Language and Power*, 2nd edition, London: Longman.

Fourie, M. (2010) Die taal sterf, sê Breyten. *Beeld* 23/3/2010 (http://www.beeld.com/Suid-Afrika/Nuus/Die-taal-sterf-se-Breyten-20100324).

Gal, S. (2010) 'Language and political space', in P. Auer and J.E. Schmidt (eds) *Language and Space: An International Handbook of Linguistic Variation*, Berlin: Mouton de Gruyter.

Heller, M. and Duchêne, A. (2007) 'Discourses of endangerment: Sociolinguistics, globalization and social order', in A. Duchêne and M. Heller (eds) *Discourses of Endangerment: Ideology and Interest in the Defence of Language*, London: Continuum.

Herring, S. (2001) 'Computer mediated discourse', in D. Schriffrin, D. Tannen and H. E. Hamilton (eds), *The Handbook of Discourse Analysis*, Oxford: Blackwell.

Hine, C. (2000) *Virtual Ethnography*, London: Sage.

Irvine, J.T. and Gal, S. (2000) 'Language ideology and linguistic differentiation', in P.V. Kroskrity (ed.) *Regimes of Language: Ideologies, Polities and Identities*, Santa Fe: School of American Research Press.

Johnson, S. and Ensslin, A. (2007) 'Language in the media: Theory and practice', in S. Johnson and A. Ensslin (ed.) *Language in the Media: Representations, Identities, Ideologies*, London: Continuum.

Johnson, S. and Milani, T.M. (2010) *Language Ideologies and Media Discourse: Texts, Practices, Politics*, London: Continuum.

Kelly-Holmes, H. and Milani, T.M. (2011) 'Introduction: Thematising multilingualism in the media', *Journal of Language and Politics*, 10(4): 467–89.

Lave, J. and Wenger, E. (1991) *Situated Learning: Legitimate Peripheral Participation*, Cambridge: Cambridge University Press.

Milani, T.M. and Johnson, S. (2008) 'CDA and language ideology: Towards a reflexive approach to discourse data', in I.H. Warnke and J. Spitzmuller (eds) *Methoden der Diskurslinguistik Sprachwissenschaftliche Zugaenge zur Transtextuellen Ebene*, Berlin: Mouton de Gruyter.

Milani, T.M. and Johnson, S. (2010) 'Critical intersections: Language ideologies and media discourse', in S. Johnson and T.M. Milani (eds) *Language Ideologies and Media Discourse: Texts, Practices, Politics*, London: Continuum.

Milani, T.M. and Jonsson, R. (2012) 'Who's afraid of Rinkeby Swedish? Stylization, complicity, resistance', *Journal of Linguistic Anthropology*, 22(1): 44–63.

Milani, T.M., Davies, B.L. and Turner, W. (2011) 'Unity in disunity: Centripetal and centrifugal tensions on the BBC Voices website', *Journal of Language and Politics*, 10(4): 587–614.

Milton, V. C. (2008) '"Local is lekker": Nation, narration and the SABC's Afrikaans programmes', *Communicatio*, 34(2): 255–77.

Ord, M. (2005) *Project Director's Presentation of Overview Summary – BBC Voices*, Cardiff: British Broadcasting Corporation.

Orman, J. (2008) *Language Policy and Nation-Building in Post-Apartheid South Africa*, Amsterdam: Springer.

Otsuji, E. and Pennycook, A. (2010) 'Metrolingualism: Fixity, fluidity and language in flux', *International Journal of Multilingualism*, 7(3): 240–54.

Painter, D.W. (2009) *Tongue Tied: The Politics of Language, Subjectivity and Social Psychology in South Africa*, Ph.D. Dissertation, Pretoria: UNISA.

Patton, P. (2010) *Deleuzian Concepts: Philosophy, Colonization, Politics*, Stanford: Stanford University Press.

Pavlenko, A. and Blackledge, A. (2004) *Negotiations of Identities in Multilingual Contexts*, Clevedon, UK: Multilingual Matters.

Rampton, B. (1995) *Crossing: Language and Ethnicity among Adolescents*, London: Longman.

Roberge, P.T. (2006) 'Afrikaans', in A. Deumert and W. Vandenbussche (eds) *Germanic Standardizations: Past to Present*, Amsterdam: John Benjamins.

Rose, A. and Mowbray, F. (n.d.) The UK Speaks (working title), Cardiff: BBC Cymru Wales.

Shaikjee, M. (2011) '"It's time for Afrikaans to go": Metalinguistic commentaries on a blog', Unpublished Honours Essay, Johannesburg: University of the Witwatersrand.

Shohamy, E. (2006) *Language Policy: Hidden Agendas and New Approaches*, London: Routledge.

Stroud, C. (1999) 'Portuguese as ideology and politics in Mozambique: Semiotic (re)constructions of a postcolony', in J. Blommaert (ed.) *Language Ideological Debates*, Berlin: Mouton de Gruyter.

Stroud, C. (2001) 'African mother tongue programs and the politics of language: Linguistic citizenship versus linguistic human rights', *Journal of Multilingual and Multicultural Development*, 22(4): 339–55.

Stroud, C. (2003) 'Postmodernist perspectives on local languages: African mother tongue education in times of globalisation', *International Journal of Bilingual Education and Bilingualism*, 6(1): 17–36.

Sunderland, J. (2004) *Gendered Discourses*, Basingstoke: Palgrave Macmillan.

Thurlow, C. (2007) 'Fabricating youth: New-media discourse and the technologization of young people', in S. Johnson and A. Ensslin (eds) *Language in the Media: Representations, Identities, Ideologies*, London: Continuum.

Williams, Q. and Stroud, C. (2013) 'Multilingualism in transformative spaces: Contact and conviviality', *Language Policy*, 12(2).

Wodak, R. (2009) *The Discourse of Politics in Action: Politics as Usual*, London: Sage.

Woolard, K.A. (1998) 'Language ideology as a field of inquiry', in B.B. Schieffelin, K. A. Woolard and P.V. Kroskrity (eds) *Language Ideologies: Practice and Theory*, New York: Oxford University Press.

6

LANGUAGE IDEOLOGY AND CONVERSATIONALIZED INTERACTIVITY IN *VOICES*

Will Turner

Introduction

This chapter explores the language ideological and political implications of the way the authors of the BBC *Voices* website represented what they described as 'the language of the UK'. Those concerns are language ideological in that they deal with the social values and ideas that people attach to different forms of language (e.g. Schieffelin *et al.* 1998; Woolard 1998) and they become political at the point where those values are purposefully manipulated in the strategic interests of a particular group or organization – in this case the BBC. Specifically, the following sections will show how the *Voices* website promoted a particular set of values surrounding the language(s) used by its audience, and moreover, how it did so in a way that was designed to serve the institutional interests of the BBC in 2004/5.

Given that the BBC's contemporary influence is largely a matter of what, how, and to whom it communicates, these overlapping issues come together as a matter of rhetoric. This is in the sense that rhetoric represents 'the politics of communication' and 'politics' describes 'the attempt to shape and regulate social relations by means of power' (Kress 2010: 45). The approach adopted here, therefore, can be seen to derive from a tradition of discourse analysis which pays critical attention to the underlying ideological and political significance of contemporary media representation (e.g. Fairclough 1995; Fowler *et al.* 1979; Kress and Hodge 1979). However, it follows recent developments in the field to take additional account of the multimodal and interactive character of such representations (e.g. Johnson *et al.* 2010; Kress 2010; Kress and van Leeuwen 2001; Machin 2007; Machin and van Leeuwen 2007; Malinowski 2006; O'Halloran 2004; Ventola *et al.* 2004). The following analysis, accordingly, attends to the website's *interactive* design as well as its graphic and written texts.

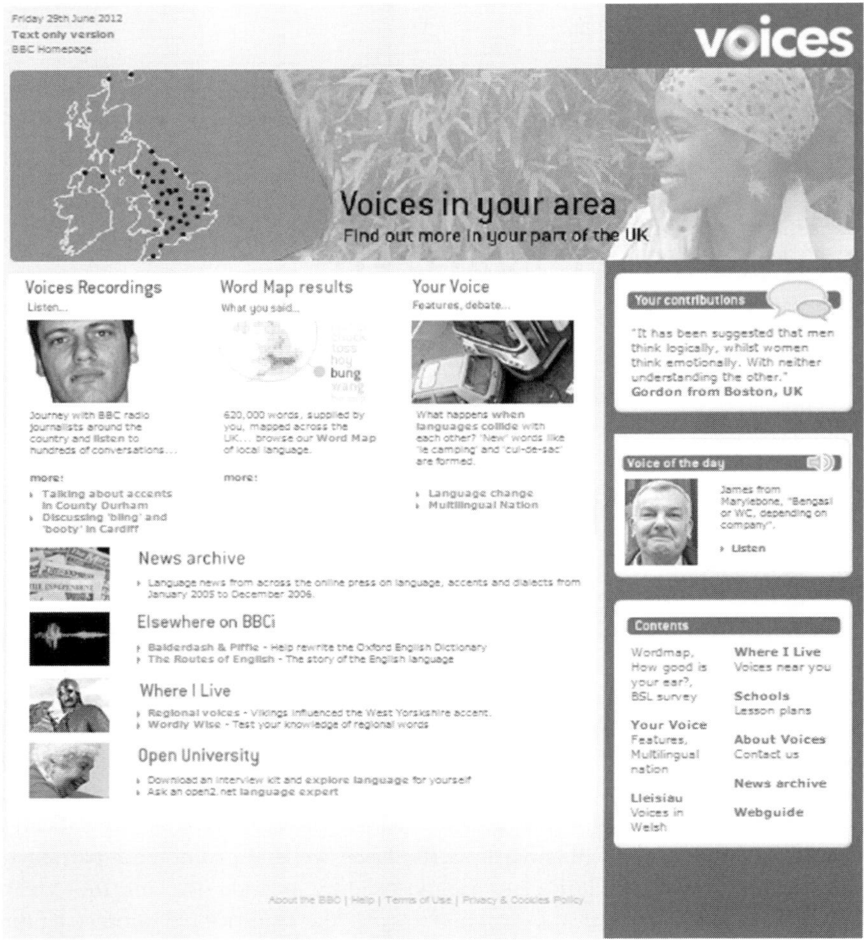

FIGURE 6.1 The BBC *Voices* homepage

In short, I'm dealing with language ideology from the perspective of online rhetoric with a particular interest in interactivity. In this analysis, I show how (1) the presentation and management of interactivity on the website sets up a relation between the site and its users, (2) how this is intrinsic to the strategic promotion of a particular set of values about different language varieties and their speakers and (3) how this reflects and articulates a broader political agenda on the part of the BBC.

Data that shed light on these concerns are taken from the explicitly interactive *Your Voice* section of the website, and from three prominent elements on its homepage (Figure 6.1): an image of 'cartoon' speech bubbles, the visual-verbal composite that introduces the *Your Voice* section, and the animated headline banners that dominate the homepage. These textual analyses are additionally informed by attention to the editorial practices that gave rise to them.

This last point reflects an ethnological concentration on the website (e.g. Androutsopoulos 2010; Cotter 2010; Georgakopoulu 2003; Warnick 2007). Thus my focus is on how the various affordances of hypertext were mobilized by the website's authors so as to achieve particular metalinguistic effects amongst the people using the site.

Metalanguage

I share the view of Coupland and Jaworski (2004) who reject the notion of a completely 'innocent' metalanguage that somehow floats free of the social world it describes. Such an appreciation can be mobilized at any number of levels (cf. Jaworski *et al.* 2004; Jakobson 1960; Silverstein and Urban 1996; Woolard 1998), but my specific concern is the way *Voices* was designed to advocate a liberal, inclusive, democratic, and celebratory view of linguistic diversity (Davies *et al.* 2012; Johnson *et al.* 2010; Milani *et al.* 2011). That is, it was established in order to promote a particular *regime of language* (Kroskrity 2000). Moreover, the way that different language varieties may be taken as indexes (and determinants) of particular social positions (e.g. Irvine 1989; Woolard 1992, 1998) allows that such a specifically linguistic regimentation may articulate an underlying and more general political programme (e.g. Blommaert 2005; Lippi-Green 1997; Milani 2008). In the case of the BBC, this can be summarized as a wholly inclusive, egalitarian treatment of its domestic audience.

Relatedly, I view the BBC as what Michael Silverstein has described as a power-laden 'centering institution' (sic) (Silverstein 1998; see also Blommaert 2005), capable of determining the indexical order which shapes the linguistic norms of the wider public. The status achieved by 'BBC English' as a prestige variety has repeatedly been described in terms that support such a contention (e.g. Lippi-Green 1997; McCrum *et al.* 1992; Milroy and Milroy 1999). From this perspective, the indexical ordering offered by *Voices* as an explicitly metalinguistic exercise is an inescapably ideological concern. That the project was (in part) assessed on the basis of whether or not it was 'thought provoking' and to what extent it made users 'think differently about the way people speak' (Burgess 2005) additionally points to the political intent within this rhetorical scenario. Inevitably, this goes beyond a straightforward matter of 'language about language' (Johnson and Ensslin 2007; Johnson and Milani 2010; Thurlow and Mroczek 2011).

Rhetoric and participation

The view of rhetoric that I am adopting here is intended to acknowledge that beyond its text-internal metadiscourse (Hyland 2005) the website articulates a more general relationship between the BBC and its audience (cf. Cotter 2010). On this basis, the presentation of discursively 'interactive' opportunities as design resources (Aiello 2007) within the website must be seen as important components of its delivery (Cotter 2010; Kress 2010; Mangen 2006; Warnick 2007). However, as writers from a variety of disciplines have shown, there is a considerable difference between 'interactivity' as the provision of a technological channel for communication, and 'interaction' as the accomplishment of such communication (Cyr *et al.* 2009; Domingo 2008; McDonald 2007; Quiring 2009; Talbot 2007). Recognising this distinction is an important first step in unpacking the implications of the website's interactive design.

More generally, Kress and van Leeuwen have (amongst others) identified a historical 'move away from decontextualized representation and imaginary identification towards participation, community and co-creation' in contemporary media (2001: 110). Audiences, they contend, are no longer simply addressed as passive consumers; they increasingly contribute to, and participate in, media productions as well (cf. also Lievrouw and Livingston 2006). The World Wide Web has, of course, become the defining example for this participatory emphasis (Warnick 2007). Kress (2010: 73) has drawn on Foucault (1982) to account for this macro-social shift in terms of a horizontal (democratic), rather than a vertical (authoritarian), (re)distribution of power.

The participatory trend is reflected in the design of the *Voices* project which was, from the outset, based on audience contributions, and which was, in the words of its Project Director, Mick Ord, 'grassroots', 'bottom up', and 'all about the audience' (Ord 2004). *Voices'* emphasis on public participation thus stands in sharp contrast to the early BBC's authoritarian promotion of standard language ideologies (e.g. Lippi-Green 1997; McCrum *et al.* 1992; Milroy and Milroy 1999).

In what follows, however, I want to show that, for all this historical shift, there remains a critical gap between participation and the sort of 'imaginary identification' referred to above (cf. also Anderson 2006 [1983]; Warner 2002). In other words, the distinction between journalistic *interactivity* and linguistic *interaction* is a key issue. As Cotter points out:

> *interaction* means the evolving, emergent, community-based activities of exchanges between and amongst participants [whereas] journalistic *interactivity* means the use of technologies like the web to achieve information exchange, and in the process establish positions of professional identity and interaction.
>
> (2010: 126)

Interactivity relates to hypertextual infrastructure whilst interaction describes the exchanges that take place between people across that infrastructure. As Cotter stresses, these two sides of participation represent a subtle but analytically important distinction. In the current context, it is one that needs to be appreciated in order to get to grips with the rhetorical significance of the BBC's representation of its 'interactive' relationship with its audience and their language.

Conversationalization

The contemporary relevance of the historical optic described above is summed up in Norman Fairclough's identification of the linguistic 'conversationalization' of contemporary public (and particularly media) discourse: the modelling of public discourse on the model of 'everyday life' (Fairclough 1994). However, Fairclough is at pains to point out that conversationalization does not 'arise with its cultural value and significance predetermined' (1994: 266). Rather, he insists on its ambivalent status. This is in the sense that, on the one hand, conversationalization is 'a focus of struggles to substantively democratize society', and, on the other, it is an attempt to 'maintain existing hegemonic relations through a *semblance* of democratization' [emphasis added]. He adds, 'its ambivalence is a symptom of the complexity and unresolved and contradictory nature of the current social settlement' (1994: 266).

In the following sections I expand this critical appreciation in order to see how, and with what effects, 'participation, community and co-creation' are offered and delivered in terms of visual and interactive design resources. In effect, what I am proposing is an extension of the scope of conversationalization that takes into critical account the way multiple modes of communication can be combined to engineer a *conversationalized* sense of informal intimacy, or 'immediacy' (O'Sullivan *et al.* 2004), between the user, the text, and its source. It is on this basis that I will draw on Fairclough's terminology to point to the *synthetic* quality (e.g. Fairclough 1989) of the apparent interaction on offer within the *Voices* website.

The politics of participation

As outlined above, the *Voices* project was conceived in terms of the scale of the potential public feedback that a website, rather than a more traditional media vehicle, could deliver (BBC 2004). The provision of devices enabling users to submit regional lexis, play an 'accent recognition game', identify regional sign language variants, and take part in a series of linguistically-themed 'debates', stand as the realization of those plans. Whilst the first four of those mechanisms stand as academically grounded exercises in data capture, the *Your Voice* section which framed those debates cannot.[1] The question of what purpose it did serve is therefore pertinent. By extension, an important element of the strategic program underlying the entire website is also brought into question.

My concern with these issues can thus be seen as a refinement of the more general treatment of media–user relations as a kind of 'pseudo-dyad' (Cotter 2010) by which media claim to engage in two-way communication with their audiences. The point of this is to highlight the synergy between the website's language ideological delivery as a matter of 'content' and its (hyper-)textual realization. The decision to anchor the project around a website (rather than one of the BBC's more established media) is, thus, a fundamental aspect of its projection (cf. Georgakopoulou 2003). My analysis hinges on what, exactly, 'interactivity' means in such a context. As the wealth of recent attention devoted to the subject amply demonstrates, this is not a straightforward matter (e.g. Cyr *et al.* 2009; Domingo 2008; McDonald 2007; McMillan 2000, 2002a, 2002b; Quiring 2009; Warnick 2007).

In terms of the *Your Voice* section of the website, a key issue is the way in which user contributions were re-entextualized to synthesize a sense of lively interaction in the form of 'debate'. This is an important aspect of the project authors' declared intention to 'get personal' with their community of coverage (Ord 2004, 2005a, 2005b) and, more generally, to foster a 'national conversation' (Mowbray 2005) around the subject of language. On this basis, it is wholly appropriate to treat the website as a profoundly conversationalized entity: that is, as evidence of the professional technologization of media discourse (e.g. Fairclough 1994, 1999) and as the textual realization of deeper ideological tensions (cf. also Cotter 2010; Kress 2010).

Interactivity

In order to provide a break-down of what can otherwise be an analytically problematic concept (Quiring 2009; Warnick 2007), I adopt the three-part descriptive taxonomy of interactivity offered by McMillan (2002a). McMillan distinguishes between 'user-to-system' interactivity, 'user-to-user' interactivity, and 'user-to-document' interactivity. In brief, user-to-system interactivity accords with the notion of navigational control and is of only marginal interest here.[2] User-to-user interactivity describes the ability of users to respond to earlier messages and for those messages to be responded to in turn. Instant messaging or a conventional open-access message board therefore fits the description of user-to-user interactivity. Importantly, in so doing, they afford the greatest measure of direct, uninterrupted *interaction* (Cotter 2010: 126). As a distinction, user-to-document interactivity reflects the ability of users to merely submit material that changes the content of the host site. This idea has been summarized in terms of users' ability to 'vote in online polls, submit questions to be answered ... or post messages and photos that become part of the website text' (Warnick 2007: 76). It therefore allows for only the most limited and indirect interactive potential. *Voices* is characterized by considerable use of such user-to-document interactivity. Necessarily, the recognition of different types of interactivity allows for markedly different rhetorical effects to be addressed.

Interactivity in Voices

The explanatory potential of McMillan's typology becomes clear once the production processes that lead to the publication of the messages within the *Your Voice* section are considered. The views of (then) Production Assistant Philippa Law, who was directly involved in the process, are revealing:

> The comments section … can't be called a message board; it's much more basic than that. It's just a selection of comments we received at the time. The system was premoderated – slowly – and it didn't allow messages to appear in threads, so it discouraged users to have an on-going conversation.
> (Law 2010)

First, user contributions were subject to mandatory editorial scrutiny (i.e. 'premoderated') before being added to the site (BBC 2005). Importantly, in terms of the published 'debate', this meant that there was a delay in messages being uploaded – often longer than a week. Second, messages were added according to the approximate order of their submission rather than brought together according to their content (i.e. 'threaded'). This 'disrupted turn adjacency' (Herring 2001: 618) made two-way exchanges (i.e. interaction) difficult. Third, these difficulties were exacerbated by the way in which the posts were ordered on the site, with newer messages placed above older ones. Consequently, any turn-taking sequences were effectively presented in reverse order. This is all the more problematic as, in the absence of any time or a date marks, this reverse ordering is not immediately evident (cf. Davies *et al*. 2012).

These factors combined to make it progressively more difficult to link arguments across posts as increasing numbers of contributions were submitted and published. Law's summation of the effects of this arrangement is usefully concise: 'It's not dynamic and it's not an open forum. It's essentially flat, dead text'. In other words, interactivity, as realized in this section of the website, is unambiguously user-to-document in character rather than the more dynamic user-to-user form that is suggested. How this *semblance* of dynamic user-to-user interactivity is promoted in verbal and visual terms is set out in the following sections.

Verbal claims to interaction

First, the verbal (written) title of the section makes what Fairclough (1989) calls the 'synthetic' and 'personalized' sense of direct interaction I am describing explicit: *Your Voice*. This title appears on the homepage, as a banner headline throughout this section, and as a link within the site's ubiquitous sidebar menu. The synthetic personalization (Fairclough 1989) in *Your Voice* forms a direct call on the reader in terms of second person address, and it does so whilst asserting the democratic element described above as a possessive quality – hence the possessive pronoun. This is in the widely used metonymic sense of 'voice' as a universal democratic attribute. Of course, it simultaneously connotes the website's linguistic theme, and it is precisely this linguistic and political/ideological overlap that is of interest here.

The conflation of *Your Voice* with the promise of 'debate' sets up a powerful expectation that some form of interaction is being made available. Moreover, this is wholly in key with the democratic, 'grass roots' emphasis of the overall project. The realization of this expectation in the subsequent prompts to submit a contribution is, thus, part of an overall delivery that affords users apparently equalized ('horizontal') relations with each other and with the text producers (Cyr *et al*. 2009).

From a grammatical perspective, the widespread use of interrogative and imperative moods and ungrammatical strings in the editorial texts across the site gives further emphasis to this apparent dialogicality – e.g. '*Journey with* BBC radio journalists around the country and *listen to* hundreds of conversations…'; 'Fireman, firewoman or fire fighter? Calling each other names is natural, but do they lead to discrimination?' Even allowing for the tendency towards such informality in online material generally (e.g. Crystal 2001), the website is marked by its strikingly conversationalized and directly personalized use of language.

Your Voice: The offer of interactivity

Reflecting the important distinction between 'interactivity' and 'interaction' described above, I will use the term *synthetic interaction* in what follows to summarize the way that the interactional potential of the website is systematically exaggerated. This ties back to the idea of conversationalization since what is at issue is the distinction between a *semblance* of democratization and its substantive delivery.

My specific interest at this point is the presentation of the written submissions which constitute the proffered 'debate'. As we have seen, despite exaggerated suggestions of interaction, the structural features and editorial processes determining the publication of messages were highly restrictive. In effect, they restricted the exercise to a user-to-document exchange, resulting in what we have seen described as 'flat dead text'.

There are, however, features in the presentation of these messages which can be seen to militate against such a reading. And it is the disjunction between this limitation to user-to-document interactivity and its presentation as seemingly unmediated user-to-user interactivity that opens up the question of synthetic interaction. Specifically, this applies to the layout and presentation of the messages themselves. I will deal with the question of layout first.

The posts are presented together on pages that require the user to scroll down as many as ten screen lengths to be able to see them all (depending on screen size and browser settings). This extended page length contrasts with the bulk of the website which delivers pages that span a more conventional two or three screen lengths (e.g. Lynch and Horton 1999). The effect of the extended pagination in *Your Voice* is to signal an uninterrupted public participation, thereby demonstrating a claim for the project as a 'grass roots' exercise (Ord 2005a). The absence of any editorial comment means they are separated only by 'empty' white space. As a result contributions appear to share an open, unmediated terrain (Davies *et al*. 2012), and since they are presented in an entirely linear arrangement, one beneath the other, they appear to realize the progression of a unitary 'debate'. The institutional nature of the exercise is downplayed whilst equivalence between messages (and hence users) is promoted.

The editorial treatment of individual messages adds to this impression of vernacular authenticity. Typically, each message is marked with the name (or chosen identifier) of the correspondent and their location. Additionally, many of the messages show non-standard spellings, inconsistent punctuation, and/or irregular spacing. This stands in marked contrast to the editorial material on the site. Whatever the production process involved in uploading the messages, the impression this delivers is of public submissions arriving untouched by any intervening hand. In effect, the identifiable yet 'messy' quality of the messages promotes a sense of unmediated authenticity (Coupland 2003) whereby contributors express themselves in their own words (Jaffe 2011). As we have seen, however, for all its ideological consistency with the democratic ethos of the website, this impression is at odds with the careful 'premoderation' involved in actually approving messages for inclusion within the site.

Thus, in keeping with the overall layout of the messages, their internal textual realization can be seen to offer precisely the *semblance* of a democratic delivery that Fairclough identifies as a feature of conversationalization. Likewise, as the unacknowledged editorial processes demonstrate, this democratized delivery is in tension with the BBC's control over which messages actually appeared, and when and how they did so.

We do not have access to the messages that were rejected, although they would undoubtedly prove informative. However, the inclusion of messages that were antithetical to the entire process is revealing. As in the example below, they can be seen as both a warrant for the apparently open, democratic forum the website provides, as well as evidence for the way that users accepted it as such. For example, an offering from the 'Language change' thread reads,

> What a load of rubbish! Is this all people have to worry about these days? Lucky them!

At this point it seems entirely relevant to point to Fairclough's observation that one of the consequences of conversationalization is that 'it is becoming increasingly difficult to differentiate informative discourse from persuasive discourse (or "telling" from "selling")' (1994: 257). The BBC's celebratory promotion of its language ideological agenda in *Voices* seems to offer a case in point, even if not all of its readers bought into it. As I have hinted at here, and as I will substantiate in the following section, this persuasive thrust is not a matter of linguistic representation alone.

Visual claims to interaction

Various graphic elements combine to signal that the website offers a dynamically interactive arena. I draw attention to two of these elements here, and show how they inform the reading of a third. All three are highly salient aspects of the website's visual design and consequently they also have a significant bearing on its language ideological delivery.

Speech bubbles

FIGURE 6.2 Speech bubbles

The two-part cartoon 'speech bubbles' that appear on the homepage and throughout the *Your Voice* section are the most straightforward of the three examples. This design is shown in Figure 6.2. First, their status as low modality (i.e. non-naturalistic), 'cartoon' style images suggests an informal, entertainment-oriented genre (Kress and van Leeuwen 2006: 166). Second, they not only provide a graphic representation of 'speech' (Johnson *et al.* 2010), but in their paired, overlaid, and bi-directional arrangement they can be seen to encode speech as a process of on-going two-way exchange.

From a more directly ideological perspective, the absence of any identified speakers or any actual 'content' within the bubbles effectively render the design universal. This is the familiar trope whereby, because it is not about anyone in particular, it can be read as being about everyone in general. What is conveyed is a visual metaphor for a dynamic, plural, and wholly egalitarian process of exchange. And moreover, it is one that is offered as a generic form of casual entertainment. The accompanying verbal text, 'Your contributions', operates on a similarly personalized basis as the *Your Voice* title already discussed, but this is inescapably added to by the dynamic to and fro suggested by the image. Additionally, the use of the second person possessive pronoun here can be seen as an ambiguous reference to either the user and/or the audience as a whole. In either case, however, user contributions are represented as forming part of an ongoing process of interaction.

'Your Voice' *introductory infobite*

The issue of debate is explicitly introduced in the prominent infobite (Davies *et al.* 2012) section of the homepage that introduces the *Your Voice* section. It is shown in Figure 6.3. What is pertinent here is how the opposing (hegemonic and democratizing) ideological tensions identified by Fairclough as the critical dimensions of conversationalization are realized as overlapping questions of synthetic interactivity and language ideology.

In the first instance, both verbal and visual components of the infobite draw on a metaphor of collision. By this means two significant motifs are established. First, the 'debate' highlighted in the title is presented as a dramatic clash

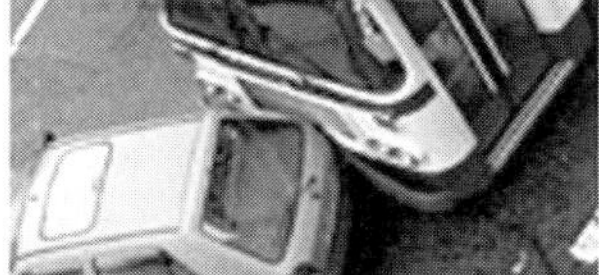

FIGURE 6.3 Infobite introducing the 'Your Voice' section

of opinion (cf. Arnheim 1997) and, as such, a form of spectacle that may be both informative and entertaining (cf. Fairclough 1992). Second, the subject of language contact is presented in similarly vivid terms. In effect, the 'crash' image effectively operates as a form of visual pun (e.g. Kress 1988) on this idea of different sorts of collision. This has a number of effects.

First, a general motif of factuality arises from the rendering of the image in the form of a documentary-style photograph. In Kress and van Leeuwen's (2006) terms it is rendered with a 'high modality' (2006: 154ff). This recognizably real-world scene, however, is one from which the viewer is put at one remove by means of an extended 'social distance' (2006: 124 ff) (i.e. a photographic long-shot) and an almost vertical camera angle which renders a flat, 'neutralized' background (2006: 144). The decontextualization that this delivers is exaggerated by the close cropping of the image such that its physical context is elided. Consistent with the 'Features, debate…' heading, the scene is offered to the viewer as an almost abstract spectacle.

This is entirely in key with the detached, objective, and above all, serious basis for the discussion introduced by the headline text. However, as an identifiably metaphorical representation, it is not contingent on any specific point of argument, or indeed any human participant. The effect thus matches that of the anonymous and 'empty' cartoon speech bubbles, albeit with a sense of greater complexity and gravitas.

The second suggestion the image is called on to deliver derives from the text immediately beneath it: 'What happens **when languages collide** with each other?' Clearly, this reflects a more explicit linguistic focus, and in this relation the depicted car and bus evidently symbolize different languages, albeit in the most general terms. The point I want to make here is that the various elements that make up this aspect of the infobite are, in effect, out of synch.

First, the disjointed angularity of the image graphically evokes uncomfortable and chaotic associations (cf. Dondis 1973: 46). The prominence of sombre greys and black (Kress and van Leeuwen 2002: 355) and the use of quite drab, heavily saturated (2002: 357) shades of colour only adds to this impression. In Kress and van Leeuwen's terms the picture makes use of 'symbolic suggestive' processes which de-emphasize detail in favour of 'mood' or 'atmosphere' (2006: 106). From a rhetorical perspective, such a markedly affective presentation is significant since it has a direct bearing on users' engagement with the material being discussed (Kress 2010). As visually represented here, contact is uncomfortable, unpredictable, and cheerless.

In terms of its depiction of language contact, the image conveys an ideologically loaded set of presuppositions, not the least of which is that distinctions between language varieties are somehow clear-cut (Irvine and Gal 2000; Pennycook 2007). A second, more affective suggestion is that contact between them may be somehow damaging or unsettling. As an opening move in the promotion and celebration of cross-linguistic fusion this is hardly very helpful. The productive potential described in the 'pidgins and creoles' section, to which the emboldened text forms a hyperlink (and which echoes the site's overall celebration of diversity), is entirely at odds with this depiction.

These tensions become increasingly evident in the text which effectively answers the interrogative ('new' words like 'le camping' and 'cul-de-sac' are formed') since the affective tone of this wording is at odds with the negativity described above. Indeed, it seems to suggest that something positive is generated (assuming that newness and formation connote positively). Likewise, the emboldened phrase appears to draw on a parodic genre of cheerful theatricality (e.g. 'when worlds collide'), even if it is somewhat watered down by the tautologous 'with each other'.

At the same time, as the use of scare quotes around the adjective signals (cf. Fairclough 1989: 89), the status of those examples as 'new' is itself questionable. The use of such familiar examples as the well-established 'cul-de-sac'[3] and 'le camping' (a stereotypical French borrowing from English) represent highly relative illustrations of 'newness'. In other words, any suggestion of novelty is displaced either temporally ('it was new then') or geographically ('it is new there'). As a result, this careful wording can be seen to argue for linguistic innovation in a way that is entirely without consequence for contemporary British English. It sets up a forum in a way that avoids triggering the familiar complaint tradition (Milroy and Milroy 1999) on any specific point of contention (the depicted car and bus could represent any two languages, after all). Consequently, this arrangement appears to pose no direct challenge to (Anglophone) standard language ideologies or their underpinning ideas of historical fixity (Cameron 1995; Lippi-Green 1997; Milroy and Milroy 1999).

Consequently, the promotion of the 'debate', as introduced here, is uninterrupted by any actual point of controversy. That is, because 'cul-de-sac' and 'le camping' are so manifestly banal, they are most unlikely to prove contentious or provoke any dramatic clash of opinion.

Homepage headline banners

The third visual element to be considered is the animated banner that headlines the homepage. Although there is much that could be said of the way this device affectively stimulates the user's engagement with the page in terms of its steady, relaxed rhythm, its use of photography, and 'solid' blocks of unmodulated colour (Johnson *et al.* 2010), my interest is more specifically concerned with the way these aspects of its presentation combine to accentuate the sense of dialogicality. In particular, this is delivered by the shifting left–right organization of the photographs and the angular blocks of colour in each of the banners. As the different designs appear, so the user's eye is rhythmically directed one way and then the other. These banners are shown in Figure 6.4.

It is possible to view the shifts in the represented 'social distance' (Kress and van Leeuwen 2006: 124) between the viewer and the represented participants in these banners in the same light. That is, the sense of left-to-right 'movement' described here is added to by a backwards-and-forwards suggestion of perspectival depth as those participants are represented as closer to, and further away from, the viewer. In sequence, they can be described in terms of a 'medium shot', an 'extreme close-up', two successively less intimate 'close-ups', and a repetition of the 'extreme close up' (ibid.). Once again, the user's visual relation to the represented participants and to the text is subject to continual fluctuation.

FIGURE 6.4 *Voices* homepage headline banners in sequence

The animated design can be seen to encode the same underlying message as the cartoon bubbles and the car crash image. The description of language as speech within a design that alternates back and forth, and that draws attention to different perspectives, stands as a powerful symbol for the apparently vibrant, interactive, and egalitarian space which is being introduced. The photographic representation of different people from different generations and different ethnicities in what are clearly different physical environments is thus entirely in keeping with this invocation of multiple contexts and perspectives.

Fundamentally, the way these 'differences' are presented as balanced, engaging, and even attractive can be seen as an articulation of the ideological current resonating throughout the project. Just as we have seen the claim made that language contact is positive and productive, the bringing together of different viewpoints can be seen as equally valorized in this affectively engaging arrangement.

Elsewhere on the homepage there are conspicuous instances where the relatively static user-to-document nature of the interactivity on offer is acknowledged, e.g. the infobite on the homepage entitled 'Word Map What you said…620,000 words supplied by you…'.[4] However, even here, the verbal delivery is offered in a highly conversationalized manner. Thus, 'What you said' is a somewhat artificial description of what might be re-rendered as 'what other people have submitted in writing'. The suggestion that some sort of conversational move has actually been made clearly exaggerates the degree of interactivity that has taken place. The point is that the directly personalized nature of these written extracts is entirely in keeping with the depiction of interactivity within the site as though it were a form of lively, dynamic interaction.

In sum, user contributions are frequently referred to, either directly or indirectly, as forming components of an ongoing series of exchanges. They are repeatedly represented as examples of dynamic user-to-user interactivity – and hence some form of direct interaction – rather than the static user-to-document interactivity which the website overwhelmingly delivers.

Conclusion

In this chapter, I have highlighted three highly salient aspects of the *Voices* site's visual presentation, as well as the way it sets up a synthetic sense of interaction with its users through its linguistic choices. This has gone some way towards addressing the question of how the site's overall rhetoric bears on its ideological delivery. Needless to say, these examples represent only a small part of that overall effect. For example, the numerous photographs that can be seen of 'ordinary' people throughout the site can be seen to have been arranged in such a way that, by 'looking the viewer in the eye', they synthesize a similar 'pseudo social bond' (Kress and van Leeuwen 2006: 118) and a wholly democratized relation between the site and its users. Likewise, closer attention to user-to-system interactivity would draw attention to the phenomenological engagement that a concentration of links can generate (e.g. Mangen 2006, 2008). The question of online rhetoric, then, is one that necessarily extends beyond a discretely linguistic approach. What is offered here can only provide an indication of the semiotic complexities involved in a website like *Voices*.

In doing so I hope to have shown that just as different communicative modes can be synchronized so as to deliver a concerted rhetoric of immediacy, there is no guarantee that such a synchronization will be achieved. This is the evidence of the example of the *Your Voice* infobite. Moreover, it is precisely this cross-modal disjuncture that exposes the divide between the *semblance* of democracy and the political basis underpinning it.

To put this in terms of the indexical ordering touched on earlier, what *Voices* argues for is a flat, indexical equivalence between varieties. Notwithstanding the editorial adherence to standard written English, political distinctions between varieties are conspicuously dismissed, as in, for example, the projection of a unitary multilingual nation (Milani *et al.* 2011). In keeping with the broader historical movement towards a more 'horizontal' distribution of power, what is projected is a collapse (or erasure) of indexical ordering so as to render all varieties (and speakers) seemingly equal.

The conversationalized character of *Voices* means that the BBC is included in this egalitarian scenario. Of course, the promotion of this apparently democratic drive is in and of itself every bit as politically and ideologically grounded as the authoritarian regime that historically promoted BBC English. The linguistic impact may be less conspicuous, and the implementation of control may be persuasive where it was once didactic ('selling' rather than 'telling'), but the exercise of indexical determination is nonetheless common to both. To echo Fairclough's summation of conversationalization, whilst there is a very strong semblance of democratization, the BBC's hegemonic attempt to regiment linguistic indexicalities remains.

A key aspect of this scenario is that *Voices* was produced at a time when the BBC's executives were going to considerable lengths to justify the corporation's level of public funding on the basis of the 'public value' which the BBC delivers to 'everyone' (e.g. Grade 2004). That is, there is a direct corollary between the corporation's executive strategy of universal inclusion and the regime of language promoted within *Voices*. Detailed analysis of the *Voices* project archive, and the testimony of those involved, shows the marked extent to which *Voices* was conceived as a means to articulate this executive strategy (Turner 2011).[5]

At a time when academic departments in the United Kingdom are subject to similar budgetary pressures to those faced by the BBC, it seems pertinent to point out that an awareness of conversationalized institutional positioning is as relevant to those involved in the study of twenty-first-century English as it is to the BBC. And in neither case is such positioning either apolitical or ideology-free. Reflecting what we have seen as the 'unresolved and contradictory nature of the current social settlement' (Fairclough 1994: 266), there is very little between 'educating' and 'informing', as wholly enriching processes, and persuading people to 'think differently', as a hegemonic one.

Notes

1 The project records show an early intention to use this section as a means to formally assess 'language attitudes', however this initiative foundered amidst a complex of ethical and practical difficulties.
2 This is not to deny the ideological implications of navigational arrangements in hypertext, e.g. see Aarseth (1997) and Iedema (2003) for detailed discussions.
3 The Oxford English Dictionary dates the first use of the term in English to the mid-eighteenth century.
4 This infobite is arranged alongside the *Your Voice* infobite described above. It links to a graphic display showing the geographical distribution of 'local language' tokens.
5 See McNicholas (2004) for a comparable example.

References

Aarseth, E. (1997) *Cybertext: Perspectives on Ergodic Literature,* Baltimore, MD: Johns Hopkins University Press.

Aiello, G. (2007) 'The appearance of diversity: Visual design and the public communication of EU identity', in J. Bain and M. Holland (eds) *European Union Identity: Perceptions from Asia and Europe,* Baden-Baden: Nomos.

Anderson, B.R.O. (2006 [1983]) *Imagined Communities: Reflections on the Origin and Spread of Nationalism,* London: Verso.

Androutsopoulos, J. (2006) 'Introduction: Sociolinguistics and computer-mediated communication', *Journal of Sociolinguistics,* 10, 419–38.

Androutsopoulos, J. (2010) 'Localising the global on the participatory web: Vernacular spectacles as local responses to global media flows', in N. Coupland (ed.) *Handbook of Language and Globalization,* Oxford: Wiley-Blackwell.

Arnheim, R. (1997) *Visual Thinking,* Berkley, CA and Los Angeles, CA: University of California Press.

BBC (2004) *UK Speaks*, unpublished 'project spec', Cardiff: BBC Cymru Wales.

BBC (2005) *Editorial Guidelines 15: Interacting with our Audiences.* Online. Available HTTP: <http://www.bbc.co.uk/guidelines/editorialguidelines/edguide/interacting/gamesusergenera.shtml> (accessed 22 August, 2010).

Blommaert, J. (2005) *Discourse: A Critical Introduction,* Cambridge: Cambridge University Press.

Burgess, K. (2005) *Voices Evaluation Report for BBC Nations and Regions*, London: MC & A Audience and Consumer Research.

Cameron, D. (1995) *Verbal Hygiene,* London: Routledge.

Cotter, C. (2010) *News Talk: Investigating the Language of Journalism,* Cambridge: Cambridge University Press.

Coupland, N. (2003) 'Sociolinguistic authenticities', *Journal of Sociolinguistics,* 7: 417–31.

Coupland, N. and Jaworski, A. (2004) 'Sociolinguistic perspectives on metalanguage: Reflexivity, evaluation and ideology', in A. Jaworski, N. Coupland and D. Galasiñski (eds) *Metalanguage: Social and Ideological Perspectives,* Berlin: Mouton de Gruyter.

Crystal, D. (2001) *Language and the Internet,* Cambridge: Cambridge University Press.

Cyr, D., Head, M. and Ivanov, A. (2009) 'Perceived interactivity leading to e-loyalty: Development of a model for cognitive-affective user responses', *International Journal of Human-Computer Studies,* 67: 850–69.

Davies, B.L., Milani, T.M. and Turner, W. (2012) 'Multilingual nation online? Possibilities and constraints on the BBC Voices website', in M. Martin-Jones and S. Gardner (eds) *Multilingualism, Discourse and Ethnography,* London: Routledge.

Domingo, D. (2008) 'Interactivity in the daily routines of online newsrooms: Dealing with an uncomfortable myth', *Journal of Computer-Mediated Communication,* 13: 680–704.

Dondis, D.A. (1973) *A Primer of Visual Literacy,* Cambridge MA: MIT Press.

Fairclough, N. (1989) *Language and Power,* London: Longman.

Fairclough, N. (1992) *Discourse and Social Change,* Cambridge: Cambridge Polity Press.

Fairclough, N. (1994) 'Conversationalization of public discourse and the authority of the consumer', in R. Keat, N. Whitely and N. Abercrombie (eds) *The Authority of the Consumer,* London: Routledge.

Fairclough, N. (1995) *Media Discourse,* London: Arnold.

Fairclough, N. (1999) 'Global capitalism and critical awareness of language', *Language Awareness,* 8: 71–83.

Foucault, M. (1982) *The Archaeology of Knowledge and the Discourse on Language,* London: Tavistock Press.

Fowler, R., Hodge, B., Kress, G. and Trew, T. (1979) *Language and Control,* London: Routledge & Kegan Paul.

Georgakopoulou, A. (2003) 'Computer-mediated communication', in J. Verschueren, J-O Östmann, J. Blommaert and C. Bulcaen (eds) *Handbook of Pragmatics,* Amsterdam: John Benjamins.

Grade, M. (2004) *Building Public Value: Chairman's Prologue*, London: BBC.

Herring, S.C. (2001) 'Computer mediated discourse', in: D. Schiffrin, D. Tannen and E. Hamilton (eds) *The Handbook of Discourse Analysis*, Oxford: Blackwell.

Hyland, K. (2005) *Metadiscourse: Exploring Interaction in Writing,* London: Continuum.

Iedema, R. (2003) 'Multimodality, resemiotization: Extending the analysis of discourse as multi-semiotic practice', *Visual Communication,* 2: 29–57.

Irvine, J. (1989) 'When talk isn't cheap: Language and political economy', *American Ethnologist,* 16: 248–67.

Irvine, J. and Gal, S. (2000) 'Language ideology and linguistic differentiation', in P. Kroskrity (ed.) *Regimes of Language: Ideologies, Polities and Identities,* Oxford: James Currey.

Jaffe, A. (2011) 'Sociolinguistic diversity in mainstream media: Authenticity, authority and processes of mediation and mediatization', *Journal of Language and Politics,* 10: 562–86.

Jakobson, R. (1960) 'Closing statemement: Linguistics and poetics', in T.A. Sebeok (ed.) *Style in Language,* Cambridge MA: MIT Press.

Jaworski, A., Coupland, N. and Galasinski, D. (eds) (2004) *Metalanguage: Social and Ideological Perspectives,* Berlin: Mouton de Gruyter.

Johnson, S. and Ensslin, A. (eds) (2007) *Language in the Media: Representations, Identities, Ideologies,* London: Continuum.

Johnson, S. and Milani, T.M. (eds) (2010) *Language Ideologies and Media Discourse: Texts, Practices, Politics,* London: Continuum.

Johnson, S., Milani, T.M. and Upton, C. (2010) 'Whose Voices? A hypermodal approach to language ideological debates on the "BBC Voices" website', in S. Johnson, and T. M. Milani (eds) *Language Ideologies and Media Discourse: Texts Practices, Politics,* London: Continuum.

Kress, G. (1988) *Communication and Culture: An Introduction,* Kensington, NSW, Australia: New South Wales University Press.

Kress, G. (2010) *Multimodality: A Social Semiotic Approach to Contemporary Communication,* London: Routledge.

Kress, G. and Hodge, G. (1979) *Language as Ideology,* London: Routledge.

Kress, G. and van Leeuwen, T. (2001) *Multimodal Discourse: The Modes and Media of Contemporary Communication,* London: Edward Arnold.

Kress, G. and van Leeuwen, T. (2002) 'Colour as a semiotic mode: Notes for a grammar of colour', *Visual Communication,* 1: 343–69.

Kress, G. and van Leeuwen, T. (2006) *Reading Images: The Grammar of Visual Design,* London: Routledge.

Kroskrity, P.V. (ed.) (2000) *Regimes of Language: Ideologies, Polities and Identities,* Oxford: James Currey.

Law, P. (2010) 'Re: BBC Voices follow up'. Email (6 March 2010).

Lievrouw, L. and Livingston, S. (2006) *Handbook of New Media: Social Shaping and Social Consequences,* London: Sage.

Lippi-Green, R. (1997) *English with an Accent: Language, Ideology, and Discrimination in the United States,* London and New York: Routledge.

Lynch, P.J. and Horton, S. (1999) *Web Style Guide: Basic Design Principles for Creating Websites,* New Haven: Yale University Press.

Machin, D. (2007) *Introduction to Multimodal Analysis,* London: Arnold.

Machin, D. and van Leeuwen, T. (2007) *Global Media Discourse: A Critical Introduction,* London: Routledge.

Malinowski, D. (2006) 'Authorship in the linguistic landscape: A multimodal-performance view', in E. Shohamy and D. Gorter (eds) *Linguistic Landscapes: Expanding the Scenery,* New York: Routledge.

Mangen, A. (2006) 'New Narrative Pleasures? A cognitive-phenomenological study of the experience of reading digital narrative fictions', unpublished thesis, Norwegian University of Science and Technology.

Mangen, A. (2008) 'Hypertext fiction reading: Haptics and immersion', *Journal of Research in Reading,* 31: 404–19.

McCrum, R., Cran, W. and McNeil, R. (1992) *The Story of English: New and Revised Edition,* London: Faber and Faber.

McDonald, M. (2007) 'Television debate, "interactivity" and public opinion: The case of the BBC's "Asylum Day"', *Media Culture & Society,* 29: 679–89.

McMillan, S.J. (2000) 'Interactivity is in the eye of the beholder: Function, perception, involvement, and attitude toward the web site', in M.A. Shriver (ed.) *Proceedings of the Conference of the American Academy of Advertising,* East Lansing, MI: Michigan State University.

McMillan, S.J. (2002a) 'Exploring models of interactivity from multiple research traditions: Users, documents, and systems', in L. Liewrouw and S. Livingston (eds) *Handbook of New Media: Social Shaping and Social Consequences,* London: Sage.

McMillan, S.J. (2002b) 'A four-part model of cyber-interactivity: Some cyber-places are more interactive than others', *New Media & Society,* 4: 271–91.

McNicholas, A. (2004) 'Wrenching the machine around: EastEnders, the BBC and institutional change', *Media Culture and Society,* 26: 491–512.

Milani, T.M. (2008) 'Language testing and citizenship: A language ideological debate in Sweden', *Language in Society,* 37: 27–59.

Milani, T.M., Davies, B.L. and Turner, W. (2011) 'Unity in disunity: Centripetal and centrifugal tensions on the BBC *Voices* website', *Journal of Language and Politics,* 10: 587–614.

Milroy, J. and Milroy, L. 1999. *Authority in Language: Investigating Standard English,* London: Routledge.

Mowbray, F. (2005) *Voices Launch: Project Manager's Presentation*, London: BBC.

O'Halloran, K.I. (2004) *Multimodal Discourse Analysis: Systemic Functional Perspectives,* London: Continuum.
Ord, M. (2004) 'Voices: How to audio gather' (Instructions to fieldworkers), Cardiff: BBC.
Ord, M. (2005a) 'Project director's presentation of overview summary – BBC *Voices*', Cardiff: BBC.
Ord, M. (2005b) '*Voices*: Some details from the creative brief for marketing campaign', unpublished memo to BBC Managing Editors.
O'Sullivan, P.B., Hunt, S.K. and Lippert, L.R. (2004) 'Mediated immediacy: A language of affiliation in a technological age', *Journal of Language and Social Psychology,* 23: 464–90.
Pennycook, A. (2007) *Global Englishes and Transcultural Flows*, London: Routledge.
Quiring, O. (2009) 'What do users associate with "interactivity"? A qualitative study on user schemata', *New Media & Society,* 11: 899–920.
Schieffelin, B., Woolard, K.A. and Kroskrity, P.V. (eds) (1998) *Language Ideologies: Practice and Theory,* Oxford: Oxford University Press.
Silverstein, M. (1998) 'Contemporary transformations of local linguistic communities', *Annual Review of Anthropology,* 27: 401–26.
Silverstein, M. and Urban, G. (1996) 'The natural history of discourse', in M. Silverstein and G. Urban (eds) *Natural Histories of Discourse,* Chicago: University of Chicago Press.
Talbot, M. (2007) *Media Discourse: Representation and Interaction,* Edinburgh: Edinburgh University Press.
Thurlow, C. and Mroczek, K. (eds) (2011) *Fresh perspectives on new media sociolinguistics,* New York: Oxford University Press.
Turner, W. (2011) 'Language ideologies and the BBC *Voices* website: Hypermodal and practice-oriented perspectives', unpublished thesis, University of Leeds.
Ventola, E., Charles, C. and Kaltenbacher, M. (eds) (2004) *Perspectives on Mulitmodality,* Amsterdam: John Benjamins.
Warner, M. (2002) *Publics and Counterpublics,* London: MIT Press.
Warnick, B. (2007) *Rhetoric Online: Persuasion and Politics on the World Wide Web,* New York: Peter Lang.
Woolard, K.A. (1992) 'Language ideology: Issues and approaches', *Pragmatics*, 2: 235–49.
Woolard, K.A. (1998) 'Language ideology as a field of enquiry', in B. Schieffelin, K.A. Woolard, and P. Kroskrity (eds) *Language Ideologies: Practice and Theory*, Oxford: Oxford University Press.

7

MAPPING THE WORD

Local vocabulary and its themes

Susie Dent

Introduction

Lexis and lexicology have long been the Cinderella of dialectology. In the popular imagination, any conscious notion of dialect is defined by its sounds. Academic study, too, has concentrated largely on morphology and pronunciation at the expense of lexis. The BBC's *Voices* project was an inclusive one; its field researchers collected local vocabularies as well as phonologies. It returned highly valuable data on the extent to which regional lexis still exists – a notion that has long attracted even more pessimism than that expressed over the health of locally individualized sounds. Moreover, beyond the findings on the volume of 'non-standard' vocabulary used in modern Britain, the word maps produced by *Voices* inform in less predictable ways: from them we can make some speculations about the catalysts for regional variation and notably about the subjects around which that variation collects. For like slang, dialect's closest neighbour, regional vocabulary can be seen to favour particular areas of discourse, and its themes are illuminating.

A lack of focus on the vocabulary of dialect is evident in many of the more recent discussions of the subject. In Trudgill (1999) for example, dialect words come last and decidedly least after matters of phonology, morphology and syntax. When lexis has been studied, one recurrent theme has been the clustering of dialect variation around particular categories of vocabulary. Such categories lie at the heart of Trudgill's own discussion, and of the lexical element in the *Survey of English Dialects* ([SED] Orton *et al.* 1961–72) and *An Atlas of English Dialects* (Upton and Widdowson 2006). They are equally central to Dent (2010), which was drawn largely from SED and the material collected by the BBC's *Voices* project. Such focus on particular vocabulary groupings was not always the case. In 1905, the greatest monument of British dialect lexicology, the *English Dialect*

Dictionary ([*EDD*] Wright 1898–1905) was completed, and it displays a distinct non-thematic inclusivity. Everything is there: from the tools of specific rural industries (like the *becket*, a turf-cutting spade from East Anglia) to rainbow-like patterns made by the sun's shadow on the walls of children's bedrooms (such as *bosie*, recorded in Berkshire). *EDD* may be the last concerted effort among dialectologists to aspire to such breadth of subject matter. The subsequent development of academic linguistics drew dialectology along a new path, and linguistics was to become self-consciously scientific in its approach.

One result of this new direction may be that thematic sways within the lexis of dialect are in part an artifact of linguistic 'ideology'. Dialectologists now tend to be interested in lexis in its geographical dimension. While this produces clear maps, it ignores the fact that lexis is often complicated, involving the interplay of style, ranges of meaning, collocations and context. Isoglossic maps inevitably capture the larger picture: they will not, for example, reflect which section of a population (e.g. older generations or children) will be using which term, and consequently the true lexis of a region may not be fully recorded. In this chapter, I take a brief overview of the different sources we currently have in surveying the lexis of British dialects over the last century, and suggest both how thematic variation appears in these sources and why that might be. Within this discussion a further important set of questions emerges, regarding the relationship between slang and dialect, and the importance or otherwise of the distinctions made between them.

Sources

My first and oldest resource is *EDD* itself, the unruly treasure cave of English dialects. The numerous county glossaries, and publications by the English Dialect Society, that *EDD* was based on are uneven in quality and frequently weakened by traces of Victorian 'time immemorial'-ism and antiquarian quaintness, meaning currency and frequency are often only to be guessed at. There can however be little doubt that the regional language of Britain has never been recorded with the same exhaustiveness as it was around 1900, and that the (sometimes rather hidden) work done by Wright's army of informers brings a much greater degree of regularity and dependability than might otherwise be assumed. The second source is SED, the Survey of Anglo-Welsh Dialects ([SAWD] Parry 1999), and other works of academic dialectology. The third is the material collected for sound archives, most obviously by the BBC *Voices* project and in the British Library, but also partial precursors such as the work done by the North-West Sound Archive in the 1970s and 1980s and published in glossary form as *Sounds Gradely* (Howarth 1984).

Finally, the fourth source is the post-*EDD* glossaries of individual regions done in the same tradition as the pre-*EDD* glossaries. These again are a mixed bag. Some are clear and scholarly, done either as side projects by SED researchers, or with the support or imprimatur of J.D.A. Widdowson and his

National Centre for English Cultural Tradition at the University of Sheffield. These give a certainty about what was collected and how. Others, like Pease's glossary of the North Riding (Pease 1928), or Scollins and Titford's glossary of the Erewash valley (Scollins and Titford 2000), are direct descendants of the nineteenth-century glossaries, made by assiduous and sensible non-academics (although now often teachers rather than parsons). Others still, often attracting opprobrium from those who fall into the previous categories, are more populist books intended to tap into the large market for things local. These glossaries often raid earlier ones (sometimes by silent transmission that can mean several centuries earlier) and conversely include contemporary slang that may or (more often) may not be regional. That fact in itself raises the question of the relationship between dialect and slang.

The slang/dialect axis

The *Oxford English Dictionary* (*OED*), amongst its definitions of the words, highlights both a possible key difference and the most important point of ambiguity between the two terms:

> dialect, n. 2: One of the subordinate forms or varieties of a language arising from local peculiarities of vocabulary, pronunciation, and idiom. (In relation to modern languages usually spec. A variety of speech differing from the standard or literary 'language'; a provincial method of speech, as in 'speakers of dialect'.)
>
> slang, n.3 1.c: Language of a highly colloquial type, considered as below the level of standard educated speech, and consisting either of new words or of current words employed in some special sense.

Dialect, according to these selected definitions, is defined primarily with relation to locality, slang in terms of informality or non-standardness. The second part of the definition of dialect, however, in also placing an emphasis on non-standardness, immediately invites ambiguity. Moreover, this point of ambiguity has become ever more the focus of our understanding of dialect. In recent decades, dialectology has considered social as well as regional lexis, as opposed to that which is circumscribed by geography alone. This tendency is doubtless in part a reflection of the spread of Standard English; we are now far less likely than previously to come across a word that is used as a standard in a particular region which is distinct from the national standard.

At this point, the motivations and choices of speakers have to be recognized as central to any separation between dialect and slang. Motivation and choice amongst speakers has always been at the root of any conception of what slang is. The word was originally used in the eighteenth century to refer to the language of 'low and despicable' (*OED*) types, such as criminals and vagabonds. Its use was a socially marked choice to describe the socially marked choices of others. From this root it grew in two directions, first referring to the jargon of a particular profession or group as visible today in academic linguistics (e.g. Adams 2003) and in studies of industrial and workplace language (e.g. Wright 1972), and second referring to the highly non-standard speech defined above by *OED*. Both of these branches deal with linguistic choices made in informal settings, and the second deals with linguistic choices which have the motivation to depart from an accepted standard. This means that as dialect became increasingly restricted to informal contexts, it was always likely to become more like slang, and for conscious motivations and choices to influence its use.

Historically, the perception of the relationship between slang and regional variation has depended to a considerable degree on the extent to which both, or either, has been viewed in a negative light. When regional dialect was seen as legitimate and acceptable, any slang within that dialect may have been overlooked, since it was slang in its broadest manifestation that was considered degraded and worthy of contempt (the *OED* gives the earliest meaning of 'slang' as 'the special vocabulary used by any set of persons of a low or disreputable character; language of a low and vulgar type'). This radically different perspective on the two forms, particularly as English became more standardized, may have falsely dichotomized the two. In his 1785 Preface to the *Classical Dictionary of the Vulgar Tongue*, Grose (1785: 2) is morally apologetic for including those terms which could be called 'indelicate' and 'immodest'. In a *Provincial Glossary* he writes of his collection's usefulness 'to all persons desirous of understanding our ancient poets' (Grose 1787: iii). Yet the two categories which inspired such different judgements come together in Grose's own work: his *Dictionary* includes such items as the Northumbrian *burr*, a local use of *butter* ('that commodity being sold in Oxford by the yard'), *dowdying* from Salisbury and the Irish *bugaroch*. Conversely, the *Provincial Glossary* includes material that might be classed as slang, such as *cobbs*, 'testicles', which he traces to Cumberland.

In this chapter, I restrict 'dialect' to its now primary, geographical sense. Within that category I then attempt to analyze some of the tendencies and themes in local vocabulary. I further categorize them with respect to the motivations and choices of the people that use them and the formality and informality of the contexts in which they are used, thereby giving some indication of the extent to which regional vocabulary can now be characterized as indistinct from slang. To take an example, the slang sense of *bird* meaning 'girl' or 'woman' is recorded in the form *berd* as a Scouse use in the 1960s (Speigl 1966), and as part of *Proper Brummie* some three decades later (Chinn and Thorne 2001). The *OED* documents this sense as arising, like many bits of slang, in the army slang of the First World War (viewing it as a linguistically distinct revival of an earlier use paralleling the Middle English *burd* ,'a maiden', which was restricted to Scottish use by the eighteenth century), and to Orkney and Shetland by the nineteenth century. But the authors of the urban regional glossaries are happy to see it as distinctive of the dialects they cover. Similarly, the slang phrase *the full monty* is first recorded in Morecambe (Howarth 1984); its slightly earlier use in the names of fish and chip shops in the Manchester Yellow Pages leaves us with the picture that the term is probably in origin one specific to the North-West, but that its history has been lost. Are these examples of the phenomenon of 'stray' slang words occurring in dialect glossaries, or are they in fact statements of genuine regional slang preferences? From these questions flow two more. How far is dialect now a matter of regional slang preferences? And insofar as there remain regional uses distinct from slang, what types of use constitute that distinction?

In some cases, the distinction between dialect and slang is straightforward. Take the term *cool*, the slang use of which has been around for at least a century. The modern affirmative use seems to originate with the 1890s Etonian slang *a cool fish*, one who was cocky and self-possessed; the term was then greatly popularized by the cool jazz movement of the 1940s. Records of *cool* show a take-up that was national in its breadth, demonstrated also in more recent affirmative adjectives, such as *bad* and *sick*. With many other terms, however, a differentiation may be arbitrary, for when we speak of 'dialect' we may simply be talking about 'style', a label that can equally apply to slang. The *OED* defines 'style' in this sense as 'a manner of discourse, or tone of speaking, adopted in addressing others'. The *Voices* recordings returned thematic collections of words that meet this criterion exactly, and that comfortably straddle both dialect and slang.

Stylistic choices

In tracking and describing the vocabulary of dialect, sound archives are enormously helpful, for they provide an opportunity to study academically which words are commonly used by dialect speakers while also allowing a greater inclusivity than academic dialect lexicology has typically done before. We find the standard dialect (or Standard English) increasingly more likely to be used in any situation, fitting in with the picture of diminished regional variation that Trudgill (1999) presents, but we also see that non-standard dialect is more than ever a matter of style in the sense of the *OED* definition, and specifically of informal style. In one *Voices* interview, four ex-dockers from Liverpool are asked about words they use to describe getting angry or upset. One suggests *narked*, a second *got a cob on*, before a third chimes in 'well, you lads might, but I just get upset' (cue laughter). Although expressed humorously, the point underlying this quip is a crucial one for dialect lexicology. A particular term may be chosen for a desired effect rather than as an instinctive and intrinsic part of the speaker's vocabulary. There is a great deal of difference, for example, between *bairn*, which has for centuries been the northern standard for *child* and which remains the usual term in informal speech, and the range of words used as local terms for a 'hedgehog', such as *hedgepig*, *furzepig* and *urchin*, where it is not clear even in those areas where *urchin* is widely recorded that that word is the natural choice over *hedgehog*. Moreover, even if it is not now, but once was, it is almost impossible to plot when that change might have happened: if *urchin* has become restricted to informal use, when did that shift from regionality pure and simple to regional informality happen?

This problem of interpreting the speaker's intentions is generally found within categories whose regional variations were largely fixed in traditional dialect areas prior to standardization. For example, most regional words for alleys, like *ginnel*, *vennel*, *loan* and *twitchel*, are very old, dating from Middle English. These words must have functioned for centuries as local standards, informal only inasmuch as any common piece of everyday vocabulary is informal (i.e. *cup* or *bread* have a degree of informality that *vicissitude* and *chloride* do not, even though they are entirely standard words). Now, however, they are very much restricted to informal contexts. In the *Voices* material they are preserved fairly robustly, but anecdotal evidence suggests that such words may now be disproportionately used with the definite article and commonly in variation with *alley*. A newcomer to an area might happily interpret 'the twitchel' as the proper name for a local landmark; they would not be likely to take up the term as a general description in preference to *alley* or their own regional variant.

Another thematic category where questions of style may be more important than those of regionality is words for 'drizzle' or light rain. To take two examples, we have *hadder* and *smurr*. *Hadder* is recorded in *EDD* from 1876 onwards in Cumberland, Westmorland, Durham and Yorkshire, and was registered by the *Voices* survey in Kirkoswald in Cumbria. *Smurr* is recorded from 1790 in Scotland and Ulster by both *EDD* and (at the headword *smirr*) the *Scottish National Dictionary* (Grant and Murison 1971), and also by *EDD* in East Anglia, Hertfordshire and Hampshire. *Voices* found it in Scotland, Northern Ireland and East Anglia. There are over forty words in *EDD* defined as 'to drizzle', and less than a quarter emanate from south of Derbyshire and Nottinghamshire – with most of those rooted in East Anglia. To that extent they form an obvious climatological group, with which the *Voices* material is completely consistent. Furthermore, most are of uncertain origin, and are quite possibly imitative or onomatopoeic. Again, *Voices*' *hadder* and *smurr* seem a plausible fit with this picture. What is most striking, though, is how recently the words appear. They do not seem to be ancient regionalisms, but rather are modern expressive formations, indicating perhaps that both their relative newness and their possible imitativeness point in the same direction. What is more, reading the style of the uses collected by *EDD* for this kind of word is highly difficult: for *hadder*, *EDD*'s 'it hadders and rains' (from Durham) and 'it keeps haddering and raining' (from Cumberland) perhaps suggest a degree of standardness, being co-ordinated as they are with *rain*, but 'it hadders and roaks' (from Yorkshire) does not fit that picture. It may well be that these were in fact functioning as words of colour rather than local denotation right from the start. My point here about the importance of style is to emphasize that the variation which marks out dialect areas need not be the variation that actually constitutes the regional linguistic identity of those areas' speakers. It is likely that, very often, our vocabulary choices are stylistic ones rather than those that are instinctively local.

'Instinctive' dialect

I would like to distinguish between two types of lexical variation within dialect, both of which are informal. The first type occurs where there is no agreed standard, and where it is highly unlikely that users have any conscious sense that a use is regional. What tends to distinguish these is not that the usage is informal, but that the object or context is. The set of local synonyms for 'plimsolls' returned by the *Voices* project offers an example (that term itself being the closest thing to a standard, dominant in the South-East, but far from a national label). In Scotland, *sandshoe* prevails, but the rest of Britain is filled up with a variety of terms. Respondents to the word map survey conducted on the *Voices* website offered, among others, *pumps*, *gollies*, *daps*, *gutties*, *kicks* and *sannies*. All of these will be the everyday words with which their speakers grew up. The lexicon of children's games offers a further example of terminology absorbed in childhood as an assumed standard. The wealth of localized words for a 'truce' include *King's, faynights, pax, Barleys, Barrels, Bees, Checks, Peas, Pearls, creamy olivers, ollyoxalls, olly-olly-ee, double queenie, breather Tibs, Tubs* and *Dubbies* (Dent 2010). (In both of these thematic categories there were clear signs of lexical erosion: the US imports of *sneakers* and *trainers* are contending as an eventual standard term for plimsolls, while *Voices* suggests that *time out* is gathering momentum to call a halt to a playground game.) There are a number of other examples which work this way. One is the act of pillion-riding on a bicycle. This is a *backie* in much of southern England, but is recorded in glossaries and in *Voices* in a number of other regional forms, including *croggy* in the East Midlands. But perhaps the deepest, least-remarked upon and most robust in the *Voices* material is terms of endearment, or familiar terms of address. There is *hen* in Scotland, *pet* and *hinny* in the North-East, *duck* and *youth* in the Midlands, *boy* in East Anglia, and so on.

Many of these themes relate to childhood and recall Brook's (1965: 27) suggestion that the accidents of childhood environment are decisive in forming and preserving dialect. Wales (2006:198) discusses this idea and gives a vivid memory of the world of her own north-eastern childhood. But to concentrate exclusively on childhood is arguably too reductive. It may be simply a fact that, in a very mobile society, many people's memories of dialect stem from their childhood. I would suggest that what matters is more the very fact of localness, or perhaps an intimately local psycho-geography. Of course, childhood is an important facet of this: for example, in Derbyshire, you might, as a child, *tag off*, buy a *cob*, catch a *croggy* from a friend and eat furtively in the *twitchel*. But Wales's picture also includes local things, like *pace eggs* and *stotties*. Local nomenclature was required to reflect things that were themselves local, such as the historical variety of types of bread across Britain, especially the different types of bread roll, as opposed to a full loaf. These things are either present or they are not, and their survival is not linked to their association with childhood. In fact, the names of local breads are vanishing along with the breads themselves, and the words that survive are under pressure from the fact that most bread is now bought in supermarkets, labelled with standard words. Ultimately, to return to Wales's Durham, *stotties* will survive as long as stotties themselves survive. This importance of the local might also help explain how an old, traditional category such as alley words can still be productive in modern urban contexts, the *jiggers* and *ennogs* of Liverpool among them.

Conscious variation

The second main category of informal use brings us closer to the category of slang. In today's lexis, such vocabulary can be found regionally in both of the principal categories in which slang more generally occurs: in the jargons of particular groups and in intentionally non-standard language, language which is marked, positively or negatively, with more connotation than denotation, and where a more standard or more neutral term is available but avoided. Here, speakers appear to be aware of the standard or neutral alternative, and to have made the decision to depart from it (regardless of whether they appreciate their departure as regional, or whether their beliefs about its regionality are in fact correct). In almost every case, users of these non-standard terms are capable of code-switching back if necessary. The catalysts for this apparent departure from a norm are many – it may be a useful shorthand, a deliberate defiance of a conventional standard, or it may function as a marker of group identity, acknowledging an in-crowd for whom this different vocabulary may be fashionable, subversive or simply practical. It is in this area of lexis that the lines between dialect and slang become exceedingly blurred.

Conscious variation from a standard term may occur predominantly in two contexts, the first being within the world of work, and the second in discourse that involves social positioning and/or the policing of behaviour. In the first case, the *EDD* and SED are rich resources of the vocabulary of rural crafts and agricultural labour: SED in particular reflected the contemporary scholarly interest in documenting the vanishing vocabularies of the 1900s for the purposes of historical language study. It is true that many of the terms included in both projects were so specific to their local trade that no real standard existed: they were the everyday vocabulary of those from whom it was collected (for example Cornwall's *atchett*, as cited by Trudgill (1999:16), signifying a pole slung across a stream to stop cattle passing). To some degree, however, the language from these trades is conceptually little different from workplace slang in subsequent urban contexts. The terminologies in some cases provided both an important industry shorthand as well as a social unifier, as in the documented vocabulary of Northumbrian Pitmatic (Griffiths 2007) which was almost manufactured to preserve the tight social structures of self-sufficient pit villages.

The coal mining industry is, I think, the only non-agricultural and urban industry to have been studied dialectologically with the attention that *EDD* and SED/SAWD have given agricultural labour, in Wright's (1972) work in the 1950s and 1960s. This research showed not only that this kind of workplace slang could produce exactly the same kind of regional variation as intimately local or childhood vocabulary, but also that it could, perhaps fittingly, mass produce it. To take one of 53 examples he documented, a haulage road in a mine could be known as a *causey* in the Scottish coalfield, a *jig* in Shropshire, a *ginny* in Yorkshire and Gloucestershire (this seems to be related to the alley word, *ginnel*, which is widely recorded for an alleyway in Yorkshire), a *rope road* in Nottinghamshire and an *incline* in Ebbw Vale. Other industries undoubtedly had their regional vocabularies, but few others, if any, are well-recorded. Spiegl (1961, 1966), Howarth (1984) and other sources such as the words of the dying ex-docker George, in Alan Bleasdale's *Boys from the Blackstuff* (1982), give us some insight into what was clearly the thriving and wide-ranging workplace slang of the Liverpool docks, of *bunce*, *welt*, *growlers*, *griffins*, *Mary Ellens* and *scalers*, but we still feel that what we learn most is how little we know. As with the case of agricultural labour, only some of these terms are likely to have been a conscious workplace code. Still, as the world of mass industry is now almost as lost as that of ploughboys and turf-cutters, it would be valuable to know whether modern office slang is producing any kind of regional variation. The fundamental similarities between such vocabularies are sometimes hidden by surface differences, so that what appears now as the colourful, rural language of ploughing seems of a piece with the other quaint terminology of rural yore rather than with the denigrated management-speak of the modern office.

Accentuating the negative

Regional vocabulary that is selected as a marker of social position, as an act of rebellion against a perceived authority, or simply as a deliberate choice of expressiveness, brings it closer still to slang. The question here is whether regional differentiation is itself a form of 'counter-language' or, perhaps more accurately, a lexis of counter-synonymy. The results are not as dramatic as one might think, and involve everyday vocabulary. They occur in situations where a standard description does exist, but where that standard is not an immediately available alternative, either because it is too formal (as opposed to merely standard) or because it is itself marked in a way that the user of the regional term would want to avoid. The act of playing truant is a well-attested subject in the *Voices* material. It shows that no self-respecting truant is likely to describe him- or herself as 'playing truant'; instead, they might prefer to *sag off* on Merseyside, *tag off* in Derbyshire, *plunk* in Scotland, *twag* in parts of Yorkshire, *wag* in London and *mitch* in the South-West and Wales (it may be that within this theme *bunk off* and *nick off* will become cross-regional surrogate standards). Such cases once again blur the boundaries between what is termed slang and what is viewed as purely regional or non-standard dialectal.

In terms of lexical themes, some of the most productive responses to the *Voices* enquiries came out of subjects that invite informality. The work of the slang lexicographer Jonathon Green has consistently revealed that his subject deals in universal preoccupations. As Green (2011) sees it, 'the basics remain consistent in slang as in much that is human: sex, money, intoxication, fear (of others), aggrandizement (of oneself)'. For Green it is this 'humanity' that dictates slang's linguistic themes:

> It subscribes to nothing but itself – no belief systems, no true believers, no faith, no religion, no politics, no party. It is the linguistic version of Freud's id, defined by him in 1933 as 'the dark, inaccessible part of our personality'.
> (Green 2011)

Within local lexis the driving force would seem to be similar: it is human to gossip, to criticize and to compartmentalize, and regional vocabularies are full of descriptors for such unhappy states as splay-footedness, ugliness, drunkenness, promiscuity and temporary poverty. Spoken language is largely referential: we speak of ourselves, and, most frequently, about other people. The act of gossip itself is a particularly fertile source of local lexis, and one that appears to be thriving. It is worth noting its lexicon in depth (although there will undoubtedly be some items excluded here) to illustrate its range. The range of verbs includes:

> *chopse* (Berkshire, Staffordshire, Gwent), *clonc* (West Wales), *jaffock* (Lancashire), *hamchammer* (Somerset), *housing* (Cornwall), *labbing* (South Wales), *magging* (Yorkshire), *nattering* (South, esp. South-East), *newsbagging* (Somerset), *newsing* (chiefly South-West), *newsmongering* (Somerset), *tick-tatting* (Norfolk), and *yaddering* (Cumbria). Synonyms for the person doing the gossiping are no less numerous, and cover *blatherskite* (Durham), *cagmag* (Gloucestershire, Sussex), *call* (Yorkshire), *caller* (Yorkshire, Lincolnshire), *canter* (South-West Midlands), *chatterbag* (South-West), *chatterbox* (various bits of the South), *chattermag* (South-West), *clat* (Lancashire), *clat-can* (Lancashire), *gabber* (Berkshire), *gad* (Yorkshire), *gallivanter* (Cheshire), *gasbag* (Berkshire, Shropshire), *houser* (Cornwall), *magger* (Gloucestershire), *natter* (Oxfordshire), *natterer* (Sussex), *news-bag* (chiefly South-West), *news-canter* (Gloucestershire), *newser* (South-West), *newsmonger* (South, esp. South-West), *newsmongerer* (Devon), *newspad* (Wiltshire), *nosey parker*, *rattlebox*, *scandalmonger* (chiefly South-East), *taler* (Dorset), *tattler* (Essex), *tongue-wag* (Worcestershire), and *yapper* (Essex).
> (Dent 2010)

When such gossiping occurs, its focus seems to invite equally prolific expression. Two further subjects which feature in most or all of the types of source outlined at the beginning of this chapter, from *EDD* to *Voices*, are words for being left-handed or pigeon-toed. These are descriptive, but frequently also judgemental, or if not explicitly judgemental at least revealing of and conveying an implicit sense of social norm and expectation. Geographically-specific words such as *kay-fisted* (north) and *twilly-toed* (East Midlands and Yorkshire) might well be functionally identical to modern, national, urban slang formulations for 'ugly', such as *mingin*, *obsocky* and *butters*. (Indeed, *EDD* includes several regional words for 'ugly', including *rodger* and *zidle-mouth*). If there is a difference, it may be that the older and more traditional examples are more likely to be instinctive choices. The more obviously neutral descriptions of basic anatomical matters would support such a supposition. Terms for 'to pant' such as *bellows* (in Suffolk), *heave* (Essex), *pump* (Staffordshire), *huff* (East Anglia), *tift* (North-West), *bussock* (Gloucestershire) and Yorkshire's *waff* (Dent 2010) are equally likely to be entirely instinctive choices for an entirely basic act, probably because they are learned in domestic, intimate settings and acquired before the standard *pant*, just as *kay-fisted* may be (or have been) absorbed before *left-handed*. But as that standard is learned, and as the child grows into an adult, such terms are likely to be restricted to informal contexts, or to contexts where some extra expressiveness is sought.

The fairly recent range of epithets answering the description of what the *Voices* researchers described as A YOUNG PERSON IN CHEAP TRENDY CLOTHES AND JEWELLERY are a comparable cluster of terms, this time from an urban slang context. The responses to the survey demonstrate that the subject would seem to follow the pattern of the first category discussed, whereby the lack of a standard word for an observable cultural phenomenon has caused a proliferation of 'bottom up' terms for it, which in turn has given rise to regional variety. Equally, however, the terms fit the model of slang which is geographically restricted. Both *chav* (in its recent incarnation) and *charver* were first recorded, according to the *OED*, in local internet newsgroups, while the earlier *ned* (particularly favoured in Scotland) is also found in its earliest guise within a dialect story. They are joined in *Voices* by the *bazza* or *fly boy* (North East), *gudgeon*, *hood* (Northern Ireland), *nob*, *ratboy*, *skanger*, *steek*, *stig* or *townie* (Lancashire and further afield), *trev* (the South) and *yarco* (East Anglia). Far from showing signs of attrition, the *Oxford English Corpus* demonstrates that the repertoire of such local labels has shown significant increase in the twenty-first century. There is, at least linguistically, the sense that the *duck-nebbed* (Northumberland) or *Wednesday-and-Thursday* (Norfolk) feet of yesterday are the *charvers* and *yarcos* of today. Many items recorded by the *Voices* project straddle the same divide – they are dialectal because they are local, but they are also slang, and it can once again be argued that the definition of 'dialect' or 'local slang' is more of a tactical choice than a taxonomic one.

Epithets such as these synonyms for *chav* underscore the fact that many of the themes within local lexis take a negative stance. They are not, perhaps, as extreme as unlocalized slang, which, to use Green's (2011) description, form 'an oral history of marginality and rebellion, of dispossession and frustration', but they are noticeably low on terms of approval, congratulation, or kindness. They focus instead on physical handicaps and misfortunes, while the widest dialectal variation for things connected to health and the body tends to dwell on the more unsavoury aspects such as blisters.

Conclusion

To view all modern dialect as a local subset of slang would be over-simplistic and un-nuanced. Yet the parallels between its chosen themes and their terms of reference would seem to undermine the collision of two separate discourses that is sometimes inferred. The results of the *Voices* survey suggests that, rather than conflicting with and subsuming local terminology, slang is often co-existing with it, and in many cases there is little distinction between the two categories. The dichotomy established in the eighteenth and nineteenth centuries, when standardization pushed slang towards the preserve of journalists, pornographers and the disreputable, while regional glossaries became a matter of conservation, is losing its relevance today. Instead, the picture is a far more complex one, with opposing forces at work – the de-regionalization of a locally-based item of slang can today, for example, take place at high speed thanks to the opportunities of web-based media. In 2004, *chav* moved in the span of a few months from being a distinct regionalism to, effectively, a national standard and an almost daily discussion point in the media. In the process, the focus of the word's use became explicitly sociological, to the exclusion of any lingering possibility of regionality (which was restricted to the folk etymology that *chav* was itself a contraction of 'Chatham average').

It may be that unconscious regionalisms will fade from view, overtaken by more explicitly chosen terms which operate as local slang or are simply viewed as no longer regional. Should this be the case, local vocabulary, as it is currently understood, will acquire a very new identity, one which it will be important to recognize and research and not dismiss as the product of anti-dialectal forces. Such research will be different from traditional dialectology: linguistic geography will need to be less a 'linguistic geology' of bedrocks and unique formations, and more a 'linguistic ecology' of shifting, dissipating and reforming regional tendencies, preferences, and innovations.

Sound archives, and particularly the results of the *Voices* project, present a picture which supports the notion of the attrition of distinctive regional isoglosses within traditional dialect areas, but which also suggests that attrition is only one side of a complex image, one which involves both highly productive areas of vocabulary and others that appear more vulnerable. After two centuries as a national pastime, it seems unlikely, for instance, that people of the East Midlands will stop *mashing* their tea in favour of a new standard. They will similarly continue to dismiss sullen, sulky people as *mardy*, even though that word may complete its journey out of the East Midlands and become a national word, having already conquered many parts of the North (Elmes 2005: 184,

208, 264). They may well go down *twitchels* less often than they used to, but even if they stop giving their children *suckers*, that does not mean that they will necessarily give them *ice lollies*, nor that they will not substitute another term which is unknown in other parts of the country. What strikes most about *Voices* (and herein lies its immense value) is that it recalls *EDD* in the range and vagaries of what turns up: a Cornish person might not wash up, but *stream the clome*, while someone from Ulster finds this least popular of household chores not even appalling but *cat melodeon*. With such results as these the *Voices* survey strongly suggests that people's desire to use language expressively will ensure that new regional words will always be found, and that at least some of the categories for regional language will remain productive. What seems very likely is that far fewer of those categories are likely to provide markers of clearly defined dialect areas, and that the traditional notion of local vocabulary will need to reflect that change. Most importantly of all, studies of regional dialect today need to consider slang and look for regional variation within it, while studies of slang must become more sensitive to regional differences.

Acknowledgement

I would like to acknowledge the assistance and ideas of Andrew Ball of the *Oxford English Dictionary*.

References

Adams, M. (2003) *Slayer Slang: a Buffy the Vampire Slayer lexicon*, New York: Oxford University Press.

Bleasdale, A. (1982) *Boys from the Blackstuff.* TV broadcast, London: BBC.

Brook, G.L. (1965) *English Dialects*, 2nd edn, London: André Deutsch.

Chinn, C. and Thorne, S. (2001) *Proper Brummie*, Studley: Brewin Books.

Dent, S. (2010) *How to Talk Like a Local*, London: Random House.

Elmes, S. (2005) *Talking for Britain: A Journey Through the Nation's Dialects*, London: Penguin.

Grant, W. and Murison, D., eds. (1971) *The Scottish National Dictionary*, Volume VIII, Edinburgh: The Scottish National Dictionary Association.

Green, J. (2011) 'Taking slang seriously, thoughts of a slang lexicographer', private transcript of a lecture given to the British Library, London.

Griffiths, B. (2007) *Pitmatic: The Talk of the North East Coalfield*, Newcastle: Northumbria University Press.

Grose, F. (1785) *A Classical Dictionary of the Vulgar Tongue*, London: S. Hooper.

Grose, F. (1787) *A Provincial Glossary: With a Collection of Local Proverbs, and Popular Superstitions*, London: S. Hooper.

Howarth, K. (1984) *Sounds Gradely: A Collection of Dialect and Other Words Used in Lancashire Folk Speech*, Clitheroe: North West Sound Archive.

Orton, H., Halliday, W., Tilling, P. and Walkelin, M. (1961–1972) *Survey of English Dialects*. Introduction and 4 volumes, Leeds: E.J. Arnold.

Oxford English Corpus (n.d.) Oxford: Oxford University Press. Online. Available HTTP: <http://oxforddictionaries.com/words/the-oxford-english-corpus> (accessed 12 July 2012).

Oxford English Dictionary (n.d.) Oxford: Oxford University Press. Online. Available HTTP: <http://www.oed.com> (accessed 12 July 2012).

Parry, D. (1999) *A Grammar and Glossary of the Conservative Anglo-Welsh Dialects of Rural Wales*, Sheffield: National Centre for English Cultural Tradition.

Pease, A. (1928) *A Dictionary of the Dialect of the North Riding of Yorkshire*, Whitby: Home and Sons Ltd.

Scollins, R. and Titford, J. (2000) *Ey Up Mi Duck! Dialect of Derbyshire and the East Midlands*, Newbury: Countryside Books.

Spiegl, F. (1961) *Lern Yourself Scouse: How to Talk Proper in Liverpool*, Liverpool: Scouse Press.

Spiegl, F. (1966) *Lern Yourself Scouse*, Volume 2, Liverpool: Scouse Press.

Trudgill, P. (1999) *The Dialects of England*, 2nd edn, Oxford: Blackwell.

Upton, C. and Widdowson, J. (2006) *An Atlas of English Dialects*, 2nd edn, London: Routledge.

Wales, K. (2006) *Northern English: A Social and Cultural History*, Cambridge: Cambridge University Press.

Wright, J. (ed.) (1898–1905) *The English Dialect Dictionary*, 6 volumes, Oxford: Henry Frowde.

Wright, P. (1972) 'Coal-Mining Language: A recent investigation', in M.F. Wakelin (ed.) *Patterns in the Folk Speech of the British Isles*, London: Athlone Press.

8

VOICES IN WALES

A new national survey

Rob Penhallurick

Introduction

This chapter considers the *Voices* project in Wales. It assesses the data collected and reflects on their future potential for the analysis of Welsh English. In particular, I compare *Voices* with the only other national survey of regional spoken English in Wales, the Survey of Anglo-Welsh Dialects (SAWD). The aim here is to gauge the compatibility of the two surveys and to determine how far they can be used in concert to provide a historical perspective on Welsh English from the mid-twentieth to the early twenty-first century. The chapter is therefore also concerned with the design and methodology of both *Voices* and SAWD as the two examples in Wales of a national dialect survey. (The Welsh-language material collected for *Voices* by Radio Cymru is not examined in the present chapter.)

Fieldwork for SAWD took place between 1968 and 1987. The *Voices* audio field-recordings were made in 2004–5, and online responses to the *Voices* Language Lab were gathered in 2005–7. In both *Voices* and SAWD, data were collected from across Wales, and appear to offer the possibility of a chronological overview of Welsh English during the last half-century. In fact, the overview could stretch back further, because the focus of SAWD in its early stages was on the speech of the elderly age-group, in their 60s, 70s, and 80s when interviewed, and much of this material consists of traditional linguistic features. But are the two surveys similar enough in character to permit such an overview?

The design, methods, and execution of *Voices* and SAWD

SAWD was founded in October 1968 by David Parry, of University College, Swansea, University of Wales (now Swansea University). It was initially a project infused with the character of philological dialectology.

Parry had been a postgraduate student under Harold Orton at the University of Leeds between 1959 and 1961. He had done fieldwork for the Survey of English Dialects (SED) in Monmouthshire in 1960, and, as he says in his 'History' of SAWD,

> I was eager, on securing my teaching-post at Swansea in 1966, to try to set up a similar investigation of the English spoken in Wales – seeking, as had SED, to record the oldest living varieties of folk-speech, and using a questionnaire resembling as closely as practicable the one prepared by Professors Dieth and Orton for the work of the SED.
>
> (Parry 2008)

The SAWD questionnaire (Chesters, Upton and Parry 1968) was for the most part the Dieth/Orton SED questionnaire (Orton 1962), with around 35 of the original questions edited out and about 25 new ones added. Parry aimed ultimately to make direct comparisons between the material collected by the SED and that collected by SAWD, including the construction of composite maps. Parry's choice of the label *Anglo-Welsh* rather than *Welsh English* for his survey perhaps reflects the tradition of use of the term in Wales, for example, as a descriptor in 'Anglo-Welsh literature' and as a name for the English-speaking community of Wales.

The aims and methods of SAWD mirrored those of SED. The questionnaire was lengthy and designed to elicit a large number of vocabulary, grammatical, and pronunciation features. The focus was on rural Wales, with a judgement sample of SED-type elderly speakers being sought. Between 1960 and 1982 nearly 120 localities were investigated. A number of these, especially those visited early on, were excluded from the final network of 90 rural localities. Up to a handful of informants per locality were interviewed, the questionnaire being asked once in each locality. Parry (1999: 1) lists the criteria for SAWD's ideal informant: '(i) aged over 60; (ii) knowledgeable about agricultural life and work; (iii) not formally educated beyond the age of 15; (iv) resident in the native area without significant interruption; (v) free from speech impediments.' The most troublesome of these was (iv), especially given that most of the target-group had lived through two World Wars, a number of them doing military service. Some leeway was therefore necessary, but lengthy absence from the locality would nonetheless disqualify a speaker from inclusion in the survey. (Details of informants can be found in the three original-data publications of SAWD: Parry (1977, 1979) and Penhallurick (1991).)

Parry was admirably self-sufficient in his direction of the survey, remaining steadfastly unbothered by the distractions of funding applications and publishers' deadlines. Thus, his first major volumes were self-financed and SAWD's fieldworkers were research students and occasionally undergraduate students, inspired by Parry and meticulously trained by him in fieldwork and phonetics. The first were Anne Chesters and Clive Upton, who collected material in South

Wales between 1969 and 1970. The last was me. Between 1980 and 1982, I did fieldwork for SAWD in rural North Wales.

Voices presents quite a contrast. The project originated in the New Media department at BBC Wales. Its primary aim was to gather material to fuel the broadcast needs of the BBC. The project would tap into the linguistic and cultural diversity of Britain, making productive use of the BBC's regional resources. Scholars from dialectology and sociolinguistics were consulted, the preliminary discussions taking place in Cardiff. The team at the BBC needed the advice and guidance of academics about survey design, and the academics started to dream of having scores of BBC journalists doing their fieldwork for them. The project offered the opportunity to collect a substantial amount of data in a small period of time – a goal beyond the means of previous national surveys. But as well as a contrast, there is also continuity between SAWD and *Voices*, precisely because the latter project was shaped by dialectologists and sociolinguists. By the time the BBC journalists started interviewing informants in 2004, *Voices* had adopted a methodology developed by Clive Upton and others at Leeds and Sheffield Universities (Elmes, this volume). Focused on lexis, and informed by the SED questionnaire, this used a set of prompts designed to guide conversations with informants, aiming to create a more informal environment than the traditional interview. The same set of lexical prompts was used for the online *Voices* Language Lab survey, which required neither fieldworker nor interview. Even so, this approach of asking participants for their words for certain named notions is something of a return methodologically to the first systematic national dialect surveys of the late nineteenth century, which asked informants to translate standard words or sentences into the local dialect. While this method is highly practicable in the *Voices* context, other than by engaging the ready participation of informants through deployment of the Spidergram (Elmes, this volume) it makes no elaborate attempts to circumvent the well-known observer's paradox, an obstacle which for decades has been variously and inventively tackled by dialectologists and sociolinguists.

In that they contained links to many local glossaries, the resultant *Voices* web-pages were in tune with the long tradition of English dialect lexicography, but a centrepiece was cartographic, a series of Word Maps, displaying responses to a selection of the lexical prompts. In the next section, I compare the *Voices* Word Map with SAWD material. It is useful that approximately 50 per cent of the lexical notions targeted by the *Voices* methodology have an equivalent in the SAWD questionnaire.

The SAWD fieldworkers were trained in linguistics and phonetics, though the phonetics training came into its own usually after the fieldwork, as most of the interviews were recorded, quite often on lo-fi cassette tape, and were laboriously transcribed at a later date. The *Voices* fieldworkers were BBC journalists, and their interviews were less formally structured. It was the journalists who chose the localities and the informants, and in this one could say that the sampling was less rigorous than in the usual academic linguistic survey. Compared with rural SAWD in particular, there are significant differences in the informant profiles. SAWD informants were elderly, whereas *Voices* informants came from young, middle-aged, and elderly groups. While all of the *Voices* informants were recorded in their respective localities, informant criteria such as lifelong residence and their being born in the locality were less strictly applied than in SAWD. This affects the Talbot Green (south Wales) *Voices* recordings especially. The Talbot Green informants were all travelling showpersons with varying degrees of attachment to and life history in Talbot Green itself. Compared with other surveys generally, *Voices* did not attempt to ensure that carefully defined social groups (according to class, age, sex, or ethnicity, for example) were equally represented in the sampling. The method might be described as a rather informal judgement sample, though one in which the biographical details of the informants are usually amply noted. The resulting data, therefore, are relatively broadly based and at the same time somewhat sketchy in terms of coverage of different groups.

There is also a difference in the locality network. The first phase of SAWD was emphatically rural. English-language *Voices* recordings were made in 23 localities in Wales in 2004–5, as follows:

- north Wales – Bangor, Bethesda, Flint, Holyhead, Llangollen, Rhosgadfan, Rhos-on-Sea, Tal-y-Bont, Wrexham
- mid Wales – Builth Wells, Newtown, Tregaron
- south Wales – Bonymaen (Swansea), Glyn-Neath, Llanelli, Milford Haven, Newport, Pontcanna (Cardiff), Pontypridd, Risca, Splott (Cardiff), Talbot Green, Treorchy.

With the exception of Bethesda (arguably), Rhosgadfan, Tal-y-Bont, Tregaron, and Talbot Green, these are all urban localities. The network is scattered rather than evenly spaced, with an emphasis on the more highly populated south-east. Nevertheless, there is something to be gained, I believe, from a comparison of the data from these localities with those gleaned from nearby SAWD rural localities, and this has been greatly facilitated by the work of the Leverhulme-funded *Voices of the UK* project at the British Library (see Robinson *et al.*, this volume). I have had access to linguistic descriptions completed by the team in 2010 for the Welsh localities, and use these below to compare *Voices* grammatical and phonological data with those of SAWD.

This comparison is aided by two further facets of SAWD. By the mid-1980s, David Parry was keen to extend the Survey into urban areas and to integrate a more sociolinguistic approach into this work. A grant from the British Academy was obtained to fund fieldwork, and I was employed as fieldworker between 1985 and 1987. A short phonological questionnaire was compiled by Parry, and a more casual style was used for the rest of the interview, centred upon discussion of the personal histories of the informants and their perceptions of local speech in relation to other varieties. There were three main aims of the urban interview: to obtain basic material that would enable phonemicization; to accumulate material that might be suitable for intonation analysis; and to elicit non-standard grammatical features. Four broad age-groups were interviewed in each locality visited: teenagers; 20–30 years old; 30–60 years old; and over 60 years old. In total, 54 informants were interviewed, with ages ranging from 12 to 82. All were natives of the locality in question, and very few had gone through higher education. Total interview time of the resulting audio recordings was nearly 24 hours. The localities were Caernarfon and Wrexham in the north, and Carmarthen and the Grangetown district of Cardiff in the south. The recordings remained unexploited until Paulasto (2006), which focused on the syntax of Welsh English. The SAWD urban phase interviews are thus much closer in format to those of *Voices*, and Paulasto's research, which also included new material collected between 1995 and 2000, provides a valuable chronological bridge between the SAWD and *Voices* grammatical data.

Parry's most recent major work also facilitates a comparison between SAWD and *Voices*. A 'tentatively-proposed phonemicization' (Parry 2008) was devised. Heedful that the SED/SAWD questionnaire was not designed with this kind of phonological analysis in mind, Parry is modest in his claims. Yet the reader can see that the one-hundred-page breakdown of the sound-systems of rural Welsh English in Parry (1999) is an important achievement. It includes complete sound-systems for each of the 90 localities, and shows the regional distribution of each phonemic unit and its realizations in 144 keywords. Although the *Voices* recordings focused on elicitation of lexis, 13 of the *Voices of the UK* linguistic descriptions also list all non-standard grammar used by informants in the interviews, and give vowel inventories and notes on non-standard consonants, using standard lexical sets. Therefore, tentative phonological comparisons can be made between SAWD rural data and some of the *Voices* recordings.

Voices and SAWD: lexis

The simple Word Map on the *Voices* website (www.bbc.co.uk/voices) has a visually immediate format. A grid covers Wales, England, Scotland, and Northern Ireland. Each square on the grid can be filled to show that a given lexical variant is used in that area. A range of colours is used on the website maps, coded to show how often the variant occurs in the area. Empty squares indicate where the variant is not found. In addition, two columns at the base of the map show the age and gender breakdown in percentages of the total number of submissions of the variant. In the panel to the right of the map there is a brief commentary which gives the total number of submissions of variants of the notion to the Language Lab survey. Look, for example, at Figure 8.1.

The notion here is *left-handed*, and the panel at the right lists the ten most frequent variants submitted to the survey for this notion (another web page lists a further 26 variants). A total of 3,850 submissions were made for *left-handed*. I have clicked on *caggy handed* and the map shows the distribution of this variant.

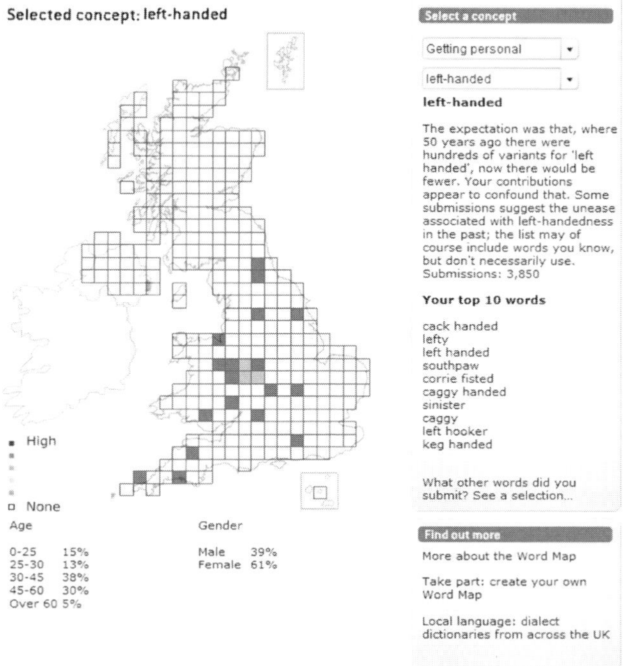

FIGURE 8.1 *Voices* Word Map, LEFT-HANDED variants *caggy* and *caggy handed*

The original colour map has mainly (dark grey here) green squares and (in the West Midlands) three (light grey here) yellow squares, which indicate a relatively restricted distribution for this variant.

The main atlas publication of SAWD is Parry's *Grammar and Glossary* of 1999, which uses a primarily isoglossic mapping format, and often (like the *Voices* Word Maps) concentrates on the limits of distribution of certain variants rather than showing all the variants for a given notion. Side-by-side comparison of a *Voices* map and a SAWD map would be illuminating, but none of the 65 lexical notions that Parry chose to map in 1999 coincides with any of the notions so far mapped by *Voices*. (Possibilities opening up by methods demonstrated by Holliday and Wieling (this volume) promise much in this regard.) However, Parry (1999) is a contribution to both of the grand traditions of dialect study (cartography and lexicography), and its 80-page glossary is a detailed catalogue of the non-standard vocabulary gathered by rural SAWD, giving etymologies and full provenance for each word. It contains distribution information for many of the lexical variants also recorded in Wales by *Voices*.

For example, *caggy handed* is listed by Parry (1999: 139) under the entry *caggy-handed/cag-handed*, which is found at seven localities in the SAWD network, in a distribution that is almost identical to that of the *Voices* Word Map. Other non-standard items recorded by SAWD for left-handed are *coochy*, *gammy-handed*, *keck-fisted*, and *left-keg* (Parry 1999: 124). Clearly there is a close relation between *cag(gy)-handed*, *keck-fisted*, *cack handed*, and *keg handed*. Considering all of these together, we find a similarity of distribution between SAWD's *cag(gy)-handed*, *keck-fisted,* and *Voices' caggy handed*, *keg handed*. *Voices' cack handed*, however, is much more widespread, and is surprisingly absent in Parry (1999). What conclusions can be drawn from this illustration?

First, the fact that a variant is not recorded by a survey does not mean that we can say conclusively that it does not occur. All we can say conclusively is that the survey did not record it. However, the rural SAWD network of localities is comprehensive, though with an informant sample that is more restricted than that of the Language Lab. The Language Lab coverage, in terms of submissions, is considerable. Therefore, when the same lexical notion is investigated by both surveys, I think we can with some measure of confidence make statements which sum up historical trends stretching between the traditional English dialects of mid-twentieth-century Wales to present-day more general non-standard Welsh English. So we could say, for example, that *caggy-handed* and its close variants have an apparently stable regional distribution in Wales; that the forms *coochy*, *gammy-handed*, and *left keg*, which were rare in the mid-twentieth century, appear to have died out; that *cack handed* now appears to be the dominant non-standard form for *left-handed* in Wales; and that the larger population sample of the Language Lab has yielded a greater number of variants. (One would also want, in this case, more information on *gamie handed*, listed on the supplementary web page for *left-handed*, in order to compare with SAWD *gammy-handed*.)

Comparing the data in more detail, one notices in the Word Map an apparent centring of *caggy handed* in the West Midlands of England, with what look like outliers at the north and south points of the Wales–England border. The seven localities in Parry (1999) which have *cag(gy)-handed* are scattered, at the north-east, mid-east, and south-east of Wales, that is, mirroring the Word Map distribution for Wales. Drawing SED data into the discussion, we find *kaggy-handed* attested mostly in the West Midlands (Upton *et al.* 1994: 228), with outliers in Hampshire and Monmouthshire. This obviously shows a connection between West Midlands dialects and Wales border dialects, and one interpretation would be that the *cag(gy)*-forms have spread to mid-east Wales from the West Midlands, spreading thence to north and south Wales. Alternatively, it is possible that *caggy handed* might once have been more widespread in mid-west England, intruding into Wales all along the border – but the evidence is not helpful for this interpretation. The SED has no widespread attestations for *kaggy-handed* and *kaggy-fisted*, and Joseph Wright (1902: 413) records only *caggy*, and only then in Staffordshire and Warwickshire. In addition, A. J. Ellis's late-nineteenth-century calculation (see Ellis 1889) of the boundary between Welsh-speaking and English-speaking localities shows a greater penetration of English-speaking in mid Wales than in the north and south (excepting Pembroke and Gower).

There is a similar potential for discussion regarding all of the lexical notions which *Voices* and SAWD have in common, which in summary are as follows: *tired, unwell, hot, cold, throw, play a game, clothes, trousers, mother, grandmother, male partner, friend, grandfather, female partner, toilet, running water smaller than a river, main room, left-handed, drunk, attractive*.

SAWD can be of further help to anyone looking to investigate the history of other *Voices* items in Welsh English. From the outset, it aimed to publish its 'incidental material' (or IM) alongside the basic responses to the questionnaire. The IM is material elicited during interviews but not forming direct answers to the questions. It tends to be more conversational or to take the form of narrative monologues by informants. Parts of the SED/SAWD questionnaire were quite efficient in prompting this kind of material. In the major SAWD publications, the pronunciation material elicited by questions is supplemented by relevant IM, and all the non-standard lexical and grammatical IM is listed. So, for example, we find that *mitch*, PLAY TRUANT, recorded by the Language Lab in several parts of Wales, especially the South Wales Valleys, and in south-west England, also occurred in SAWD IM (Parry 1999: 168) in the Gower Peninsula and south Pembroke, which are long-anglicized areas of Wales whose English dialects have historical connections across the Bristol Channel. It seems, then, that there are fruitful avenues to follow in comparing the lexical reserves of SAWD and *Voices*.

Voices and SAWD: grammar

In order to assess the possibilities with regard to grammar, we must use a different resource of the *Voices* project, the audio recordings, and specifically the commentaries on those recordings produced by the *Voices of the UK* team at the British Library (Robinson *et al.* 2009–2012 and this volume). As noted above, commentaries have been created for the localities in Wales. Nine commentaries have only lists of lexis: the variants elicited by the Spidergram methodology (the lexical prompts), as used also in the Language Lab. These localities are: Bangor, Llangollen, Rhosgadfan, Wrexham, Glyn-Neath, Milford Haven, Newport, Pontcanna, and Pontypridd. Tal-y-Bont has no commentary at present. The remaining 13 commentaries have the above lexical lists plus any spontaneously occurring non-standard lexis, lexical set vowel descriptions, notes on non-standard consonants and phonological variation in certain lexis, and notes on all non-standard grammar. I have already made use of these grammatical data for my contributions to Kortmann and Lunkenheimer (2011, 2012), which have also entailed comparison with SAWD data. The SAWD data come from responses to the questionnaire and from IM; the *Voices* data come from what we might call *Voices* IM. As was the case for lexis, and with some provisos, the two sets of data are eminently comparable; and Paulasto (2006) offers a useful additional perspective to the comparison.

My work on the two sets of grammatical data reveals the following categories:

i features associated with the traditional rural dialects which are attested in SAWD but not in *Voices*
ii features attested by *Voices* but which have not been found in rural SAWD
iii features which show continuity between SAWD and *Voices*, and which are usually well attested.

Most of the features in category (i) appear to be either obsolete or obsolescent. Often they are linked with influence from the traditional English dialects of western and south-western England. Features with *a*-prefixing, such as *a-cutting*, *a-coming*, *a-taking*, and *a-doing* (Parry 1999: 112, 117) exemplify this set: recorded sporadically by SAWD on the Welsh–English border, on Gower, and in Pembroke, they have not been captured by *Voices* in Wales. A further example is the use of subject pronoun forms in object function, as in *come and see we* and *never heard of they* (Parry 1999: 109) in mid Wales. An instance of this was recorded in 2004 by *Voices* in Builth Wells, but the information given (as noted by the British Library team) corroborates its obsolescence: '*"do you want to come with we?" rather than "do you want to come with us?"* – the informant says this is something she heard old farmers say when she was a child'. Because of the disparity between the type of localities investigated by the first, rural phase of SAWD and the more urban network of *Voices*, one cannot be completely certain of the obsoleteness of these features.

Similarly, it would be prudent to see the features in category (ii) as ones which either were overlooked by SAWD or its publications or eluded its field investigators, rather than to understand them as innovations. As well as occurring in Welsh English, this small set of features (relative to the other two) is associated with general non-standard British English. For example, the *Voices* data for Wales have 26 instances of *like* as a focusing device (as in *I've heard quite a few things, like*, from Llanelli), which is also well attested in British English generally. This is not a feature targeted by the SAWD/SED questionnaire, but I would be surprised were there not some examples of it in untranscribed SAWD audio recordings or unpublished SAWD field-transcriptions. And yet, one could also posit tentatively that the trend with nearly all the features in this set is that they are more common in early twenty-first-century Welsh English than they were in traditional mid-twentieth-century Welsh English.

Category (iii) is the largest set. The features here show continuity between SAWD and *Voices*, despite there being some disparity in types of locality and informant. Most of these features are not specific to Wales, though some are particularly associated with Welsh English. Among the latter is 'focus fronting', an intriguing and somewhat complex feature much discussed under a number of labels in the literature on Welsh English. Parry (1999: 119–20) calls it 'sentence-initial emphasis', and gives a number of examples from IM, such as *a weed it is*, from mid Wales. In the 13 *Voices* commentaries with grammar it turns up just once, at Bonymaen, in *worn out, I got*, and it is less attested by *Voices* than one would expect and than other features in this category are. This does add to its usefulness as an example in the present discussion, however.

First, it might be that it points towards a weakness in the *Voices* methodology: non-standard syntactic features are difficult to elicit via questionnaire, and free-flowing conversations might yield more non-standard syntax, but not necessarily anything approaching the full repertoire of an informant. Second, as Paulasto (2006: 157) notes, fronted constructions are commonplace in many other varieties of English, and it is conceivable that investigators might overlook Welsh English instances. What distinguishes the particularly local Welsh English forms is not so much a structural but an informational matter: the initial, fronted item carries the focus of the sentence, unlike other fronted constructions which preserve the end-focus (Paulasto 2006: 158). In this present sentence, we have an example of the latter. From Paulasto we get an extreme example of the former: *Very much involved with the WI* [Women's Institute] *over the years I've been* (from Llandybie in south Wales). This difference explains Paulasto's choice of label: *focus fronting* refers to a fronted construction in which the informational focus also is fronted. Paulasto's in-depth study provides us with another possible interpretation of the relationship between the SAWD and *Voices* data on focus fronting: she concludes (2006: 214–15) that the feature occurs more often in Welsh English than in English English, and that transference of Welsh-language constructions is a key cause, especially in traditional Welsh-speaking regions. She also affirms that in some anglicized areas the forms of focus fronting have been affected by English English usages, and that a reduction in the functional range of focus fronting was evident in her younger age groups. In other words, in summary, the more conspicuously Welsh forms in Welsh English seem to be showing signs of levelling with English English.

Even in this troublesome example – or perhaps especially in this troublesome example – we see the potential for updating the picture of Welsh English that *Voices* offers when used in comparison with other sources.

Voices and SAWD: phonology

There is a similar potential in the phonological data that can be gleaned incidentally from the *Voices* recordings. Most of the *Voices* localities in Wales do not coincide with SAWD localities. Nevertheless, if the data and their analysis are compatible, then there is scope for comparing the networks overall and for comparing a *Voices* locality with its nearest SAWD locality. The best way to assess this is to compare the one *Voices* locality that is also in the rural SAWD network: Tregaron, in western mid Wales.

The British Library team, in their commentary for Tregaron, provide a sketch of the vowel phoneme inventory and some analysis of non-standard consonants. From this we see that Tregaron has, for example, stressed schwa realizations in the STRUT set, variation between front and back realizations in BATH and

PALM, and variation between diphthongal and monophthongal realizations in both FACE and GOAT. We learn that /l/ is frequently clear in syllable coda, that /r/ is frequently flapped and occasionally rolled, and that medial consonants are often subject to gemination.

Turning to Parry's (1999: 68) phonemicization of SAWD data from Tregaron (these data were collected in 1978), we find very similar information in his equivalents to the STRUT, BATH, PALM, FACE and GOAT sets. He notes that /l/ is nearly always clear, that /r/ is always flapped or rolled, and he has two examples of medial gemination, in *shilling* and *woman*. Both surveys record occasional NG-fronting too, in *farthing* (SAWD) and *reading*, *talking*, *wedding* (*Voices*).

There are also divergences: for example, Parry (1999: 68) notes that /t/ is frequently dental (possibly due to Welsh-language influence), while this is not observed in the *Voices* commentary; the *Voices* recording, however, has occasional post-vocalic word-final /t/-glottaling, which is absent in Parry.

The analyses are compatible. In order truly to make more confident judgements about changes in progress between the two collections of data, one would wish for more tokens so as to attempt a statistical comparison, but the material does not allow this. Perhaps one cannot expect national surveys which are also concerned with lexis and grammar to collect scores of tokens of variant realizations of each phoneme. In the case of Tregaron (SAWD) and Tregaron (*Voices*), one notices some evidence of more back realizations for BATH and PALM in the later data, and no mention of (Welsh-language-influenced) rhoticity in 2005 – rhoticity was frequent in the SAWD data collected in 1978 (Parry 1999: 68). The divergences in the realizations of /t/ lead one to speculate further about decreasing Welsh-language influence and increasing general British English influence when comparing the newer data with the older. All of these issues would be worthy of deeper investigation by comparing more *Voices* and SAWD phonological commentaries. And the issues that arise out of a comparison of *Voices* and SAWD might also encourage one to return afresh to the original audio recordings and/or field transcriptions.

Conclusion

The aim here has been to appraise *Voices* in Wales as a national dialect survey, and to do so in particular by means of comparison with SAWD, thereby also in a very preliminary way looking at the prospects for updating our view of Welsh English. The signs all round are positive, I believe, bearing in mind also that much of the *Voices* Language Lab data are only now becoming available, and that a further ten *Voices* audio recordings from Wales await annotation at the British Library. At the levels of lexis, grammar, and phonology, the materials already completed and available do make possible informative comparisons, and they signal paths for further investigation, either by reference to other research on Welsh English or by deeper scrutiny of *Voices* (and SAWD) data.

References

Chesters, A., Upton, C. and Parry, D. (1968) *A Questionnaire for a Linguistic Atlas of England: Modified for Use in Welsh Localities,* Swansea: privately published.

Ellis, A. J. (1889) *On Early English Pronunciation*, Volume V, London: Trübner.

Kortmann, B. and Lunkenheimer, K. (eds) (2011) *The Electronic World Atlas of Varieties of English* [*eWAVE*], Leipzig: Max Planck Institute for Evolutionary Anthropology. Online. Available HTTP: <http://www.ewave_atlas.org/>.

Kortmann, B. and Lunkenheimer, K. (eds) (2012) *The Mouton World Atlas of Variation in English* [*pWAVE*], Berlin/New York: De Gruyter Mouton.

Orton, H. (1962) *Survey of English Dialects, (A): Introduction*, Leeds: E. J. Arnold.

Parry, D. R. (ed.) (1977) *The Survey of Anglo-Welsh Dialects*. Volume 1: *The South East*, Swansea: privately published.

Parry, D. R. (ed.) (1979) *The Survey of Anglo-Welsh Dialects*. Volume 2: *The South West*, Swansea: privately published.

Parry, D. R. (ed.) (1999) *A Grammar and Glossary of the Conservative Anglo-Welsh Dialects of Rural Wales*, Sheffield: The National Centre for English Cultural Tradition, University of Sheffield.

Parry, D. R. (2008) 'The Survey of Anglo-Welsh Dialects: History'. Online. Available HTTP: <http://www.swan.ac.uk/riah/researchgroups/lrc/awe/storyofsawd/>.

Paulasto, H. (2006) *Welsh English Syntax: Contact and Variation*, Joensuu: Joensuu University Press.

Penhallurick, R. J. (1991) *The Anglo-Welsh Dialects of North Wales: A Survey of Conservative Rural Spoken English in the Counties of Gwynedd and Clwyd*, Frankfurt am Main: Peter Lang.

Robinson, J., Herring, J. and Gilbert, H. (2009–2012) *Voices of the UK* linguistic descriptions. Online. Available HTTP: <http://sounds.bl.uk/Accents-and-dialects/BBC-Voices>.

Upton, C., Parry, D. and Widdowson, J. D. A. (1994) *Survey of English Dialects: The Dictionary and Grammar*, London/New York: Routledge.

Wright, J. (ed.) (1902) *The English Dialect Dictionary*. Volume III, Oxford: Henry Frowde.

9

VOICES OF THE UK

The British Library description of the *BBC Voices Recordings* Collection

Jonathan Robinson, Jon Herring and Holly Gilbert

Introduction

This chapter focuses on the *BBC Voices Recordings*, the digital audio archive of group conversations recorded by BBC Local Radio journalists under the umbrella of the BBC *Voices* initiative and deposited at the British Library (BL) in November 2005. We first introduce *Voices of the UK* (VoUK), a BL project designed to create a dynamic online dataset of British English vernacular speech by extracting detailed linguistic information from the *Voices* recordings, which makes the collection searchable according to linguistic criteria. Next, we outline the approach adopted by the BL-based research team and reflect on the challenges encountered in describing twenty-first century English for both an academic and a public audience. Finally, we present two case studies to demonstrate potential applications of this dataset.

Dialect resources at the British Library

The British Library has in its archives one of the largest collections of recorded sound in the world. The collection documents all aspects of life in the United Kingdom and supports a broad range of research enquiries. It exceeds 3.5 million recordings and consists of over 550,000 hours of recorded sound, a third of which is speech, predominantly in English. This spoken material encompasses commercial recordings such as speeches, drama and literature, radio broadcasts and unpublished recordings, including linguistic surveys, oral history interviews, and public talks and lectures. The recordings, which capture spoken English in a variety of forms and settings spanning more than 100 years, represent an extremely rich resource for linguistic researchers. Recent BL experience has, in particular, noted considerable academic, popular, and media interest in the Library's unique collection of sound recordings of vernacular speech. In 2004, the BL online dialect archive *Sounds* (http://sounds.bl.uk/) made sound recordings from the internationally acclaimed Survey of English Dialects ([SED] Orton *et al.* 1962–71) and the BBC's *Millennium Memory Bank* (MMB) available to a worldwide audience for the first time. Its extraordinary popularity encouraged the Library to increase its online portfolio, creating *Sounds Familiar* (http://www.bl.uk/soundsfamiliar) in 2007. This educational resource celebrates and explores regional speech across the UK through short extracts from SED (BL shelfmark C908), MMB (BL shelfmark C900), and the Survey of Anglo-Welsh Dialects ([SAWD] Parry 1977–79, 1999, BL shelfmark C1314) recordings, and these are presented alongside accessible linguistic analysis.

The impact of the two websites, *Sounds* and *Sounds Familiar*, together with ongoing enhancement of BL sociolinguistic resources and services, can be measured in a number of ways. First and foremost, the two existing websites achieve consistently high user figures: *Sounds Familiar*, for instance, remains the most popular BL learning resource by a considerable margin, with 292,000 individual visitors in 2011. This represents an impressive 24,000 users per month and over one million distinct users since its launch. Furthermore, both resources are widely incorporated into school and Higher Education syllabuses in the United Kingdom and overseas, informing and supporting best practice. In 2006, for example, the AQA A-Level English Language examination paper (11 January 2006) featured a question deriving from an article published in the *Daily Mirror* (Borrows 2004) which was, in turn, inspired by the launch of *Sounds*. Also, since 2011, at the request of the American Institutes for Research, an assessment based on content from *Sounds Familiar* has been included in the Ohio Graduation Test, the material selected 'because of its high quality, appropriateness, accessibility, and appeal for high school students'.

Publishing the SED and MMB online cemented existing relationships between the Library and the University of Leeds and the BBC respectively, and coincided with the Leeds–BBC collaboration on the *Voices* enterprise. A natural extension of this close co-operation was the inclusion of the BL as the principal repository for the recorded output of *Voices*, not only to secure the legacy of such an important collection of sound recordings, but also to ensure that they would be immediately and permanently available to the worldwide academic research community and to the general public. This fulfilled two of the Library's strategic priorities, namely (i) guaranteeing access for future generations, and (ii) enabling access for researchers (British Library 2010). The *Voices* recordings were deposited at the BL in November 2005 and are archived alongside equally prestigious nationwide language surveys, such as the *Berliner Lautarchiv British & Commonwealth Recordings* (BL shelfmark C1315), SED, SAWD, and the *British National Corpus* (BL shelfmark C897). The subsequent implementation of the VoUK project described below addresses the Library's other strategic priorities, namely (iii) supporting research communities in key areas for social and economic benefit, (iv) enriching the cultural life of the nation, and (v) leading and collaborating in augmenting the world's knowledge base (British Library 2010).

BBC *Voices* recordings

The *Voices* audio archive constitutes the most extensive survey of recorded linguistic fieldwork yet undertaken across the British Isles. The intention was to capture how we speak at the turn of the twenty-first century by encouraging contributors to talk about the languages and language varieties they use, their styles of talk, and their attitudes to language. Recordings were made in 303 locations involving 1,293 people. The vast majority of conversations were conducted in English, but the collection also includes ten recordings in Welsh, five in Scottish Gaelic, three in Irish, and one each in Manx and Guernsey French. Thirty-one conversations in Scotland include either whole groups or individual participants who define themselves as speakers of Scots, and three recordings in Northern Ireland include contributors who identify themselves as Ulster Scots speakers. These identities are based on responses provided by speakers to a biographical questionnaire in which they were asked to 'describe their English accent'. The conversations, recorded between late 2004 and mid 2005, were guided by BBC journalists based at local and national BBC radio stations and the independent Manx Radio. It was acknowledged from the outset that this exercise could not be representative of all vernacular speech in the UK, so interviewers chose groups of people who between them offered some illustration of the variety and richness of accent and dialect in their region. In most cases, all members of an interview group knew each other well and were either chosen from similar geographic, social, and/or ethnic backgrounds or shared the same interests. Most recording sessions lasted between one and two hours and took place in a location that was familiar to the group. The overall goal was to capture relaxed, unselfconscious conversation within the group in as natural an environment as possible, with minimal interference from the interviewer.

To ensure the recorded conversations were comparable, every discussion followed the same loose structure and used the same set of prompts. In advance of the recording session, each participant was sent the Spidergram (see Elmes, Crystal, this volume). Interviewers used the Spidergram as a starting point from which to discuss any alternative words and to establish in what circumstances these might be used. They also explored words and phrases specific to the group itself, by initiating conversation about the place they came from, their work, or their shared interests. The third source of prompts was a list of questions concerning the participants' attitudes to language: the reactions of others to the way they speak, their reactions to other accents, the language of their parents and/or children, the role of education in language use, the influence of the media/popular culture, and attitudes to swearing and 'bad language'.

Selected excerpts from the recordings were broadcast on BBC local and national radio in programmes scheduled throughout 2005, and formed the basis of *Word4Word*, a seven-part series on BBC Radio 4 exploring language use across the country in greater depth. A set of illustrative audio-clips from most conversations is available at http://www.bbc.co.uk/voices/recordings/, and the entire set of full-length recordings is available at the British Library. English-language recordings were also deposited at the University of Leeds, and recordings made in Wales, Northern Ireland, and Scotland were deposited at The Museum of Welsh Life at St Fagan's, The Ulster Folk and Transport Museum, and Glasgow University respectively. The collection, known as the *BBC Voices Recordings* (BL shelfmark C1190), is catalogued at http://cadensa.bl.uk/cgi-bin/webcat. Entries include details of speakers, recording location and date, and a summary of the conversation, with links providing direct access to the corresponding audio file for onsite users in the BL Reading Rooms at St Pancras and Boston Spa. In 2009, the BL made a successful joint application with Clive Upton to The Leverhulme Trust to fund a three-year project, VoUK, to develop remote access to the collection and enable sophisticated interrogation of the data by linguists.

Voices of the UK

As sound files alone the *Voices* recordings, though valuable, present challenges for linguistic research. A linguist wishing to compile evidence of the survival of traditional features or the diffusion of innovations, for example, faces the daunting task of auditing up to 500 hours of recordings in the hope of locating useful material. VoUK creates a searchable linguistic dataset, deriving initially from all 283 recordings in English and Scots/Ulster Scots, to assist linguists in identifying relevant content. Inspired by the foresight of the late Harold Orton in publishing the comprehensive SED *Basic Material* (Orton *et al.* 1962–71), thereby facilitating research far beyond the Survey's original diachronic focus, VoUK presents significant amounts of linguistic data with only minimal editing. As with the SED *Basic Material*, there is no attempt to evaluate the features identified. Rather, the intention is to present detailed linguistic information in a set of descriptions, one for each recording, to be interpreted, analyzed, and compared according to need.

VoUK descriptions record the presence and/or quality of an extensive set of linguistic features presented in three categories: lexis, phonology, and grammar. Lexical descriptions have been created for the entire set, from which a subset of 130 recordings has been further audited to extract phonological and grammatical data. Examples of features included in each category, with a rationale for inclusion, are given below.

Descriptive methodology

The template for VoUK linguistic descriptions is a refined version of the format devised for the comparative study, *Sounds*, and combines elements of previously published dialect datasets. A comprehensive inventory of phonological and grammatical variables was compiled by Robinson, modelled on the analysis used in Kortmann *et al.* (2004), and expanded to include additional features encountered when creating the earlier BL descriptions of SED and MMB sound recordings. We draw on elements of the SED and on the style of dialect data presentation used in Hughes *et al.* (2005) and Foulkes and Docherty (1999). A close audit of each recording focuses on the Spidergram lexical stimuli, a set of 55 phonological variables (with 191 possible values), 33 grammatical variables (with 126 possible values), and additional 'incidental information'.

Edited descriptions are arranged by recording and presented as Word documents. The corresponding data were transferred to Excel spreadsheets, enabling the creation of an online discovery and access resource. While we deliberately seek a neutral presentation, additional information is occasionally included to distinguish, for instance, between linguistic forms that are clearly 'performance' or imitation, and those which represent more natural, authentic usage. Recordings which feature speakers from very different linguistic backgrounds are also clearly identified. In order to maintain a theory-neutral framework, we occasionally present the same phenomenon in more than one linguistic category. For instance, a pronunciation of the first person singular possessive pronoun with a weak vowel is recorded both as a potential phonetic process and as a possible grammatical variant:

> ***my*** (0:17:19 *if I lose my* [mɪ] *temper*; 0:17:31 *if something like I'd whacked my* [mɪ] *thumb or something*; 0:39:02 *I get in the habit of saying my* [mɪ] *'grandkids'*)
> **possessive *me*** (0:17:19 *if I lose me temper*; 0:20:30 *if something like I'd whacked me thumb or something*; 0:39:02 *I get in the habit of saying me 'grandkids'*)
> BBC London interview (BL shelfmark C1190/03/02)

Similarly, where we are aware of a strong local consensus or speaker intuition supported by reliable published evidence, we record some items as lexical entries with a cross-reference in the relevant phonological section:

> ***dae*** = *to do* (0:05:44 *aye, lots of other jobs to dae*; 0:57:51 *always had their names on my list afore I start to dae the report*)
> ***do*** (0:05:44 *aye, lots of other jobs to do* [dɪə]; 0:57:51 *always had their names on my list afore I start to do* [dɪə] *the report*)
> BBC Radio York interview in Helmsley (BL shelfmark C1190/35/03)

Researchers seeking data from a variety of theoretical perspectives can thus locate examples relevant to their enquiry via different routes.

A considerable strength of the *Voices* recordings is the prominence afforded to lexical data collection compared with most post-SED studies. Considered problematic to collect, since elicitation devices such as questionnaires formalize responses and can fail to distinguish effectively between a respondent's active and passive vocabulary (Beal 2006), lexical data also present a particular challenge for documentation. Consideration was given in VoUK to the possibility of an SED-inspired treatment, involving close phonetic transcription of every response. This was rejected on several grounds. First, this approach, although justified for SED fieldworkers with limited access to sound-recording technology, was less appropriate here given that sound recordings featuring all the elicited items are available for researchers to transcribe should they so wish. Second, detailed transcription would not have allowed sufficient time for attention to be given to the phonological and grammatical data contained in the spontaneous 'incidental material' arising during the course of the conversations. Finally, an important aspect of the *Voices* initiative as a whole is public engagement. Lexis is to the fore in popular notions of vernacular speech, and the popularity of commercial publications such as slang and dialect glossaries, and online platforms such as the *Urban Dictionary* (http://www.urbandictionary.com/), demonstrates the broad appeal of repositories of regional and/or sociolectal vocabulary. Consequently, the lexical data are recorded using conventional orthography, itself not a straightforward task, as discussed below.

Lexis

Lexical items elicited in response to the Spidergram are presented as lists of variants for each of the prompt terms, or variables. The number of responses differs from variable to variable, and the amount of time spent exploring alternatives depends on group interest and interviewer style. There is frequently animated discussion within the group, and interviewers often probe for clarification. Where this additional reflective information is linguistically revealing, we include it. SED editorial practice was to include such contextual information in square brackets, by quoting or paraphrasing an informant's remark, such as ["regarded as Scots"], ["older"], ["modern"], ["broader"], or by using a set of descriptive terms to summarize, e.g. [used by older farmers], [rare], [less frequent]. We adopt similar conventions and present the responses provided in italics in the order in which they occur within the conversation and in the form given there. Hence a verb might appear as a lemma or in its inflected form. If more than one speaker supplies the same response, we record this as one entry, unless a second response is markedly different (e.g. in a different grammatical form or contained within an extended phrase). Relevant supplementary information follows in round brackets. The following example from a group responding to the stimulus variable UNATTRACTIVE illustrates this approach:

> **unattractive** *minger* (of female, learnt from TV, *"in-word"*, *"word of the moment"*); *moose*, *munter*, *back end of a bus*, *plain*, *plain Jane* (of female); *ugly* (avoided in past); *loser* (of male).
>
> BBC Radio Berkshire interview in Purley (BL shelfmark C1190/06/04)

The information supplied in brackets above relates to the immediately preceding response(s). Commas separate responses which share the bracketed information; semi-colons distinguish between responses with unique or no additional information. Italicized entries in double quotation marks indicate a speaker's insight or observation on a given usage. The entry above, therefore, shows that the speakers consider the variants *minger*, *moose*, *munter*, *back end of a bus*, *plain,* and *plain Jane* more likely to be applied to female referents, while *loser* might be more commonly used to describe a male. *Minger* is thought to have risen to prominence recently, and the group attribute their own use to hearing it on television.

Orthography follows conventional sources where available, and entries indicate whether a word or phrase has been found in an authoritative publication. The following are consulted to establish spelling precedent: *Oxford English Dictionary* ([*OED*] online edition), *Brewer's Dictionary of Phrase & Fable* (Rockwood 2009), *English Dialect Dictionary* ([*EDD*] Wright 1898–1905), *Survey of English Dialects Basic Material* (Orton *et al.* 1962–1971), *Dictionary of the Scots Language* (online edition), Dalzell and Victor (2006), Green (2010), *Urban Dictionary* (online edition); and specialist glossaries and/or sources as appropriate, such as *Dictionary of Caribbean English Usage* (Allsopp 1996), Griffiths (2011), Roud (2010), and Baker (2002). Reliance on precedent allows us to choose more consistently between potentially competing alternatives, as in the case of the response of an *Evening Standard* seller recorded by BBC London (BL shelfmark C1190/03/02) to the prompt ANNOYED, *got the zig*. The speaker explains the phrase *got the zig* derives from *got the Sigmund Freud*, but that the conventions of rhyming slang require the rhyming component ('Freud' rhymes with 'annoyed') to be omitted and, in this instance, the initial component 'Sigmund' is also abbreviated to *zig* [zɪg]. Without previous evidence we might have chosen to spell *zig* with initial <s> to reflect the spelling of the personal name from which it derives. Furthermore, we might also have considered the relative merits of capitalizing <S> to reflect that the underlying form is a proper noun. An entry with initial <z> in Dalzell and Victor (2006) including citations from other publications prompts us to adopt this spelling.

Where no previous written evidence has been found or legitimate alternatives exist, decisions regarding appropriate spelling are made on a case by case basis. As noted above, there is no attempt within the lexical description to include a comprehensive set of phonetic realizations, as the corresponding phonological description provides sufficient guidance and audio files are available online for clarification. We do phonetically transcribe a small number of responses where pronunciation is unclear from the spelling or obscure in the phonological description. Where items supplied appear to result from misunderstanding, we preface the entry with a question mark. Words and phrases in languages other than English are noted, although it has not been possible to transcribe all such items in an appropriate orthography or indeed to provide a Roman transliteration. It is expected that, ultimately, crowd sourcing will enable us to record these responses more appropriately.

Phonology

Although there is clearly considerable scope for intra- and inter-speaker variation in pronunciation within the course of the recorded conversations, VoUK phonological descriptions present a record of a whole recording rather than of individual speakers. The aim is to record the presence and/or quality of a set of phonological features to enable users to locate these for their own analysis, rather than to provide detailed sociolinguistic interpretations. Consonantal and vowel realizations are recorded comprehensively. We selectively identify significant connected speech processes (e.g. intrusive /r/) and prosodic features (e.g. uptalk) where relevant. Where individuals within a group come from markedly different linguistic backgrounds, or use pronunciations that are deemed ‘performance’, we provide additional comments.

Vowel realizations are arranged according to lexical set (Wells 1982). An auditory assessment is made of common realizations for each set, and broad transcriptions are provided. Stress marks are not used unless necessary to avoid ambiguity or to indicate a pronunciation that contrasts with conventional stress patterns. Sample utterances are provided, cited in context and time-stamped within the relevant recording. Systemic and distributional variation is also noted, with examples cited and transcribed accordingly. The following extract illustrates the presentation of vocalic data:

> STRUT [ə]
> (0:04:52 *everyone lives in a different part of the country* [kəntɹi]; 0:8:00 *for a film or something* [səmθɪŋ]; 0:09:56 *OK we're going to start with ‘drunk’* [dɾəŋk])
>
> FOOT [ʊ]
> (0:05:33 *putting* [pʊʔɪn] *the Welsh accent with the English word*; 0:05:56 *uh they don't think I speak um very good* [gʊd] *Welsh because I do it*; 0:19:59 *you end up looking* [lʊkɪn] *stupid*)
>
> GOAT [oː ~ ou]
> (0:05:56 *uh they don't* [doːn] *think I speak um very good Welsh because I do it*; 0:06:51 *it's just we have so* [soː] *many, like, English influences around us*; 0:12:33 *we do know* [nou] *the Welsh … correct Welsh word for the words just we use them because it sounds more cool*; 0:15:55 *‘to throw’* [θɾou] *uh ‘llechio’*; 0:35:43 *I hope* [oːp] *so*)
>
> BBC Wales interview in Bethesda (BL shelfmark C1190/41/02)

The examples above show that the group interviewed in Bethesda distinguish consistently between words in the STRUT and FOOT sets, using [ə] and [ʊ] respectively. For GOAT they vary between [oː] and [ou]. We do not assess quantitatively whether the two variants result from inter-speaker variation or reflect systemic variation for the group as a whole, but as both occur relatively frequently during the recording we include several examples by way of illustration. Given the location, we suspect that some, or possibly all, of the speakers show evidence of the GOAT–SNOW split reported for some varieties of Welsh English (Penhallurick 2008: 112–13), this entry alerting researchers to the suitability of the recording for further investigation.

Although we seek to provide a comprehensive description of consonant production for each recording, it is considered superfluous to record predictable realizations that reflect most, possibly all, varieties of English (e.g. /m/ with [m]). Pronunciations considered marked in some way are presented by phoneme, using conventional labels where available (e.g. 'L-vocalization'). An example of each variant is cited in context (multiple examples for very high frequency phenomena), with time reference and phonetic transcription. We also document salient connected speech processes and prosodic features such as 'Yorkshire assimilation' (Wells 1982: 366–7) and 'uptalk' (Liberman 2006). In cases where we have been unable to establish a consensus on taxonomy we either make use of precedent, such as 'linking V' (Wales 2006: 170) to describe the process in the north-east of England and elsewhere whereby, for instance, *to* preceding a vowel might surface as /tɪv/, or we devise a transparent term, such as 'ablaut negative', to describe West Midlands negation forms such as doPASTNEG as /dɛɪ/.

We arrange consonantal data using conventional terminology for groups of consonants (e.g. 'fricatives', 'glides') or phonetic processes (e.g. 'elision', 'liaison'). As with the lexical data, some entries are repeated elsewhere in our descriptions. So, for instance, the utterance *she 'with child'* [ʧʌɪɫ], *yeah, she's 'with child'* [ʧʌɪɫ] recorded in Reading (BL shelfmark C1190/06/05) is transcribed elsewhere as *she 'with chile', yeah, she's 'with chile'*, as an entry in Allsopp (1996) suggests 'chile' as a lexicalized form. Likewise the statement recorded in Oldham (BL shelfmark C1190/04/04) *and if the other* [tʊðə] *one was the* [ʔ] *kitchen* is transcribed elsewhere as *and if tother one was t' kitchen*, as *OED* includes 'tother' as a headword and describes 't' as a northern English dialect form of the definite article. These multiple entries ensure that researchers can locate features in a variety of ways. They also enable non-specialist audiences, such as those in schools, to interpret some of the data which might otherwise be beyond their level of expertise.

Grammar

Cheshire and Edwards (1993: 35) note the traditional paucity of data on morphology and syntax. There is undeniable difficulty in obtaining grammatical material naturally and in sufficient quantity to make meaningful comparisons, particularly as many features that are known to vary (e.g. past tense forms of rare verbs) are relatively low-frequency phenomena. It is a matter of chance whether a verb produced in spontaneous speech occurs in a form that is open to variation (e.g. present *I drink* occurs uniformly in most varieties of English, although past forms potentially include *I drank*, *I drunk*, *I drinked*, *I've drank*, *I've drunk* and *I've drinked*). VoUK, however, creates a significant new dataset for researchers in this area.

It would be possible to create a comprehensively tagged corpus from the recordings to support morphosyntactic research, but our desire to give equal focus to lexical, phonological, and grammatical issues has shaped our approach to presenting grammatical data. VoUK descriptions record the presence in a recording of constructions that we consider to deviate from 'mainstream' usage. We share with Hughes *et al.* (2005) an understanding of Standard English as the socially prestigious variety of written and spoken English usually used in the UK for teaching in schools and universities, most widely represented in the British press and broadcast media, and the model used for teaching British English to foreign learners. Our sense of its linguistic characteristics matches the outline contained in *A statement about Standard English* (Committee for Linguistics in Education 2010), such that we feel there is sufficient consensus on the grammar of Standard English in its broadest, most inclusive sense to enable us to use that as a benchmark for our notion of mainstream usage. However, occasionally, judgements have to be made as to whether individual constructions meet our criteria. Some forms clearly deviate significantly from universally accepted notions of Standard English (e.g. negative *ain't*); other forms that are indisputably Standard we include as potentially revealing in terms of significant change and/or variation (e.g. *have* with 'do-support'). We also include forms that exist in most varieties of English, including Standard varieties, but which are the focus of considerable academic and popular debate (e.g. pragmatic *like*). An inventory of features to be included was compiled principally from those listed in Kortmann *et al.* (2004), and this was supplemented by phenomena encountered in other descriptions, notably the SED and previous BL studies by Robinson (2004, 2007). Forms are categorized according to conventional terminology where available, cited in context, and time stamped. The following excerpt illustrates our presentation of grammatical data:

Pronouns
possessive *us* (0:19:06 *so we never used to wear us lamp on us cap*)

Verbs
past
be – frequent *were* generalization (0:01:29 *all he wanted to do were come into the business*; 0:01:37 *he'd been working since he were eight*; 0:08:15 *so it were all ready for sale the next morning*; 0:08:49 *but that's how it were done in them days*; 0:08:54 *it were bitterly cold darling*; 0:08:54 *yeah, but the wholesale market*

were there as well; 0:12:16 *you had to have somebody to take it to your motor to wherever it were parked*; 0:16:23 *he were a farrier*; 0:17:11 *but sometimes when I were on nights*; 0:19:20 *and that were because we had a lad trapped in the shaft*; 0:20:58 *and by this time the manager were down the pit*; 0:26:52 *when your grandad were learning his trade*; 0:31:42 *the toilet were down the yard*; 0:47:03 *she'd a stick like that it were no bigger than that*; 0:53:22 *I used to go regular when I were a child*; 0:57:10 *and as soon as she said it I were off*)

Discourse

utterance-internal *like* (0:12:33 *did you have, like, vans like we do now?*; 0:49:45 *or if you, like, burned half the school down or something you'd get expelled*; 0:59:14 *why didn't he just wake up at, like, seven in the morning?*)

emphatic tag (0:59:47 *I went to the bonfire, me*)

BBC Radio Leeds interview in Castleford (BL shelfmark C1190/19/01)

The entries above give a sense of the range of features included. Again, we do not evaluate the forms used. Rather, we highlight constructions that researchers might especially wish to quantify and analyze for their own purposes. The examples selected here include constructions that previous studies suggest reflect localized or supra-regional variation (e.g. 'possessive *us*' and '*were*-generalization'), or forms which are socially marked but geographically widespread (e.g. utterance-internal *like*). Entries also include phenomena that have only occasionally received attention in previous studies: the construction recorded here as an 'emphatic tag' is one of a number of variants of right dislocation available to speakers of different varieties of English. We do not include forms we consider comparatively mainstream, albeit marked for emphasis (e.g. *he's always late for work, David* and *he's always late for work, David is*), but variants such as the form recorded in Castleford, and equivalent constructions used by speakers of other varieties, are considered sufficiently distinctive to be noted (e.g. *he's always late for work, him*; *he's always late for work, is David*; or *he's always late for work, so he is*).

As some constructions are clearly morpho-phonological, we create entries for these under both grammar and phonology. For speakers of most varieties of English the auxiliary verb forms *is*, *was*, *has*, and *does* produce negative forms *isn't*, *wasn't*, *hasn't*, and *doesn't* respectively, most commonly realized with word final /z/ + /nt/. A spelling <wadn> (Orton and Barry 1971: IX.7.6) reflects a phonetic process that occurs in some varieties, notably in the south and west of England, as captured in the recording in Knowle West (BL shelfmark C1190/07/02) in the phrase *not for me there wadn*. The use of 'wadn' in our grammatical description is intended as comprehensible to audiences unfamiliar with the pronunciation itself or with phonetic transcription. However, by recording the same utterance within the section on phonology as *not for me there wasn't* [wɒdnʔ], we also satisfy linguists for whom this is a more appropriate representation.

Case studies

The following are two case studies of how the VoUK resource allows researchers to examine the *Voices Recordings* data in some detail. First, we explore issues of connotation and usage surrounding a selection of responses to the lexical prompt PREGNANT across a geographically and socially varied sample of recordings. Second, we look at how the resource can serve as a foundation for a fuller quantitative analysis of specific grammatical variables, using speakers from two English locations who exhibit non-standard use of simple past forms of 'to be', *was*- and *were*-generalization.

Lexis

Comments and discussion surrounding the elicitation of lexis provide a wealth of information about the participants' use of, and attitudes towards, a small part of their active and passive vocabulary. By including this reflective information in the VoUK descriptions on the *Sounds* website, either as direct quotations or as summaries, we aim to assist researchers interested in locating lexical data for a variety of purposes. The descriptions also contain biographical data, including age, gender, and occupation of participants, as well as additional information about parents and how long speakers have lived in their current place of residence, thereby allowing social factors to be taken into consideration.

The following observations focus on the supplementary information collected for a selection of responses to one prompt word on the Spidergram. Closer inspection of a subset of responses provided for the concept PREGNANT illustrates how these additional comments from speakers provide insights into the range of connotative meanings and how these connotations relate to attitudes towards pregnancy. This survey also demonstrates how VoUK data can potentially be used to explore further how differences in opinion relate to age, gender, social background, and geographical location.

Many participants simply provided *pregnant* as a variant. It seems like an obvious choice, but closer observation allows a fuller understanding of what it connotes for these speakers:

> I would never say anything other than 'pregnant' because that to me is the proper term for it and I wouldn't want to upset anybody by using anything else.
>
> (BL shelfmark C1190/14/01)

> I would just say 'pregnant' I wouldn't say anything else it would be offensive.
>
> (BL shelfmark C1190/43/17)

> I don't think there's any need to replace 'pregnant' with anything else.
>
> (BL shelfmark C1190/31/02)

This contrasts with the way in which some speakers describe the use of *pregnant* in the past, suggesting that it has become a more socially acceptable word or that younger speakers are more comfortable using it more openly:

> They would never say she was 'pregnant' because it was absolutely the term, you could sort of hide behind [...] euphemisms, [...] 'pregnant' was, you know, sort of like the condition that people never used to admit to.
>
> (BL shelfmark C1190/14/01)

> I don't think I knew what the word 'pregnant' meant till I was quite old.
>
> (BL shelfmark C1190/43/23)

> People didn't speak about being 'pregnant', you know, it was never even mentioned.
>
> (BL shelfmark C1190/43/23)

A number of frequently elicited variants that clearly derive from *pregnant*, such as *preggers*, described as "modern cultural shorthand" (BL shelfmark C1190/14/01) and *preggy*, described as "used now" (BL shelfmark C1190/12/05), are widely held by participants to be recent innovations. In many conversations *preggers* is offered without further comment; occasionally it is even considered a polite or approved form (BL shelfmark C1190/03/04). However, it is a word that often divides opinion, as some speakers indicate negative connotations of *preggers* in the comments they make about the word, describing it for example as a "slang term" (BL shelfmark C1190/11/02), "rude", or showing "no respect for the baby" (BL shelfmark C1190/17/02). It is also revealing that many speakers suggest they only use *preggers* about someone they do not know (BL shelfmark C1190/35/05). Equally revealing are comments such as the recognition that *preggers* and *preggy* are words one group recalls using as teenagers in the past but which they now consciously avoid (BL shelfmark C1190/04/02).

Several of the collected variants are clearly euphemisms, figurative expressions used in order to avoid embarrassment for the speaker or offence to the listener (Allan and Burridge 2006). Examples in this category, with varying connotations, are:

> *carrying* (BL shelfmark C1190/43/19)
> *caught on* (BL shelfmark C1190/28/01)
> *expecting* (BL shelfmark C1190/32/02)
> *in the family way* (BL shelfmark C1190/14/01)

Sometimes these are explicitly acknowledged as euphemisms by the speakers, showing an awareness of social etiquette in linguistic choice. Comments and discussion about such usage suggest that they were used more frequently in the past, for example:

> When I was young it was always 'expecting' and it was said in a whisper it was never said, you know, you didn't say things like that about ladies.
>
> (BL shelfmark C1190/43/13)

> It was 'in the family way' when I was little the word 'pregnant' was never ever used.
>
> (BL shelfmark C1190/14/01)

Contrasting with the tendency towards euphemism are variants such as *up the duff* and *bun in the oven* (see also Upton, this volume). Both expressions occur extremely frequently in the data, but the prevailing attitude towards *up the duff* is overwhelmingly negative, with comments including: "sounds derogatory" (BL shelfmark C1190/14/01), "horrible" (BL shelfmark C1190/31/02), "rude" (BL shelfmark C1190/43/17), "awful" (BL shelfmark C1190/35/05), and "disrespectful" (BL shelfmark C1190/40/03). Also, more discursively:

> I've had two children but I would never have called myself 'up the duff' I think that's a horrible expression.
>
> (BL shelfmark C1190/43/25)

> You wouldn't go up to congratulate someone 'oh well done you're up the duff'.
>
> (BL shelfmark C1190/43/22)

In addition to registering comments about the phrase itself, some informants discuss speakers they associate with using the expression, for example: "I think it's more a man's expression" (BL shelfmark C1190/43/25) and "the school ground one" (BL shelfmark C1190/43/17), acknowledging the importance of social context in lexical choice. One speaker thinks that it implies that the pregnancy was a mistake (BL shelfmark C1190/14/01; compare *she's got some bad news* (BL shelfmark C1190/30/01)), and another comments that it would be used to describe an unwanted pregnancy or is more likely to be applied to a particularly young pregnant woman (BL shelfmark C1190/35/05). One group discusses the fact that male speakers use *up the duff* in the company of male friends but *expecting* when with women (BL shelfmark C1190/43/13). *Up the duff*, and by implication other variants such as *bun in the oven*, clearly connote for many a range of negative ideas in terms of what the phrase communicates both about the pregnancy or person being described and the contexts in which they would use it. However, *bun in the oven*, though attracting such comments as "awful" (BL shelfmark C1190/32/05), "horrible" (BL shelfmark C1190/31/02), and "crude" (BL shelfmark C1190/32/05) from some, is considered by others to be somewhat more positive than *up the duff*. For example, it is described as "polite" (BL shelfmark C1190/43/13), "nicer than 'up the duff'" (BL shelfmark C1190/43/31), "light-hearted", and "not offensive" (BL shelfmark C1190/34/01) by some speakers.

Many of the variants for PREGNANT show linguistic playfulness and creativity. *Stacking the hatch* or *a stack in the hatch* are described as "barging slang" and regarded positively (BL shelfmark C1190/02/04). No other reference to these phrases has been found, so it is difficult to confirm if they are in fact well-known barging terms or simply used by a particular group of Essex bargemen, although the metaphor is transparent. Also suggested is *got a belly full of arms and legs*, categorized as Romani by the speakers who use it (BL shelfmark C1190/17/01). Again, it is difficult to ascertain if this phrase does indeed come from Romani, as no supporting reference has been found. Also elusive is *nipped*, claimed to be used frequently in Annalong, Northern Ireland (BL shelfmark C1190/44/01), but for which no substantiating record has been found. Other examples of the imaginative, that provoked much hilarity during the conversations, are: *baking a sprog* (BL shelfmark C1190/04/03) and *pimple under your pinny* (BL shelfmark C1190/29/02). Less positive but equally innovative variants include *caught bending in Woolworths* (BL shelfmark C1190/29/02). Sometimes these suggestions are overtly labelled as humorous by the speakers themselves, but at other times it is the reaction of the rest of the group that indicates they are not intended to be taken seriously. That they might best be considered as designed to ameliorate the experience of child-bearing is suggested by the fact that such variants are predominantly the province of female participants.

Quite universally provoking strong disapproval, however, are those variants which associate human pregnancy with the animal world. Interestingly, these responses are predominantly found in rural areas, and examples include:

in pig (BL shelfmark C1190/24/01)
in calf (BL shelfmark C1190/12/03)
in lamb (BL shelfmark C1190/29/01)
in kid, labelled as "agricultural" (BL shelfmark C1190/21/03)
in foal, considered to be impolite (BL shelfmark C1190/26/03)
pupped, described as "not particularly pleasant" (BL shelfmark C1190/43/25)
calfit, described as "dreadful" (BL shelfmark C1190/43/17)

Place is seen to be of the essence in the occurrence of particular types of variant, including those regarded almost universally negatively. The correlation of lexical variables with other social variables such as age and gender and, to the extent that it can be deduced, social background, is possible through the *Voices* recorded data, as it is from the material submitted online (see both Upton and Thompson, this volume).

Grammar

Here we take a description of simple past forms of *be* as the basis for a case study of how the data can be used to provoke grammatical exploration. This is an area of grammatical variation (and potential change) in both British and World

Englishes that has received considerable attention in sociolinguistic research over the past two decades (see for example Tagliamonte 1998; Cheshire and Fox 2009; Moore 2011).

There are long-established patterns in the dialects of British English where non-standard inflected forms are used (variably or categorically, depending on the speaker) across all person–number combinations. That is, for some speakers, singular *was* replaces Standard British *were* alongside full noun third person plural (3pl) subjects and plural pronouns *we*, *they*, and *you*:

> ***was* generalization** (0:58:41 *I knew Newcastle before you was even born!*)
> BBC Radio Newcastle interview in Seaham
> (BL shelfmark C1190/23/05)

For other speakers, plural *were* replaces Standard *was* after the singular pronouns *I* and *he/she/it*, and full noun third person singular (3sg) subjects:

> ***were* generalization** (0:14:19 *Hilary were four-eyed I should've been but I darena wear them*)
> BBC Radio Derby interview in Swadlincote
> (BL shelfmark C1190/12/05)

As the descriptions of each sound recording were compiled, *was*-generalization and *were*-generalization (also referred to as '*was/were* levelling' in the literature) were two of the 126 grammatical variables noted by the team. For this case study, we take two recordings from the database: one from the Radio Kent region, indexed as containing instances of *was*-generalization; and one from the Radio Leeds region, having frequent instances of *were*-generalization.

As explained above, the purpose of the VoUK indexing is simply to note the presence or absence of potential linguistic features, along with a selection of clauses containing those features. In order to demonstrate the potential for more detailed and quantitative analysis once the recordings had been picked out by the indexing system, we re-listened to the two recordings mentioned above in their entirety. All instances of simple past forms of *be* were extracted, along with their clausal context. While the focus is to be on non-standard levelled forms, we also extracted the Standard occurrences of *was* and *were*. Below, we present the distribution of the Standard and non-standard forms in each recording and discuss the linguistic and extra-linguistic factors we observe to be associated with them.

Was-*generalization in Boughton Monchelsea, Kent*

The recording taken from the Radio Kent set was of M and R, a married couple who have lived all their lives in Boughton Monchelsea. On the date the recording was made (January 2005) M was 72 and R 70. They did not supply details of their former occupations. Both left school at 13. The occupations of their parents are given as farm worker, quarryman, waggoner, and parlour maid.

The 32-minute recording was made by a 39-year-old female BBC journalist and the interview took place in the main room of the informants' cottage. Of 45 tokens of past tense *be*, only two are spoken by R, and they occur in the same clause:

> 00:20:52 *that was the bog when it was down the garden*
>
> BBC Radio Kent interview in Boughton Monchelsea
> (BL shelfmark C1190/17/02)

Although R uses Standard agreement morphology here, we cannot say for sure that *was*-generalization is or is not in his linguistic repertoire, given the lack of evidence. M's use of the simple past forms of *be* is summarized in Table 9.1.

There are no second person forms in Table 9.1. Other data show clearly that third person singular (3sg) forms are the most common in M's speech (occurring on average about once a minute during the interview). This is not a potential environment in which *was*-generalization occurs. The frequency of occurrence of one person-number form over another can correlate with the type of discourse that occurred naturally in the conversation. The format of the *Voices* recordings has two main types of question: to draw out lexical variation ("What other words would you use for ___?") which tend to elicit responses with present tense or conditional forms ("We usually say ___"; "I think I'd say ___"); and requests for subjects to elaborate on their memories and experiences of how language was used in the past. Hence it is quite natural that 3sg forms are dominant in this and other conversations.

Looking more closely at the potential environments for *was*-generalization, the data for 1pl and 3pl instances are reproduced in Table 9.2 to show the relative incidence of non-standard forms.

The sample size for potential slots for *was*-generalization in M's speech is too small to make a meaningful quantitative analysis, but it is possible to give a more qualitative reading of all of the contexts in which they occur and any patterns observed.

The four instances of Standard *they were* occur in rapid succession in one closely linked set of clauses that together form a coherent discourse unit:

> 00:02:39 *they said they were body builders*
> 00:02:44 *they were like two matches with wood scraped off, they were, honest*
> 00:02:48 *they were, honest*
>
> BBC Radio Kent interview in Boughton Monchelsea
> (BL shelfmark C1190/17/02)

Since the Standard *were* forms occur at the beginning of the interview, this intra-speaker variation can be accounted for in terms of the observer's paradox

TABLE 9.1 Number and relative distribution of all simple past forms of 'be' in M's speech, interview C1190/17/02, Radio Kent, Boughton Monchelsea

	No. of all tokens	*% of all tokens*
1sg was	7	16.2
2sg.pl	0	0
3sg was	27	62.8
1pl was	2	4.7
1pl were	1	2.3
3pl was	2	4.7
3pl were	4	9.3
Total	43	100

TABLE 9.2 Proportion of non-standard simple past forms of 'be' as a percentage of all instances for speaker M, interview C1190/17/02, Radio Kent, Boughton Monchelsea

	No. of all tokens	*% use of 'was' in standard 'were' context*
1pl was	2	66.6
1pl were	1	
3pl was	2	33.3
3pl were	4	

and speech accommodation. M is speaking to a BBC journalist with a digital recorder and large microphone in front of her, so it is reasonable to assume that in her earliest utterances she is least relaxed and most likely to accommodate towards her interviewer by using a Standard form (Tagliamonte 1998: 183). The three later instances (between 00:02:44 and 00:02:48) also form a set. A main verb phrase, "they were like two matches", is followed by two dependent tag forms, "they were, honest", and these obey Standard agreement rules, matching the form of the original *they were*.

The two non-standard instances of *they was* occur separately, one a little way into the interview and one shortly before the end:

> 00:04:35 *you know they was born in the cottages up the hill*
> 00:29:04 *and they was drinking brown ale and whisky*
>
> BBC Radio Kent interview in Boughton Monchelsea
> (BL shelfmark C1190/17/02)

These non-standard forms occur when, it can be argued, the effect of being observed has decreased. Both instances also occur in exchanges that are apparently topic-influenced. The later example is part of a narrative about a time when R, the husband, became sick through excessive drinking, an episode that M is still apparently embarrassed about. The wider discourse context for the earlier "they was born in the cottages up the hill" is that M was discussing other villagers who have made an effort to lose their local speech forms and accent:

> 00:04:27 *but having said that some of them they try and be different they go,* [adopts affected RP accent] *"oh hello darling! how are you today?" you know and you know what … you know they was born in the cottages up the hill sort of thing and they're no different to you their dad worked on the farm same as yours did why be ashamed of that?*
>
> BBC Radio Kent interview in Boughton Monchelsea
> (BL shelfmark C1190/17/02)

Here, M is deliberately foregrounding issues of social status; her change in accent when she quotes the (as she perceives them) affected villagers is swiftly followed by her reverting to her own accent; this coincides with the use of a *was*-generalized form, an unconscious reaction but an identity-laden one nonetheless.

The three instances (Standard and non-standard) of 1pl noun phrases with past *be* are:

> 00:03:50 *if somebody said to me … um like some if if we was at … I've had the office lady here this morning*
> 00:04:00 *like we were saying she said to me this morning*
> 00:20:56 *it was a bog bucket when we was down the garden*
>
> BBC Radio Kent interview in Boughton Monchelsea
> (BL shelfmark C1190/17/02)

Again, there are insufficient data to make generalized inferences about M's patterns of language use here. The anomalous usage comes in the middle utterance, where M uses a Standard *were* (00:04:00) only a few seconds after a *was*-generalized form (00:03:50). Repeated listening to the data suggests that an initial transcription *like we were saying* might have been misleading. There is nothing in the phonetic stream [lʌɪk wi wəsæɪɪn] that privileges *we were saying* over *we was saying*, if *was* is realized in its typical unstressed variant [wəz] and the word-final [z] assimilates to the subsequent word-initial [s] of *saying*. Hence, it could also be said that M does categorically use *was* in 1pl contexts in this recorded conversation.

Were-*generalization in South Milton, Yorkshire*

The second recording selected for its past *be* content is of D, A, and S, three generations of the same family who live in South Milton, near Castleford,

West Yorkshire. D, 70 at the time of recording in November 2004, is the father of A, 44, and grandfather of S, 11. D is a retired greengrocer and A, who began his career working for his father, is now the director of his own food distribution company. S attends a fee-paying school in Leeds. D's wife (a retired school teacher) is also present in the room.

The 62-minute recording was made by a 42-year-old female radio journalist. She shares the same surname as the speakers and may have been a member of the family, although there is no record of this in the demographic data for the recording that was deposited by the BBC. The conversation took place in the main room of D's home and was primarily between A and D, with some interjections from S. D's wife (thus A's mother and S's grandmother), for whom we have no biographical information, answers a handful of questions directed to her about specific lexical items.

There are 190 tokens of past tense *be* in this recording. Two of these are spoken by D's wife:

> 00:32:38 *a midden wasn't a water… toilet*
> 00:32:51 *yes they were middens.*
>
> BBC Radio Leeds interview in South Milford
> (BL shelfmark C1190/19/01)

These are disregarded in the presentation and discussion that follows. Table 9.3 summarizes the distribution of simple past forms of *be* for the three remaining speakers.

For all three speakers, 3sg forms are the most common, repeating the pattern observed for M (see above). This reflects the genre and discourse type of interview, two younger generations asking the eldest for anecdotes from the past. There is a higher number of 2sg forms in this recording, reflecting the fact that A asks his father a lot of questions (e.g. 00:35:20 *what would you do if you weren't going to school?*; 00:53:41 *you were confirmed at twelve?*; 00:54:24 *you were rich?*; 00:55:38 *was this a corner shop that you went to then?*).

Both male speakers, but not S, show evidence of *were*-generalization. Indeed, the most striking pattern of the data is the shift between generations in the proportional use of non-standard *were*. This progression is summarized in Table 9.4.

Less than a tenth of D's 1sg forms and less than a fifth of his 3sg forms include Standard *was*, so clearly *were* is his default inflected form for simple past *be*. There are no obvious correlations between the occurrence of Standard *was*/ non-standard *were* and the other grammatical properties of the sentence they are part of, such as the type of subject, or the polarity of the sentence. He uses *was* when the subject is a full noun or pronoun (00:16:2 *your great-grandad was a farrier*; 00:18:49 *yeah but I mean it wasn't often that uh …*; 00:53:40 *I was twelve*). He uses *were* in both declaratives and negatives (00:17:11 *but sometimes when I were on nights*; 00:39:42 *well I weren't clever enough to be educated*).

TABLE 9.3 Number and relative distribution of all simple past forms of 'be' (N=188) by each speaker in interview C1190/19/01 Radio Leeds, South Milford

	D		*A*		*S*	
	No. of all tokens	*% of D's tokens*	*No. of all tokens*	*% of A's tokens*	*No. of all tokens*	*% of S's tokens*
1sg was	1	1.0	2	3.2	5	19.2
1sg were	9	8.9	1	1.6		
2sg/pl were	0	0	13	21.0	2	7.7
3sg was	12	11.9	32	51.6	17	65.4
3sg were	62	61.3	1	1.6		
1pl were	2	2.0			2	7.7
3pl was	1	1.0				
3pl were	14	13.9	13	21.0	0	0
Total 189	101	(100)	62	(100)	26	(100)

TABLE 9.4 Proportion of non-standard simple past forms of 'be' as a percentage of all instances per speaker in interview C1190/19/01 Radio Leeds, South Milford

	D	*A*	*S*	*D*
	% use of 'were' in standard 'was' context			*% use of 'was' in standard 'were' context*
1sg were	90.0	33.3	0.0	0.0
3sg were	83.8	3.0	0.0	0.0
3pl was				6.7

A predominantly uses Standard *was* in both 1sg and 3sg environments. As observed with M in Kent (see above), his non-standard forms occur in moments of heightened emotion or at confrontational points in the conversation. There are just two instances of *were*-generalization in A's speech, at both of which he is explicitly challenging D about how well he remembers some events he is recounting:

> 00:45:01 *I were gonna say I didn't know how you rode ten bikes at once*
> 00:54:59 *or would you stay out after it were dark?*
>
> BBC Radio Leeds interview in South Milford
> (BL shelfmark C1190/19/01)

These instances occur later in the interview, when A is more likely to have let down his linguistic guard. Here he shows himself diglossic, using the Standard variety (as he would do in formal business situations or in the context of being recorded for broadcast by the BBC) but also code-switching in moments of debate or more impassioned speech.

S evidences exclusively Standard forms. There are only 26 simple past *be* instances on which to base judgements, but it appears that, with her, a social and linguistic transition set in motion by A has now been completed for this family. We can make further observations based on demographic data. D left school at 14 and worked in food wholesaling; he married a school teacher. Their son A followed D into the family business but set up his own company. S attends a fee-paying school in Leeds, some miles from the family home. This undoubtedly influences her linguistic and social milieu and helps to explain her use of exclusively Standard forms of past tense *be*.

The right hand column in Table 9.4 reveals a further aspect of D's non-standard usage. In just one 3pl context out of 14 (hence 13 per cent of the time in this dialogue) he uses *was*:

> 00:05:54 *so that they was immediately tipped on the stall to sell*
>
> BBC Radio Leeds interview in South Milford
> (BL shelfmark C1190/19/01)

This cannot be attributed to the Northern Subject Rule ([NSR] Ihalainen 1994). The NSR predicts that singular verb agreement morphology (*-s*, but in this case *was*) can be observed with adjacent plural subjects, but only when they are full nouns. If the subject is the pronoun *they*, the NSR only applies when the pronoun is not adjacent to the verb; but it is adjacent in D's usage here. For this speaker, then, we conclude that his non-standard variety allows both *was*- and *were*-generalization.

Among the high number of instances of *were* spoken by D (including some with plural subjects) but not those spoken by A, there is an additional variation in vowel quality, with articulation further back in the vowel space as [wɒ] rather than [wə(:)]. This had initially been noted in the VoUK project linguistic commentary for South Milford as an extra category, "frequent *wo*", and four examples were given in the documentation. We re-listened to all 87 of D's *were* examples and noted which were pronounced [wɒ] and which [wə(:)]. Twenty-three had the marked [wɒ] and the patterns of occurrence are summarized and further subcategorized in Table 9.5.

These forms appear to be highly indexical of urban language of the former West Riding of Yorkshire (cf. Petyt 1985:193ff.) and yet they are not attested in the SED, for example in the section eliciting past tense forms of *be*: "We drank water because we/I/she/they … thirsty" (Orton and Halliday 1963: VIII.9.5). Here *were* is frequently offered as the inflected 1sg or 3sg form across the Yorkshire sites, yet none were recorded phonetically as [wɒ] by the fieldworkers. This absence

TABLE 9.5 Number and relative distribution of all forms of 'wo' spoken by D in interview C1190/19/01 Radio Leeds, South Milford

	No. of tokens	*Example*
1sg	1	00:18:53 *I were* [wɒ] *down the pit one day*
1sg negative	2	00:39:40 *well I weren't clever enough*
3sg	16	00:25:01 *because it were* [wɒ] *so cold he caught pneumonia*
3sg + V	2	00:25:33 *it were* [wɒɹ] *a pit*
3pl	2	00:40:09 *and your hands were* [wɒ] *still swollen at twelve o'clock*
Total	23	

is noted by Petyt (1985:194): "perhaps SED failed to record [wɒ(ɹ)] because of the deficiencies of its methods". He also proposes that since Wright (1892:161) had found [wɒ(ɹ)] for the stressed variant of past *be* to be used extensively, sixty years before SED, perhaps the more marked [wɒ] form was being subsumed under [wə(:)], regardless of sentential stress/discourse prominence for all but the most working-class speakers. D's relatively high-frequency use of [wɒ] seems to recall much earlier dialectal forms. As Table 9.5 shows, D's [wɒ] is not solely restricted to sentence-final or pre-pausal environments where a stressed form would be expected.

The greater relative length of the South Milton recording means that more tokens of non-Standard past *be* forms can be extracted for further analysis here than from the Kent recording. However it was still most fruitful to use a more qualitative approach, drawing on the speakers' social and linguistic backgrounds, as revealed in the conversation itself and the biographical information collected by the journalist, to look more deeply into the patterns and use of data and what they say about the speakers.

Conclusion

Participation in the *Voices* enterprise has enhanced the BL's position as a key repository for research output and provider of resources in the field of British dialectology. The fact that the lifecycle of a single collection can be so obviously and immediately linked to the Library's core mission demonstrates the research value of the *Voices* recordings and the benefit to the Library of collaborative collection development and research partnerships. The BL has been actively engaged with students at Queen Mary University and the University of Leeds in creating phonological and grammatical descriptions of the remaining 153 recordings, and we are keen to explore the possibility of opening up this opportunity to other institutions and extending description to other collections. The two case studies here illustrate the enormous potential of this rich audio content, once described, for quantitative and qualitative research.

We have had regular confirmation of the broad appeal of the content to diverse audiences as data have already been sought by users from a wide range of disciplines. Linguists at Aston University have collaborated on issues relating to the transcription of regional speech for a lay audience; lexical data have been used to support research for a popular publication on the language used to express love, sex, and relationships; a GIS researcher (Holliday, this volume) has manipulated the data to test cluster analysis techniques; a TEFL teacher in France has requested evidence to support research on grammatical change in spoken English; and we have responded to several enquiries from academics and undergraduate and postgraduate students interested in a variety of sociolinguistic phenomena . All this interest has arisen prior to widespread knowledge of, or online access to, the content.

In April 2012 the 283 recordings in English were uploaded to the *Sounds* website, opening up the data to a worldwide audience. Corresponding VoUK descriptions will be released as .pdf files in batches, with a full set available from summer 2013. The *Sounds* website has simultaneously been redesigned and relaunched with considerably enhanced functionality. Recordings on the site can be browsed by location and by date, and summaries of individual recordings are fully searchable, so that users have numerous ways of locating appropriate content. In addition, users can now create and save their own play-list, tag recordings, and embed notes in individual audio files, allowing them to create their own bespoke linguistic corpora for research and/or teaching purposes. A discovery and access functionality to enable users to browse recordings by linguistic criteria will be implemented by summer 2013. This additional linguistic browse functionality will allow researchers to locate and cluster recordings according to a pre-determined set of criteria, for example grammatical features such as *was*-generalization (*we was late*) or phonological phenomena such as TH-fronting (*I fink so*). We are intrigued to see how users will engage with the material as it becomes more easily accessible, and how it will complement and connect with existing and future linguistic datasets.

References

Allan, K. and Burridge, K. (2006) *Forbidden Words: Taboo and the Censoring of Language*, Cambridge: Cambridge University Press.

Allsopp, R. (ed.) (1996) *Dictionary of Caribbean English Usage*, Oxford: Oxford University Press.

Baker, P. (2002) *Fantabulosa: A Dictionary of Polari and Gay Slang*, London: Continuum.

BBC (2005) *Voices*, London: BBC. Online. Available HTTP: <http://www.bbc.co.uk/voices/> (accessed 12 December 2011).

Beal, J.C. (2006) *Language and Region*, Abingdon: Routledge.

Borrows, W. (2004) 'Why Northern Accents are Worth Saving', *Daily Mirror*, 2 February.

British Library (2010) *2020 Vision*, London: British Library. Online. Available HTTP: <http://www.bl.uk/2020vision/> (accessed 16 April 2012).

Cheshire, J. and Edwards, V. (1993) 'Sociolinguistics in the classroom: exploring linguistic diversity', in J. Milroy and L. Milroy (eds) *Real English: The Grammar of English Dialects in the British Isles*, Harlow: Longman.

Cheshire, J. and Fox, S. (2009) '*Was/were* variation: a perspective from London', *Language Variation and Change*, 21:1–38.

Committee for Linguistics in Education (2010) *A Statement about Standard English*, London: Committee for Linguistics in Education. Online. Available HTTP: <http://www.phon.ucl.ac.uk/home/dick/ec/CLIE/pubs/standard-english.doc> (accessed 6 April 2012).

Dalzell, T. and Victor, T. (eds) (2006) *The New Partridge Dictionary of Slang and Unconventional English*, London: Routledge.

Dictionary of the Scots Language (n.d.) Online. Available HTTP: http://www.dsl.ac.uk/ (accessed 12 December 2011).

Foulkes, P. and Docherty, G. (1999) *Urban Voices: Accent Studies in the British Isles,* London: Arnold.

Green, J. (2010) *Green's Dictionary of Slang*, London: Chambers.

Griffiths, W. (2011) *A Dictionary of North-East Dialect*, Newcastle: Northumbria University Press.

Hughes, A., Trudgill, P. and Watts, D.J. (2005) *English Accents and Dialects: An Introduction to Social and Regional Varieties of English in the British Isles*, 4th edn, London: Hodder Arnold.

Ihalainen, O. (1994) 'The Dialects of England since 1776', in R. Burchfield (ed.) *Cambridge History of the English Language,* vol. 5, Cambridge: Cambridge University Press.

Kortmann, B., Schneider, E.W., Burridge, K., Mesthrie, R. and Upton, C. (eds) (2004) *A Handbook of Varieties of English,* 2 volumes plus CD-ROM, Berlin: Mouton de Gruyter.

Liberman, M. (2006) 'Uptalk is not HRT', Language Log. Online. Available HTTP: <http://itre.cis.upenn.edu/~myl/languagelog/archives/002967.html> (accessed 12 December 2011).

Moore, E. (2011) 'Interaction between social category and social practice: explaining *was/were* variation', *Language Variation and Change*, 22: 347–71.

Orton, H. and Barry, M.V. (eds) (1971) *Survey of English Dialects: (B) The Basic Material*, Vol. 2, Part 3, Leeds: E.J. Arnold.

Orton, H. and Halliday, W.J. (eds) (1963) *Survey of English Dialects: (B) The Basic Material*, Vol. 1, Part 3, Leeds: E.J. Arnold.

Orton, H., Halliday, W., Barry, M., Tilling, P. and Wakelin, M. (eds) (1962–1971) *Survey of English Dialects (B): The Basic Material*, 4 volumes, Leeds: E.J. Arnold.

Oxford English Dictionary (n.d.) Oxford: Oxford University Press. Online. Available HTTP: <http://www.oed.com/> (accessed 12 December 2011).

Parry, D. ed (1977–1979) *Survey of Anglo-Welsh Dialects*, 2 Volumes, Swansea: privately published.

Parry, D. ed. (1999) *A Grammar and Glossary of the Conservative Anglo-Welsh Dialects of Rural Wales*, Sheffield: National Centre for English Cultural Tradition.

Penhallurick, R. (2008) 'Welsh English Phonology', in B. Kortmann and C. Upton (eds) *Varieties of English: The British Isles*, Berlin: Mouton de Gruyter.

Petyt, K.M. (1985) *Dialect and Accent in Industrial West Yorkshire*, Amsterdam: John Benjamins.

Robinson, J.P. (2004; re-published 2007) *Sounds: Accents and dialects*, London: British Library. Online. Available HTTP: <http://sounds.bl.uk/accents-and-dialects/> (accessed 16 April 2012).

Robinson, J.P. (2007) *Sounds Familiar? Accents and Dialects of the UK*, London: British Library. Online. Available HTTP: <http://www.bl.uk/learning/langlit/sounds/index.html> (accessed 12 December 2011).

Rockwood, C. (ed) (2009) *Brewer's Dictionary of Phrase and Fable*, 18th edition, Edinburgh: Chambers Harrap.

Roud, S. (2010) *The Lore of the Playground: One Hundred Years of Children's Games, Rhymes and Traditions*, London: Random House.

Tagliamonte, S. (1998) '*Was/were* variation across the generations: view from the city of York', *Language Variation and Change*, 10: 153–91.

Urban Dictionary (n.d.) Online. Available HTTP: <http://www.urbandictionary.com/> (accessed 12 December 2011).

Wales, K. (2006) *Northern English: A Social and Cultural History*, Cambridge: Cambridge University Press.

Wells, J.C. (1982) *Accents of English*, Cambridge: Cambridge University Press.

Wright, J. (1892) *A Grammar of the Dialect of Windhill in the West Riding of Yorkshire*, London: English Dialect Society.

Wright, J. (ed.) (1898–1905) *The English Dialect Dictionary,* 6 volumes, Oxford: Henry Frowde.

10

FOCUS ON *VOICES* IN NORTHEAST ENGLAND

Ann Thompson

Introduction

From the mid-1990s, the Northeast of England was top of the government's priority list for the creation of a devolved regional assembly, having a reputation as the most clearly defined and self-aware of the English regions (Milne 2006). The rejection of that assembly in the 2004 referendum suggested a complexity in the structure and composition of the Northeast that went beyond the erstwhile popular assumption that it was a homogeneous region centred on Newcastle upon Tyne (Beal 1999). The boundaries within the Northeast proved to be more controversial than the boundary around the region (Milne 2006: 7). The three areas under review in this chapter centre on the three main rivers in the region: the Tyne, the Wear, and the Tees. They are defined by using area postcodes: NE (Northumberland, North and South Tyneside, and Gateshead centred on Newcastle upon Tyne), SR (Sunderland), and TS (Middlesbrough) (see Figure 10.1).

Although by the mid-nineteenth century there was a feeling that these three river areas should form an integrated industrial whole (Milne 2006: 72), there had been rivalries between them as far back as the seventeenth century, and by the 1930s the 'three-way split was a well-established formula' (Milne 2006: 73). There are a number of historical, social, and economic reasons for this dislocation of the three centres. For example,

- Coal mining was the main industry on Tyneside and Wearside, whereas Teesside focused on iron and steel.
- Tyneside had most inhabitants and shipped most coal.
- Until the national boundary changes of 1974, Teesside had formed the northern boundary of Yorkshire, leading to the perception that 'whilst Teesside might be *in* the North, it was certainly not *of* the North' (Milne 2006: 205).

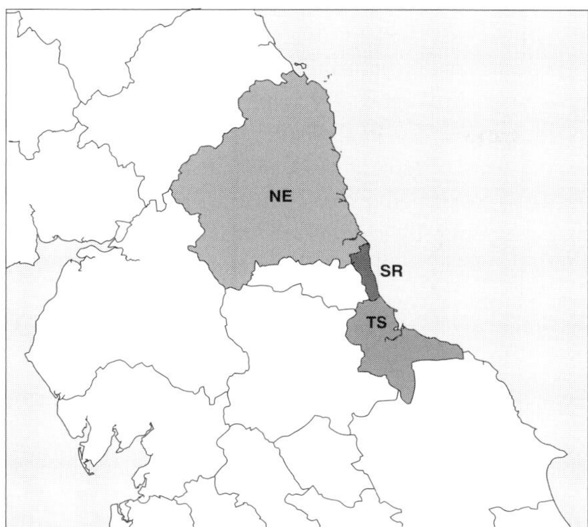

FIGURE 10.1 Outline map of postcode areas NE, SR, and TS

In 1974, formation of the controversial new metropolitan county of Tyne and Wear brought Newcastle upon Tyne and Sunderland into the same region. The Northeast was perceived by some to be an 'appropriation by Tynesiders' and essentially as 'Tyneside writ large' (Green and Pollard 2007: 222). The merger left the 'Mackems' (a 'term used to refer to people from Sunderland and which derives from the traditional Durham/Sunderland pronunciation of the words *make* and *take*, which is [mak] and [tak] respectively' (Beal *et al.* 2012: 13)) opposed to the cultural and economic dominance of Newcastle.

Present local rivalries often centre on the appellation 'Geordie' (see Beal (1999) for an in-depth discussion of this term), used by some to describe the population of the entire Northeast. Instead of representing a positive and affirming label for a homogeneous region, the term is regarded by some in Sunderland and Middlesbrough as 'Newcastle imperialism', an indication that they are 'subservient to Newcastle' (Milne 2006: 8). The cultural and economic dominance of Newcastle is clearly resented by those who perceive themselves as having distinct local identities within the wider Northeast region (Beal *et al.* 2012: 14). Today, rivalry is most overtly expressed in terms of football rivalry, but resistance to a subsumed identity is still fierce, particularly in Sunderland (Beal 1999).

Resentment, and the associated perceived importance of a separate identity for non-Tynesiders, is manifested in the retention of local lexical choices. Within the region, local, areal differences in the lexis of the three main centres highlight the divisions between them, although there is shared regional lexis too: according to Beal *et al.* (2012: 70), 'traditional regional vocabulary has been, and continues to be, a very distinctive feature of dialects in the Northeast', this including 'items which are not used anywhere else in the country and items which reflect the history of the region'. There are numerous instances of lexis that illustrate this observation including, for example, *hoy*, *netty*, and *beck*. These lexical differences and similarities are explored in this chapter. A number of studies, among them those by Beal (1999), Burbano-Elizondo (2006), Pearce (2009), Llamas and Watt (2010), and Beal *et al.* (2012), have already explored from a sociolinguistic perspective the nature of the relationships between the smaller areas that are generally seen as comprising the 'Northeast'. The aim of this chapter is to investigate whether the *Voices* lexical evidence advanced here supports the conclusions of this previous scholarship.

A Northeast dataset

When the BBC *Voices* project was launched, respondents were invited to record electronically their alternative lexical items for a total of 38 concepts offered in Standard English (Elmes, Crystal, this volume). By 2007, when the website ceased to be live to new offerings, over 730,000 submissions had been received. Respondents registered by entering details of their gender, age, place of birth, and the postcode of their current residence. They then submitted their responses for the Standard English concepts. Responses were allocated to individuals using the encoded registration details. Data can thus easily be decoded to give a full profile of each respondent and submission. The use of area postcodes enables patterns of data to emerge without the constraints of county boundaries.

The total responses submitted by respondents living in postcode areas NE, SR, and TS for all 38 *Voices* concepts have been extracted from the full database to form a discrete dataset in a series of Excel worksheets, one worksheet for each concept (see the website accompanying this book for the complete Northeast dataset). Data were initially tabled as simple counts of the numbers of respondents in each postcode area. Subsequently, these counts have been tabled as percentages so that, given the imbalance in numbers of submissions and respondents as well as the varying size of each postcode area, legitimate comparisons can be made. (Postcode area NE consistently returned greater numbers of submissions than did SR or TS.) Other imbalances must be acknowledged in the dataset in terms of those submitting data to it. The electronic dataset derives only from respondents to the on-line survey, as distinct from those completing paper-based returns: this results in there being a bias towards younger and wealthier people who have computer access. There is also a consistently higher response rate from females. However, detailed profiles of the respondents can be seen in the database, permitting evaluation of the effect on findings of any such biases.

Extracted data have been collated and lemmatized, and the three most popular lexical items noted for each concept in each of the three postcode areas. This has resulted in a total of 342 lemmatized lexical items forming the basis for this study, although some particularly interesting examples of lexical usage outside this set have also been retained, to be foregrounded at relevant points. Concepts are classified into four groups, A to D (see next section). Lexical items in each group are investigated to highlight the fluctuating 'alliances' between postcode areas, indicating which lexical items are recorded in all three areas, in two of the three or in a single postcode area. In this way, it is possible to assess the level of lexical homogeneity across the region, note any indications of levelling, and identify the lexis that is only found in a particular postcode area.

Williams and Kerswill (1999: 149) describe levelling (often the result of industrialization, the growth of urban centres, and social mobility) as reducing differences between regional varieties: 'features which make varieties distinctive disappear, and new features emerge and are adopted by speakers over a wide geographical area'. In the Northeast, Watt (2002) holds that this levelling, or supra-local, process emanates from Newcastle upon Tyne. Pearce (2009: 187), however, suggests that 'Sunderland and Middlesbrough also have a role to play'. Study of the *Voices* data addresses these hypotheses and seeks to clarify the situation regarding the competing influences of the urban centres in the region.

Investigation of the data

Group A

In this group (Table 10.1), *Voices* responses are identical across all three postcode areas. The three most popular variants offered for the variable ANNOYED illustrate the general pattern of the group: *pissed (off)* is in fact the principal UK non-standard response for ANNOYED as identified in the overall *Voices* database. In the Northeast it shows significantly higher percentage submissions than the second most popular response, *narked*. Another variant, *fuming*, is not included in the overall UK top ten responses for this concept, but is here reported across all three postcode areas in third most popular position, and can be considered as a regional variant. It is noticeably more popular in SR than in NE or TS.

TABLE 10.1 Concepts in Group A

Group	*Concept*	*NE*	*SR*	*TS*
A	ANNOYED	Pissed, narked, fuming	Pissed, narked, fuming	Pissed, narked, fuming
A	PREGNANT	Up the duff, preggers, bun in the oven	Up the duff, preggers, bun in the oven	Up the duff, preggers, bun in the oven
A	LEFT-HANDED	Cack-handed, leftie, left-handed	Cack-handed, leftie, left-handed	Cack-handed, leftie, left-handed
A	LACKING MONEY	Skint, broke, poor	Skint, broke, poor	Skint, broke, poor

TABLE 10.2 Concepts in Group B

Group	*Concept*	*NE*	*SR*	*TS*
B	TIRED	Knackered, shattered, exhausted	Knackered, shattered, brayed out	Knackered, shattered, worn out
B	RICH	Loaded, minted, rolling in it	Loaded, minted	Loaded, minted, well off
B	UNATTRACTIVE	Minging, ugly, dog	Minging, ugly, rank	Minging, ugly, dog
B	MALE PARTNER	Boyfriend, lad, bloke	Boyfriend, lad, bloke	Boyfriend, lad, husband
B	FEMALE PARTNER	Lass, girlfriend, wife	Lass, girlfriend, bird	Lass, girlfriend, wife

Group B

The five concepts of Group B (Table 10.2) share two of their most popular responses. For example, the two most popular choices for TIRED across all three postcode areas are *knackered* and *shattered*. These two lexical items are responsible for around 50 per cent and 12 per cent respectively of the responses in each postcode area, whereas the third most popular responses, *exhausted* (NE), *brayed out* (SR), and *worn out* (TS), demonstrate some variation but ultimately only account for a small percentage of the submissions from each postcode area.

Of these third most popular responses, *brayed out* from SR is a notable local variant. In the Tyneside Linguistic Survey (TLS), *bray* is recorded as being widely used in NE (Beal *et al.* 2012: 84). It is therefore interesting that it should be recorded in SR rather than NE, which returned the more standard term *exhausted* instead. The *English Dialect Dictionary* ([*EDD*] Wright 1898–1905) shows *bray* as originating in the 'North Country' with the meaning 'to beat; to bruise or grind to powder'. *Paggered*, for TIRED, was submitted from SR by a respondent who was born in NE. There are three further instances of *paggered* in the data which were submitted by respondents all born and resident in NE. This suggests that *paggered* and *bray* could both be NE lexical items that have diffused to SR, or that they have long been widespread in the region.

Lass is a regional variant for FEMALE PARTNER, significant here as it is the most popular choice across all three postcode areas. Its support puts it some way clear of the second most popular lexical item, *girlfriend*. Here, *lad* and *lass* were elicited as a variant for MALE/FEMALE PARTNER and, in this context, the responses for *lass* support the findings of Beal *et al.* (2012: 91) that, in Newcastle upon Tyne and Sunderland, 'LASS is used more than LAD in the sense "sexual partner"'. For *lad*, however, the evidence is less clear. Beal *et al.* (2012: 86) find that 'for "partner" it [*lad*] is more common than BOYFRIEND, but less common than HUSBAND'. The *Voices* data in fact show the reverse, as *lad* takes second place in the responses to the standard lexical item *boyfriend* across all three postcode areas. NE and SR respondents submitted *bloke* as the third most popular choice (according to Beal *et al.* it is a lexical item generally used for older males) whereas TS returned *husband*. (See Beal *et al.* (2012: 85–91) for an in-depth discussion of the occurrence of *lad* and *lass* in the Northeast.)

The data underpinning the Group B concepts show a level of complexity beyond that of simple lexical item correlation. The five concepts demonstrate incidences of Standard English lexis, such as *boyfriend* and *husband*, alongside national variation in lexical items such as *knackered*. There is regional variation in lexical items, such as *lad* and *lass*, and still other lexical items (*brayed (out)*, for example) that have a diachronic element to their usage. Although the third most popular responses vary between the postcode areas, they are generally, with the exception of *brayed (out)*, examples of national rather than regional variation.

Group C

The concepts of Group C (Table 10.3) have been divided into three sub-sections, based on the configuration of the submitted responses. They share a common first response and then show subsequent variation in the second and third responses.

Group C-1

Of the 15 concepts that make up Group C, the four of sub-group C-1 show the same three lexical items, but with differing levels of popularity across the three responses and the three postcode areas.

Group C-2

The six concepts in sub-group C-2 have more variation. In each of these concepts, regional or local lexical items are foregrounded by their position as the most popular submissions, or by their appearance in a particular postcode area. For instance, after *bairn*, the most popular response for BABY and a notable regional variant from the Northeast of England (see Beal *et al.* 2012: 84), the foregrounded SR submission here is *babby*, a local variant. *Babby* features significantly in submissions from SR although it is, at 11.9 per cent of offerings, well behind *bairn* at 54.8 per cent. It is well-established across all age groups, and also appears in each of the other two postcode areas, albeit at much lower levels of popularity (6.16 and 5.26 per cent). Even though there is some evidence of its use in TS, none of the respondents offering it was actually born on Teesside.

FRIEND attracted a wide range of submissions. The most popular response from the three Northeastern postcode areas, as across much of the UK, is *mate*, a well-established national variant. The meaning of *mate*, particularly when

TABLE 10.3 Concepts in Group C

Group	*Concept*	*NE*	*SR*	*TS*
C-1	UNWELL	Poorly, ill, sick	Poorly, sick, ill	Poorly, sick, ill
C-1	MOTHER	Mam, mum, ma	Mam, ma, mum	Mam, mum, ma
C-1	GRAND-MOTHER	Nana, grandma, gran/granny	Nana, gran/granny, grandma	Nana, grandma, gran/granny
C-1	LONG SOFT SEAT IN MAIN ROOM	Settee, sofa, couch	Settee, couch, sofa	Settee, sofa, couch
C-2	PLEASED	Chuffed, happy, over the moon	Chuffed, made up, over the moon	Chuffed, happy, made up
C-2	SLEEP	Kip, sleep, snooze	Kip, sleep, snooze	Kip, nap, snooze
C-2	MOODY	Mardy, huff, moody	Mardy, stroppy, miserable	Mardy, stroppy, moody
C-2	BABY	Bairn, baby, kid	Bairn, babby, kid	Bairn, baby, sprog
C-2	FRIEND	Mate, marra, pal	Mate, marra, chum/friend	Mate, friend, pal
C-2	NARROW WALKWAY ALONGSIDE BUILDINGS	Alley, path, cut	Alley, pavement, cut	Alley, snicket, pavement/cut
C-3	HOT	Boiling, roasting, lathered	Boiling, roasting, scadding	Boiling, mafted, roasting
C-3	COLD	Freezing, chilly, nippy	Freezing, chilly, frozen	Freezing, nithered, chilly
C-3	PLAY (A GAME)	Play, join in	Play, av a gan, knock about	Play, laik, have a game
C-3	DRUNK	Pissed, mortal, hammered	Pissed, mortal, wasted	Pissed, bladdered, blaked
C-3	ATTRACTIVE	Fit, lush, bonny	Fit, bonny/gorgeous/sexy, hot/lush/good-looking	Fit, bonny, gorgeous

used by the younger age groups, covers different degrees of friendship which might be classified separately as 'acquaintance', 'colleague', and 'close friend'. *Marra*, however, the second most popular response from NE and SR, and the fifth most popular from TS, is a solid regional choice. *Marra* appears to have more specific parameters than *mate* and the *Oxford English Dictionary* (*OED*) gives 'companion', 'fellow worker', and 'partner' as its principal meanings. These definitions all carry connotations of the solidarity of a (male) working environment, reflecting the intrinsic importance of the coal mining and heavy industry closely associated with the Northeast of England, dominating male working life particularly in NE and SR. Teesside was better known for its iron and steel industry than for coal, and the discrepancy between the popularity of *marra* in NE and SR and in TS may well be the result of these different historical influences. Of the 58 respondents from NE who returned *marra*, 36 are male, and there is just one female respondent each from SR and TS.

Group C-3

Five further concepts have even less uniformity. The significance of this subsection is that, although the most popular submissions are still identical and, indeed, for some are more standard-dialectal than are those in Group C-2, there is much more local variation between the postcode area responses in second and third most popular positions. Three concepts in particular highlight this local divergence between the postcode areas. NE and SR, for example, both have *roasting*, *chilly,* and *mortal* as their second most popular variants for HOT, COLD, and DRUNK, while TS returns *mafted*, *nithered,* and *bladdered* instead. Moreover, the three postcode areas each offer individual lexical items *lathered* (NE), *scadding* (SR), and *mafted* (TS) for HOT.

The polarization of the responses for these concepts can be illustrated by data for *mafted* from the three postcode areas. The majority of respondents are from TS, and the database shows that 21 of the 28 respondents who provided the 17.6 per cent *mafted* responses from TS residents were also born on Teesside. The age variable for *mafted* in TS covers an age range from 16–60 years, evidencing a long-established variant for TS that is not present in NE or SR to the same extent. *Nithered*, submitted for COLD, is similarly noted in TS but is not prevalent in NE or SR. It shows distribution characteristics akin to those of *mafted*, with TS returning 75 per cent of this variant's total Northeast submissions, in comparison with 24 per cent and 1 per cent from NE and SR respectively. *OED* classifies *nithered* as '*Eng. Regional* (*north.*)', suggesting a widespread connection that removes it from specific association with the Northeast.

Summary

Overall, the responses from Group C show instances of regional and areal variation that are a development of the more general homogeneity of Groups

A and B. Submissions of lexical items such as *play* and *sleep* reflect standard lexis, *pissed* and *kip* are examples of national variation, while *bonny* and *bairn* are regional choices from all three postcode areas. *Mafted* and *nithered* are local lexical items from TS, as is *babby* from SR. Together, they demonstrate how, although in this group of concepts there is a general correspondence of the most popular responses with national responses for the everyday concepts such as HOT and COLD, there is also a widespread use, across these concepts, of more local lexis at a lower level of popularity. The less circumscribed concepts such as PLAY (A GAME) allow for more variety of response, and this is reflected in the wider range of lexical items submitted for the concepts in this group.

Group D

Almost 40 per cent of concepts fall into Group D (Table 10.4), where there are no instances of complete correlation of responses in terms of first, second, or third most popular across the three postcode areas. The responses for many of the concepts included in this group are, therefore, the most indicative of lexical divergence between the three postcode areas. Again, as in Group C, the concepts have been sub-divided (into four sections for this group) for ease of comparison.

Group D-1

In this sub-section, the submissions have the least variation, in that they comprise identical lexical items from each postcode area, though these occur in a differing order of popularity. Crucially, the lexical correspondences are not constant, so no two postcode areas are consistently alike, and a third is always different. For YOUNG PERSON..., for example, submissions from NE and SR do correspond, while it is notable that *charva* is only the third most popular choice for TS. Significantly, Beal *et al.* (2012: 81) highlight the fact that *OED* differentiates between *charva/charver* and *chav*, categorising *charva/charver* as Northeast regional slang and *chav* as a derogatory slang term originating in the South of England, this seemingly positioning Middlesbrough outside the Newcastle upon Tyne/Sunderland enclave for this lexical item. However, while NE and TS correspond on GRANDFATHER for example, SR responses for this concept are in a different order of popularity.

Group D-2

The eight concepts that comprise this sub-section each show four different lexical items distributed across the three postcode areas as their most popular. These occur in different combinations and with different percentages. Each postcode area, therefore, necessarily has instances of a popular local lexical

TABLE 10.4 Concepts in Group D

Group	*Concept*	*NE*	*SR*	*TS*
D-1	GRAND-FATHER	Granddad, granda, grandpa	Granda, granddad, grandpa	Granddad, granda, grandpa
D-1	YOUNG PERSON IN CHEAP TRENDY CLOTHES AND JEWELLERY	Charva, chav, townie	Charva, chav, townie	Chav, townie, charva
D-1	CHILD'S SOFT SHOES WORN FOR PE	Plimsoles, sand shoes, pumps	Sand shoes, plimsoles, pumps	Plimsoles, pumps, sand shoes
D-2	THROW	Hoy, chuck, lob	Hoy, chuck, toss	Chuck, hoy, lob
D-2	CLOTHES	Clothes, claes, gear	Claes, clothes, gear	Clothes, gear, togs
D-2	TROUSERS	Pants, trousers, kecks	Pants, strides, trousers	Keks, pants, trousers
D-2	MAIN ROOM OF HOUSE	Living room, sitting room, lounge	Sitting room, living room, lounge	Living room, front room, lounge
D-2	TOILET	Loo, bog, netty	Bog, loo, netty	Loo, bog, toilet
D-2	RAIN LIGHTLY	Drizzle, spitting, shower	Spitting, drizzle, spitting on	Spitting, drizzle, shower
D-2	RAIN HEAVILY	Pouring, chucking it down, pissing down	Chucking it down/pouring, pissing down, lashing down	Pouring, pissing down, chucking it down
D-2	RUNNING WATER SMALLER THAN RIVER	Stream, burn, beck	Stream, beck, brook	Beck, stream, brook
D-3	PLAY TRUANT	Skive, wag off, bunk off	Doll off, skive, bunk off	Nick off, skive, bunk off
D-3	HIT HARD	Whack, smack, thump	Smack, crack, belt	Smack, whack, thump
D-4	INSANE	Mental, mad, crazy	Mad, loopy/mental, crackers/crazy	Mad, mental, crazy/loony

item that does not appear in the other two areas. There are clear indications both of regional lexis in the three postcode areas (*hoy*, *chuck,* and *beck*) and of foregrounded localized lexical variation (*strides*, *netty,* and *burn*) in the submissions. *Hoy* is the most popular response to THROW from NE and SR and second most popular from TS. The majority of the 183 NE residents who submitted *hoy* were in fact born in Tyne and Wear. It is recorded in *EDD* in Northumberland, Durham, and Cumberland, meaning 'to throw, heave'. As would be expected with such a clear diachronic link, the age range extends up to 75 years, but *hoy* is also popular with lower age groups too, particularly those in the 16–30-year old range. This suggests a regional adherence to this lexical item that is being maintained in NE and SR through the generations, to the extent that it now also includes TS.

Finally in this sub-section, a consideration of the lexical items submitted for RUNNING WATER SMALLER THAN A RIVER foregrounds *beck* and *brook*. *Beck* is evidenced in *EDD* from Durham, Cumberland, Westmorland, Yorkshire, Lancashire, and into East Anglia, but particularly 'not from Northumberland'. As NE covers all of Northumberland, there is evidence that, if *EDD* is to be relied upon, *beck* has now spread into the area. But it is not as prevalent here as *stream* or *burn*, a lexical item common in Scotland, Ireland, and the Northeast of England according to *EDD*. In the *Voices* data, *beck* appears as the predominant choice in TS, the second most popular in SR, and third most popular in NE. The lexical item *brook* is an interesting inclusion in the top three responses from SR and TS: according to *EDD*, it comes historically from more southerly counties.

Group D-3

The two concepts here incorporate five responses in total. PLAY TRUANT, for example, has the same lexical item, *bunk (off)*, in third most popular position for each postcode area, while the disagreement occurs in the more popular responses given within each area. Where NE returns as its most popular variant the nationally most popular *skive (off)*, SR and TS respondents have submitted the local responses of *doll (off)* and *nick (off)* respectively. The more local response *wag (off)* for NE is in second most popular position, with 23.3 per cent less support than *skive (off)*.

PLAY TRUANT is notable across the *Voices* data UK-wide for demonstrating distinctive local lexical items. It would be reasonable to assume that local lexical items have been retained by older respondents as passive vocabulary. However, the data clearly reveal that younger respondents continue to use the local variants for this concept across the three postcode areas. Where this is not the case, the popular supralocal variant is invariably *skive (off)*. In the Northeast, although the local variants seem well-entrenched in SR and TS, the potential for *skive (off)* to spread as the dominant form from NE and, in time, to overwhelm the local variants, is not to be underestimated.

Group D-4

This sub-section comprises a single concept, INSANE, which offers six different lexical items across the three postcode areas to express its inherent variation. There are a number of responses from each area for INSANE that were submitted by the same percentage of respondents, indicating that there is a wide range of equally acceptable alternative lexical items for this concept (for example *cuckoo, insane, doolally, barmpot*). This concept is therefore unusual among the *Voices* data, which generally demonstrate a clear hierarchy of choices from respondents. Many of the alternative submissions appear to be largely due to the difference in age of the respondents. In particular, *crazy* was largely restricted to the under-16 to 30-year old age group across all three postcode areas. (Twenty-four of the 29 NE respondents who submitted *crazy*, for example, were in this age range.) It would therefore be reasonable to assume that *crazy* is a modern variant that is becoming popular across the region.

Summary

Group D responses show an increase in the range of variants for each concept. The uniformity shown in the responses to concepts in Groups A, B, and C is replaced with more nuanced differences, such as *charva* and *chav*, *granda* and *granddad* or, indeed, with local lexis that speaks to an individual local area identity, such as *doll (off)*, *nick (off)*, *mafted*, and *burn*. These lexical items, dominating the responses to a concept in one of the postcode areas or suggesting a lexical alliance between any two out of the three, can be found alongside strong regional choices such as *netty*, *hoy*, and *bairn* which are common across the Northeast, and age-defined lexical items such as *crazy*.

The findings above are derived from the evidence extracted from the 2007 *Voices* database, and can usefully be compared with the lexis collected in other regional surveys such as the Diachronic Electronic Corpus of Tyneside English (DECTE). One example, *marra* (Group C-2), submitted by predominantly male respondents from NE and SR, is also to be found in interviews conducted for DECTE. Two older subjects there (in their 50s) include *marra* in a group of peculiarly 'Geordie' mining terms, alongside *cuddy* and *pit-yakka*, while subjects in their 30s and 40s described *marra* as a word that their parents and grandparents would use. It is conceivable that these lexical items specifically associated with mining are in decline with the industry itself. *Hoy*, on the other hand, is recorded as being in use by respondents from as far back as the 1960s up to the present day. The main thrust of these regional surveys is accent and dialect, but they usefully augment the data collected for *Voices* by illustrating the way in which the regional lexis is regarded and used in context.

Discussion of findings

Taking into account the three most popular responses for each of 38 concepts, there are 114 possible combinations to be extracted from the submitted lexical items (Table 10.5). From these 114 combinations,

- 42 responses are identical both in terms of the lexis and its popularity level
- there are 21 recorded examples of individual variants
- there are 23 instances of lexical correlation between NE and TS
- there are 17 instances of lexical correlation between NE and SR
- there are 11 instances of lexical correlation between SR and TS.

Instances of identical lexis across the three postcode areas are indicated by X in the table, correlation between postcode areas is indicated by a slash (for example, between NE and SR by NE/SR), and lexical variation is noted as such. The table shows that the identical lexical items (24 instances of X) are mainly to be found in the most popular response column. The fact that these submissions also correlate closely with the national most popular lexical items (see Group A) challenges the perception of the Northeast as having a 'sense of isolation' from the rest of the UK (Beal 1999: 34).

Nationally popular lexical items are more prevalent in NE than in the other two postcode areas and, as Newcastle upon Tyne is the dominant urban centre in the Northeast of England, it would be tempting to assume that it would also be the centre from which all lexical innovation and change in the region emanates. There are indeed consistently higher correlations of lexical choice between NE and SR (17) or NE and TS (23) than there are between SR and TS (11), suggesting a wide NE influence. However, some lexical items (*babby* and *beck*, for example, which are more solid local choices in SR and TS than in NE) do suggest some marked separation of these areas from NE. This offers lexical support for Pearce's (2009: 187) suggestion that the levelling of lexical choices in the region might, in some cases, be influenced by Sunderland and Middlesbrough, with 'their own distinct leveled forms spreading into their hinterlands'.

The maintenance and possible diffusion of Sunderland and Middlesbrough lexis in the face of the lexical power of Newcastle upon Tyne is a reflection of Pearce's (2009: 188) findings of a desire for identity preservation through dialectal variants, as he identifies 'real linguistic variation in space' in the Northeast. Pearce's investigations in perceptual dialectology find that there is clear evidence of sensitivity from the respondents to differences between the three centres. Lexical variation appears, therefore, not simply as a sporadic occurrence but as an important factor in the lexical choice of the Northeast. There are ten instances of local variant use in each of the second and third most popular submission columns of Table 10.5, as well as the local lexical variants in most popular position for PLAY TRUANT, these clearly evidencing a tendency towards local diversity.

TABLE 10.5 Distribution of the three most popular responses from NE, SR, and TS for each concept

Concept	*Most popular response*	*2nd most popular response*	*3rd most popular response*
HOT	X	NE/SR	VARIATION
COLD	X	NE/SR	VARIATION
TIRED	X	X	VARIATION
UNWELL	X	SR/TS	SR/TS
PLEASED	X	NE/TS	VARIATION
ANNOYED	X	X	X
PLAY GAME	X	VARIATION	VARIATION
PLAY TRUANT	VARIATION	SR/TS	X
THROW	NE/SR	NE/SR	NE/TS
HIT HARD	SR/TS	VARIATION	NE/TS
SLEEP	X	NE/SR	X
DRUNK	X	NE/SR	VARIATION
PREGNANT	X	X	X
LEFT-HANDED	X	X	X
LACK MONEY	X	X	X
RICH	X	X	VARIATION
INSANE	SR/TS	VARIATION	VARIATION
ATTRACTIVE	X	VARIATION	VARIATION
UNATTRACTIVE	X	X	NE/TS
MOODY	X	SR/TS	NE/TS
BABY	X	NE/TS	NE/SR
MOTHER	X	NE/TS	NE/TS
GRANDMOTHER	X	NE/TS	NE/TS
GRANDFATHER	NE/TS	NE/TS	X
FRIEND	X	NE/SR	NE/TS
MALE PARTNER	X	X	NE/SR
FEMALE PARTNER	X	X	NE/TS
YOUNG PERSON	NE/SR	NE/SR	NE/SR
CLOTHES	NE/TS	VARIATION	NE/SR
TROUSERS	NE/SR	VARIATION	NE/TS
PE SHOES	NE/TS	VARIATION	NE/SR
MAIN ROOM	NE/TS	VARIATION	X
SOFT SEAT	X	NE/TS	NE/TS
TOILET	NE/TS	NE/TS	NE/SR
WALKWAY	X	VARIATION	X
RAIN LIGHTLY	SR/TS	SR/TS	NE/TS
RAIN HEAVILY	NE/TS	SR/TS	VARIATION
RUNNING WATER	X	VARIATION	SR/TS

While accent differences are clear for each postcode area, Burbano-Elizondo (2006: 126) reflects that the lexical differences between NE and SR 'proved to be the hardest ones to identify for speakers'. Lexical items that are exclusive to Sunderland include *kets* for SWEETS and *doll (off)* for PLAY TRUANT.

There is comprehensive information in the *Voices* database about the place of birth of many of the respondents which suggests that there is little significant movement of population between the three postcode areas. The majority of respondents are still resident in the area in which they were born. However, respondents who have moved, from Middlesbrough to Newcastle upon Tyne, for example, tend to retain their native lexis rather than adopt the new variants, and thus spread their lexical choices from one postcode area to another.

The more localized distribution of a lexical item can in some cases be seen on maps derived from detailed postcode–district–level data. Figure 10.2 shows *nick (off),* the TS variant for PLAY TRUANT, mapped across the region at this finer *district* level of detail. It shows how the main concentration of *nick (off)* is, as expected, around Middlesbrough, with some submissions from north and east NE postcode districts in Northumberland. There are fewer instances of *nick (off)* in more central NE postcode districts, and minimal submissions from SR: SR respondents overwhelmingly submitted *doll (off)* for PLAY TRUANT, and the urban centre of Newcastle upon Tyne returned *skive (off)*. Some further, qualitative research into the socio-economic status of the residents of the postcodes that returned *nick (off)* might be valuable in drawing more defined conclusions about the context of use for this variant.

One clear example of the coincidence of national lexis with the retention of the regional and local variants is to be found for HOT (see Group C-3), where the most popular response, *boiling*, is common to all three postcode areas (reflecting supralocal lexical choice), the second most popular response, *roasting*, is common to two (NE and SR) of the three regional areas and, finally, there are three instances of local lexical variants, one from each postcode area: *lathered* (NE), *scadding* (SR), and *mafted* (TS).

It is hard to account for the differences between those concepts that have attracted a national lexical item and those that evidence some degree of local variation. For example, the four concepts that have identical and largely nationwide responses across two or three of the submission columns (Group A concepts) are not linked by any discernible common element. The pattern of the instances of lexical variation between the postcode areas, however, is rather easier to categorize, and includes groups of lexis reflecting some physical states (HOT, COLD, TIRED, and PLEASED), some social and value judgements (DRUNK, RICH, INSANE, and ATTRACTIVE), and some clothing items (CLOTHES, TROUSERS, and CHILD'S SOFT SHOES WORN FOR PE). These groups of concepts are such as might be expected to produce variation as they are to do with personal issues, and this suggests that at this personal level there are significant differences between the three postcode areas. With reference to the instances of lexical variation posited above, the three concepts for clothing, for example, could

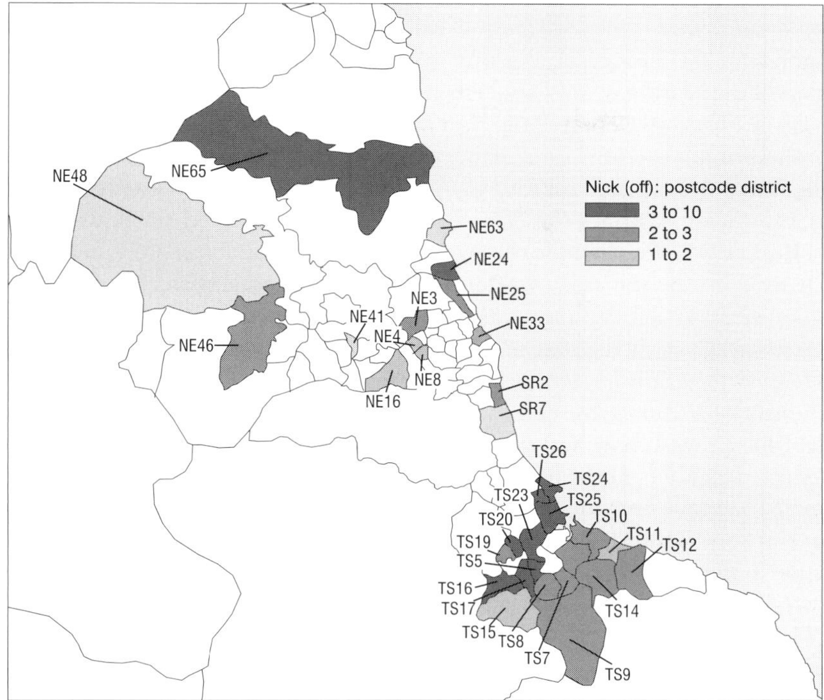

FIGURE 10.2 Distribution of *nick (off)* across the postcode districts of postcode areas NE, SR, and TS

be regarded as lexically establishing an outer image which perhaps symbolizes the perception of an inner identity (see Beal (1999: 35) on the importance of the Newcastle United football strip as a symbol of identity).

Furthermore, at the level where 'individual' becomes 'society', the boundaries between lexical identity and the more complex interactions between the three postcode areas begin. Burbano-Elizondo (2006:115) asserts that:

> the community boundary encapsulates the identity of the community and, like the identity of an individual, is called into being by the exigencies of social interaction. Boundaries are marked because communities interact in some way or other with entities from which they are, or wish to be, distinguished.

She adds (2006:127) that respondents in Sunderland are striving to dissociate themselves from the assumption that they are under the influence of the larger urban centre of Newcastle upon Tyne, and mark their opposition to the Tyneside community not only by means of ideologies, but also linguistically.

There are 23 instances of shared lexical choice between NE and TS, in comparison with the 17 between NE and SR, and it may be that, while

Sunderland respondents are resisting lexical contact, Middlesbrough respondents are, conversely, seeking to consolidate their relatively new identity as part of the Northeast (as distinct from Yorkshire) by adopting lexical items also in use in Newcastle upon Tyne. As a large urban centre with its own heritage, Middlesbrough can afford to share certain lexical items with Newcastle upon Tyne (*alley*, *plimsoles*, and *pal* for example), thus consolidating its status as part of 'the Northeast', without the element of rivalry documented (in Pearce (2006) and Beal (1999), for example) between Newcastle upon Tyne and Sunderland.

It may also be the case that Middlesbrough respondents feel that they are, unlike those in Sunderland, sufficiently differentiated from Newcastle upon Tyne because of their erstwhile Yorkshire affiliation. Individual lexical items such as *netty*, *bladdered*, *blaked,* and *snicket* are examples of differences that remain indicative of a Middlesbrough background. A particular example here is *laik*, an established Yorkshire lexical item discussed at some length in *EDD*, which was submitted by 6.9 per cent of middle-aged TS respondents as a variant for PLAY A GAME. These respondents, aged 46–55, record their places of birth as West Yorkshire and Teesside, indicating a merging of the lexical profile as well as the administrative allegiance of the city. The younger TS respondents do not appear to use this variant to the same extent as do older ones.

Llamas (2001:107), however, does detect some 'resentment towards the perceived dominances of Newcastle in the Northeast' in Middlesbrough, and suggests that this resentment reflects an ongoing sense of rivalry between the two centres and an awareness by the inhabitants of Middlesbrough of their 'border town' status. It is not possible to investigate this resentment qualitatively through the *Voices* data amassed so far, but quantitative indications are that Middlesbrough residents vindicate Llamas' observation on their heritage by retaining many local lexical variants and resisting the spread of lexis from both Newcastle upon Tyne and Sunderland.

Conclusion

The early history of the Northeast established a separation between the communities of the three areas under review here in terms of location and work patterns and, even today, there are continuing social factors maintaining this division and resisting change. The use of regional and even more local lexis throughout a social network of peer or social groups is based on a desire for solidarity, to be part of the local 'in-group'. In the Northeast, a distinct regional cohesion (which outweighs the status afforded by the use of the Standard variety) is, in turn, challenged by a desire in each postcode area to maintain an individual identity at a more local level. Beal (1999: 34) recognizes that there is this 'certain common identity' in the Northeast of England, a regional cohesion that is evidenced here by the submissions to the *Voices* survey across the three postcodes. But she adds that anyone 'mistaking a person from Sunderland or Middlesbrough for a Geordie has made an unforgivable social gaffe'. There is much lexical evidence in the *Voices* database that supports the findings of previous researchers, and scope for further, more detailed research that could illuminate the interaction, both lexical and social, between Newcastle upon Tyne, Sunderland, and Middlesbrough.

References

Beal, J. (1999) '"Geordie Nation": Language and regional identity in the Northeast of England', *Lore and Language*, 17, 33–48.

Beal, J., Burbano-Elizondo, L. and Llamas, C. (2012) *Urban Northeastern English: Tyneside to Teesside*, Edinburgh: Edinburgh University Press.

Burbano-Elizondo, L. (2006) 'Regional variation and identity in Sunderland', in T. Omoniyi and G. White (eds.) *The Sociolinguistics of Identity*, London: Continuum.

Diachronic Electronic Corpus of Tyneside English. Online. Available HTTP: <http://research.ncl.ac.uk/decte/> (accessed 2 June 2012).

Green, A. and Pollard, A.J. (2007) 'Conclusion: Finding North-East England', in A. Green and A.J. Pollard (eds.) *Regional Identities in North-East England, 1300–2000*, Woodbridge: The Boydell Press.

Llamas, C. (2001) 'Language variation and innovation in Teesside English', unpublished thesis, University of Leeds.

Llamas, C. and Watt, D. (eds) (2010) *Language and Identities*, Edinburgh: Edinburgh University Press.

Milne, G. (2006) *North East England, 1850–1914: The Dynamics of a Maritime-Industrial Region*, Woodbridge: The Boydell Press.

Oxford English Dictionary. Online. Available HTTP: <http://www.oed.com> (accessed 6 August 2012).

Pearce, M. (2009) 'A perceptual dialect map of North East England', *Journal of English Linguistics*, 37, 162–92.

Tyneside Linguistic Survey. Online. Available HTTP: <http://research.ncl.ac.uk/necte/> (accessed 2 July 2012).

Watt, D. (2002) '"I don't speak with a Geordie accent, I speak, like, the Northern accent": Contact induced levelling in the Tyneside vowel system', *Journal of Sociolinguistics*, 6, 44–63.

Williams, A. and Kerswill, P. (1999) 'Dialect leveling: Change and continuity in Milton Keynes, Reading and Hull', in P. Foulkes and G. Docherty (eds.) *Urban Voices: Accent Studies in the British Isles,* London: Arnold.

Wright, J. (ed.) (1898–1905) *The English Dialect Dictionary*, 6 volumes, Oxford: Henry Frowde.

11

BLURRED BOUNDARIES

The dialect word from the BBC

Clive Upton

Introduction

Lexis is at the centre of the *Voices* enterprise, both as it was originally conceived by the BBC and as it has evolved through the early stages of analysis. Lexical variation was appreciated as of primary interest to the radio audience who were to be mobilized to help the BBC and its academic collaborators with the project (Elmes 2005), so it was essential that words should be put in the spotlight from the outset. And for the dialectologist, collection of a mass of lexis promises to provide a great deal from which insights can be gained on linguistic variation and mechanisms of change. But lexical ordering and analysis are not necessarily straightforward, and the messages coming from careful research are certainly not clear-cut: words, never easy to gather in the mass in an orderly, structured way, are unruly and hard to codify once collected.

That is not to say that, for the specialist in English-language variation, usable English dialect lexical data are not available, especially in the form of glossaries and full-scale dictionaries (Penhallurick 2009, 2010). Online versions of seminal dictionaries in particular now have much to offer, taking the user a long way into understanding the non-standard lexicon and, crucially, making possible inter-connections between related lexical items which have often not been available in printed versions. Even the century-old *English Dialect Dictionary* ([*EDD*] Wright 1898–1905), in paper form a mine of information which could be stubbornly reluctant to yield its full riches to the user, is finally showing its impressive potential through the Innsbruck-based SPEED initiative (Markus and Heuberger 2007; Onysko, Markus and Heuberger 2009; Markus 2010; Praxmarer 2010). But dictionaries and glossaries, typically the product of questionnaire-based fieldwork or textual research, tend not to capture informal spontaneous usage. Nor do they contain quantifiable data on independent social variables relating to dialect speakers, of the kinds required by the social dialectologist. If the aim is to study language collected in an informal manner, from a range of speakers identified by such variables as location, age, or gender, usable data are not to be found in works deriving from formal interviewing and the gleaning of written sources. They will best emerge from the informally-delivered language of speakers who, as much as possible, have not been subjected to the steering of professional linguists in tightly-structured interviews. Also, lexical variants need to be gathered in quantities sufficient to offer the likelihood of reliable quantification of their use.

Strang (1968: 215) was quick to recognize the marginalization of lexis caused in large part by the difficulties attendant on its capture for modern research purposes. Rule-governed phonemic inventories and grammatical paradigms provide environments in which comparisons between variants can be readily made. Data-capture strategies are relatively unproblematic here: find a topic about which a biographied informant can talk fluently and unreservedly, record them discussing it, and a complete phonemic inventory will readily emerge, to be available for comparative social-dialectological investigation. Such recordings will also readily yield a good deal of morphosyntactic data, though other techniques, such as that employed by Schneider *et al.* (2004) relying on the existence of grammatical paradigms, have proved invaluable too. The same ease of data capture cannot be expected for lexis. A rigid, formatted questionnaire of the kind devised for the Survey of English Dialects ([SED] Orton and Dieth 1962: 37–113) will certainly permit the gathering of a great deal of valuable lexical information. But in order that comparable material will be elicited from the many people questioned, a traditional SED-type questionnaire device will inevitably be slow to deliver and quite formal in structure, with a consequent formalising influence on the kind of responses given. (A singular case in point concerns variants for DRUNK, a variable of well-known complexity for which some fifty-seven variants were collected through *Voices*, in a bewildering array of orthographic forms in 29,275 responses, but only four variants occurred in SED (Upton *et al.* 1994: 127).) If an informant's unforced lexical usage is to be documented by means of a questionnaire, a quite elaborate mechanism must be devised, and such a mechanism is likely to trigger the observer's paradox as well as being difficult to use repeatedly, for comparative purposes, across a large population in a feasible amount of time.

Breaking with convention, the word-connecting technique inspired by Aitchison's (2003) notion of a 'web of words' that was developed by Llamas for her doctoral research on Teesside (Llamas 1999; Kerswill *et al.* 1999) proved successful in prompting unforced discussion of lexis in the mass. Ultimately, through a process of paring down and revision of Llamas's 'sense relation network sheets', this produced the Spidergram (Elmes, Crystal, this volume) deployed for *Voices*. The thirty-eight concepts on this device were used by BBC journalists to encourage unselfconscious yet structured discussion with groups of people they selected for interviewing (Robinson, Herring and Gilbert, this volume). More particularly for the purposes of this chapter, the Spidergram created the Web-mounted structure designed to encourage members of the public in large numbers to register their variants on a dedicated BBC website. The underlying premise of the Spidergram, based on Llamas's experience and that of others later (Asprey *et al.* 2006), was that since people find 'the word' a readily-identifiable concept, and variation between their lexicon and that of others a source of great interest, the observer's paradox would not greatly inhibit either face-to-face or online collection exercises. And indeed the belief was substantiated in *Voices*, the aim of bulk data-collection proving a marked success with some 84,000 volunteers submitting a total of 734,000 responses to the on-line prompts. Reassuringly, this readiness to volunteer on the subject of 'words' suggests an unselfconscious enthusiasm quite at odds with any tendency to feel under test and so to offer only formal language. Information on just thirty-eight variables is of course not going to furnish the means to create a dictionary, and this was never the intention of the *Voices* exercise. However, the unparalleled volume of responses, averaging around 17,000 variants offered per variable and with some variables attracting in the region of 30,000 responses as seen above for DRUNK, provides ample opportunity for the quantification needed to permit some detailed interrogation of the working of lexis as a linguistic component in today's dialectology.

Of course, no data are perfect. It would be wrong to assume that in the *Voices* technique a way has been found to collect material for completely unproblematic analysis: caveats are bound to arise as to authenticity as representative of unselfconscious language use or absolute comparability across variants or between variables. The 'Spidergram' technique has its limitations like any other. But the amount of readily-offered information acquired through its application means that anomalies and inconsistencies are exposed as idiosyncratic to some considerable extent, permitting analysis to be concentrated on core data where appropriate. Conversely, there is interest to be found too in the exceptions to any large-scale regularly-occurring data, these upon occasion standing out starkly from the mass of tidier data as demanding of investigation.

Spelling

Orthographic representation of the non-standard is an area offering itself for immediate exploration in this latter regard, especially since standard English orthographic conventions are of only limited use when words from an essentially spoken medium come to be written down. Anyone trying to make use of a 'dialect' dictionary quickly becomes aware of this: they might well have a quite decided idea how they themselves would write such a word, but it is quite likely that at least some others will write it differently, even if they are applying quite standard spelling techniques. This being the case, just what written shape will the dictionary compiler have given to such a word? The *Voices* prompt PLAY TRUANT produces *skive (off)* as its dominant variant, at over 10,000 of the total of 27,380 responses offered to the website. This is unsurprisingly rendered overwhelmingly as <skive> by those submitting (8,179 in its simplest unlemmatized form alone). However, beyond inflected <skive> forms, the orthographic rendering of this one variant alone is remarkable: amongst others the list includes <scaive>, <scav>, <scavie>, <sceive>, <scieve>, <schive>, <schyve>, <scive>, <sckive>, <skcive>, <skeive>, <skieve>, <skiv>, <skivve>, <skyve>, and <skyvv>. The matter is not especially problematic here, of course, if one is seeking a form under which all others are to be lemmatized. Predominantly here we are in Standard English territory, with <skive> both the recognized standard spelling and by far the most dominant spelling choice for informants, while others such as <scive> and <skyve> conform to well-known spelling conventions which make apparent the reasons for their being chosen. Beyond these, some spelling variants, such as <skivve> and <skiv>, might well be mere mis-keyings. Others represent well-known English spelling difficulties proliferating variation, as in <sceive>/<scieve> and <skeive>/<skieve>. Still others, including <skcive>, might be thought to be more whimsical, or they could represent a respondent hedging their bets by not choosing between alternatives. Especially at this outer edge of readily-understandable representation we are approaching an important issue, relating to the primacy of the spoken medium in modern society and the consequent relegation of spelling to lesser status. And some variants can raise issues quite unrelated to the orthographic: the PLAY TRUANT variants *skeifio* and *skivo* see the interaction of vernacular English with Welsh to create lexical items which can do duty in both Anglo-Welsh (Penhallurick, this volume) and Welsh itself.

Problematic though the spelling issue can be when dealing with Standard English lexical variants, the problems of representation and interpretation become far greater in the non-standard realm, where informants have only their intuitions as regards normal spelling conventions to guide them in rendering their spoken usage. At its simplest, we are dealing here with such variants as <caggy> and <kaggy> for LEFT-HANDED: both initial <c> and <k> are quite reasonable offerings, and there is nothing to choose between them. As they *are* initial, however, the choice is significant for the compilation of any alphabetical listing such as that of a dictionary, a matter which I myself had to address for the dictionary of the SED (Upton *et al.* 1994). We can often go on precedent in such cases, but although that aligns our work with that of other professional practitioners it does not assist the uninitiated, especially those who have to exercise some imagination in their word-searches. Still more imagination is required in less obvious cases. *OED* provides us access to, and hence a recognized spelling form for, *boak* 'to vomit', given for *Voices* in response to the prompt UNWELL. But this is to be found within the *OED* entry for *bolk*, regarded as obsolete, and has the contending forms <boak>, <boke>, and <bouk> in both the literature cited by *OED* and the *Voices* responses. All are reasonable representations of /bəuk/, and all might therefore serve. Again, *Voices* provides a largely Scottish variant for TOILET in the forms <shunkie>,

<shunky>, <shunkey>, <shunk>, and <shonkey>, with only the slightly larger support for the first of these to suggest *shunkie* as the most representative form, there clearly being no great consensus among users on this.

In the fluidity of the orthography of vernacular language use we are here in a situation analogous to that of Middle English, with many users writing as they speak instead of being influenced by the dictates of a Standard-dialect writing convention. Remarkably, even Standard or other well-recognized spellings are registered only lightly by very many contributors to a database such as that of *Voices*. It is not that such contributors are language-unaware: after all, they have voluntarily responded to a broadcast invitation to offer up their information. But setting aside the variability to be expected in the rendering of non-standard lexis, it is manifestly the case that spelling is not a priority issue for many. Whether or not we consider this to have implications as regards 'literacy' depends of course on the definition of the term, and here even the *OED* is ambivalent. Its definition 1a for *literate*, which it marks as 'now rare' (though with a latest citation from 2002), is 'Of a person, society, etc.: acquainted with letters or literature; erudite, learned, lettered': clearly many *Voices* respondents, on the evidence of their spelling, are not to be thought wholly 'literate' by this definition. However, meaning 1b is 'In weakened use: able to read and write': simply by responding in a written medium to online written prompts, those volunteering information can now be deemed 'literate'. The perception that the notion of literacy is, to say the least, a flexible one is confirmed by information available from the National Literacy Trust (www.literacytrust.org.uk). This body, which seeks to inform debate on literacy and advises on this in the educational sphere in Britain, states in a definition which is not very prominent on its website: 'We believe literacy is the ability to read, write, speak and listen well. A literate person is able to communicate effectively with others and to understand written information'. Whilst the orthographic representations of *Voices* lexis communicate a great deal of fascinating and potentially extremely valuable information from people committed to its transmission, as regards their performance 'well' and 'effectively' are adverbs open to a range of judgements. The meanings of these words are not pursued by the Trust, which seems content by its vagueness to keep the boundaries of literacy blurred, at least as they relate to spelling. We might suggest that part of the value of the whole BBC venture has been to give a 'voice' to very many who, according to some conventional notions of literacy, might be considered not fully in command of their language.

Semantic loading

Lexicographers customarily assign style labels to non-standard and some standard lexical items, these acting both as adjuncts to definitions and as usage guides. Prominent amongst these are 'dialect', 'slang', 'colloquial', and the like. Clearly, it is necessary to offer guidance on lexical usage. However, respondents to *Voices* have invariably offered up their information on local and personal speech regardless of where it lies on a cline of formality, from the most elevated and rarefied Standard English lexis, through the everyday and the colloquial, to the most vulgar and taboo, while taking in too the obviously regional, local, and obscurely idiolectal. Sometimes, the *users* of the language, as distinct from its describers, might appear from their submissions to be as blissfully unaware of artificially-imposed stylistic distinctions in their language as they are of the niceties of English spelling. This would be to do them a disservice, however: it is abundantly clear, especially from the discussions recorded by the BBC interviewers, that speakers generally have a very sensitive awareness of the need for care over word selection. This will not be so in every case, of course, but it must be accepted that, as far as informing denotative meaning is concerned, the *Voices* database is a blunt instrument for the recording of informants' subtle stylistic decisions.

Members of the public contributing to the *Voices* website were simply asked to give their words for the thirty-eight different prompts without comment, with subtle semantic nuances being lost in consequence. So, are the 7,792 instances of *living room* for MAIN ROOM OF HOUSE analogous in every case to the 4,958 instances of *lounge*, the 2,387 of *sitting room*, and the 2,260 of *front room*? It is highly unlikely that they are, there being known distinctions by region and social group concerning this variable. And where do the 53 instances of *den* lie here, distinguished as it is by its comparatively infrequent occurrence? At the level of the bald response figures we can only speculate, at least until the recorded postcode data can be matched to census demographics, acknowledging the fuzziness inherent in such material. Still more ambiguity is likely to be enshrined in a concept which can be expected to involve wide connotative range. Such a variable is UNATTRACTIVE, for which responses relating to the opposite sex were very frequently offered. While, out of a total of 20,733 responses to this prompt, 5,739 prove to be based on Standard adjective *ugly*, variants based on the non-standard noun *minger* total virtually the same, at 5,537: the semantic loading inherent in these quite balanced choices is not to be lightly dismissed, any more than it is in more occasional though well-attested variants such as nouns referencing animals (*badger*, *beast*, *dog* …).

Uncertainty as to the proper import of terms does not end with *apparent* synonyms, of course: variants for one quite unambiguous variable will often carry distinctly different loadings. So PREGNANT yields a wide range of variants in its 15,158 total, many of which, whilst obviously having the same denotation, are known to be socially marked stylistically for less-than-polite, even somewhat taboo, connotation. Exploration among the large-scale *Voices* data of the four most popular PREGNANT variants in Table 11.1, *pregnant* (3,768 across ages <16 to 85), *expecting* (1,249), *bun in the oven* (1,379), and *up the duff* (5,045 citations), well illustrates this. (See also Robinson *et al.*, this volume.)

In a situation entirely characteristic of the on-line *Voices* submissions, which sees a preponderance of female respondents (itself a circumstance which is deserving of investigation at some future point), the norm-setting ratio across

TABLE 11.1 Four variables for PREGNANT, number of responses by gender

Variant	*Female*	*Ratio (Norm 1.40:1)*	*Male*
Pregnant (n=3,842)	2,450	1.76:1	1,392
Expecting (n=1,282)	937	2.69:1	348
Bun in the oven (n=1,407)	797	1.31:1	610
Up the duff (n=5,143)	2,726	1.13:1	2,417

all selected PREGNANT variants is F[emale]8,653:M[ale]6,177, or F1.40:M1. In Table 11.1 we see, first, a marked gender difference in the support given to each of the selected variants here. *Pregnant* itself shows an actual ratio of F1.76:M1, at 0.36 greater than the norm, indicating that it is generally more favoured by females than by males. Still more strongly indicative of female speech is *expecting*, with a twice-the-norm ratio of F2.69:M1. Conversely, *bun in the oven*, with a below-average ratio of F1.31:M1, is noticeably a variant favoured by males, and still more so is *up the duff*, with a ratio of F1.13:M1. So when we move beyond the mere fact of variant submission to consider the demographic of respondents, we have a noticeable female–male split, with females favouring Standard *pregnant* and *expecting*, and males *bun in the oven* and *up the duff*. On this evidence, of the four variants *expecting* is clearly a female variant of choice and *up the duff* the male-favoured alternative. This apparent bias across the gender boundary is as yet unremarked by dictionaries, and might be tentatively ventured as a possibility for inclusion in defining.

However, it would be quite misleading to suppose any uncomplicated male–female differentiation, even when figures carry a clear-cut gender message at a superficial level. Too-ready assumptions are fraught with pitfalls, never more so than when what might readily be thought to support well-researched stereotypes reinforces also a popular 'understanding', in this case of the appropriateness of men's and women's differing adherence to stylistically-marked lexical variants. Factoring in details of the age of respondents permits observations to be refined: Figures 11.1–4 show the age and sex data for our four chosen variants as a percentage of (sex) column.

For all four variants, it can be seen that the proportion of responses tails off to numerically insignificant levels in the later age groups, making further comment on the numbers for the older respondents problematic. Focus especially on the age groups up to 56–60 is, however, revealing, and suggests that age is quite as significant as sex in the frequency with which the variants are supported. Unsurprisingly, especially given that data were collected on-line, the heaviest response rates are in the young and younger middle-aged age groups. Across the range, for *pregnant* (Figure 11.1) especially, the figures for females and males track each other fairly consistently throughout the range, with just some female preference in the youngest years, changing to male preference

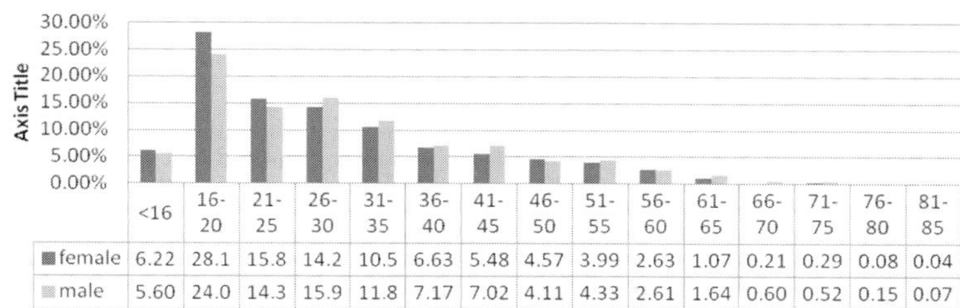

	<16	16-20	21-25	26-30	31-35	36-40	41-45	46-50	51-55	56-60	61-65	66-70	71-75	76-80	81-85
female	6.22	28.1	15.8	14.2	10.5	6.63	5.48	4.57	3.99	2.63	1.07	0.21	0.29	0.08	0.04
male	5.60	24.0	14.3	15.9	11.8	7.17	7.02	4.11	4.33	2.61	1.64	0.60	0.52	0.15	0.07

FIGURE 11.1 PREGNANT variant *pregnant*, percentage of all female and all male responses, by age group

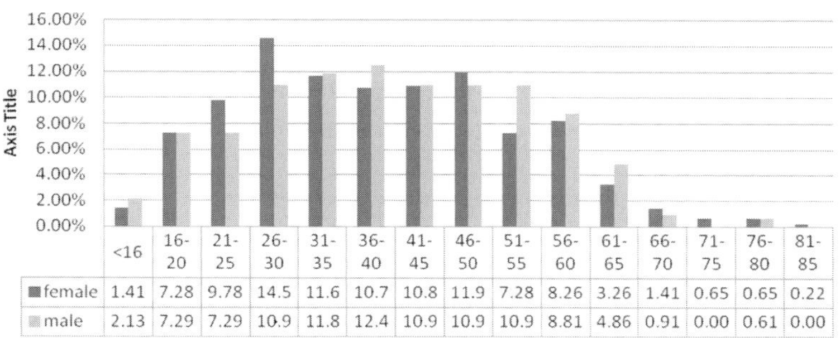

	<16	16-20	21-25	26-30	31-35	36-40	41-45	46-50	51-55	56-60	61-65	66-70	71-75	76-80	81-85
female	1.41	7.28	9.78	14.5	11.6	10.7	10.8	11.9	7.28	8.26	3.26	1.41	0.65	0.65	0.22
male	2.13	7.29	7.29	10.9	11.8	12.4	10.9	10.9	10.9	8.81	4.86	0.91	0.00	0.61	0.00

FIGURE 11.2 PREGNANT variant *expecting,* percentage of all female and all male responses, by age group

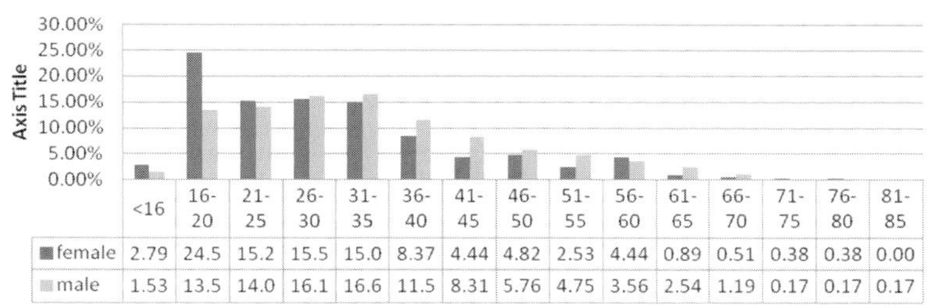

	<16	16-20	21-25	26-30	31-35	36-40	41-45	46-50	51-55	56-60	61-65	66-70	71-75	76-80	81-85
female	2.79	24.5	15.2	15.5	15.0	8.37	4.44	4.82	2.53	4.44	0.89	0.51	0.38	0.38	0.00
male	1.53	13.5	14.0	16.1	16.6	11.5	8.31	5.76	4.75	3.56	2.54	1.19	0.17	0.17	0.17

FIGURE 11.3 PREGNANT variant *bun in the oven*, percentage of all female and all male responses, by age group

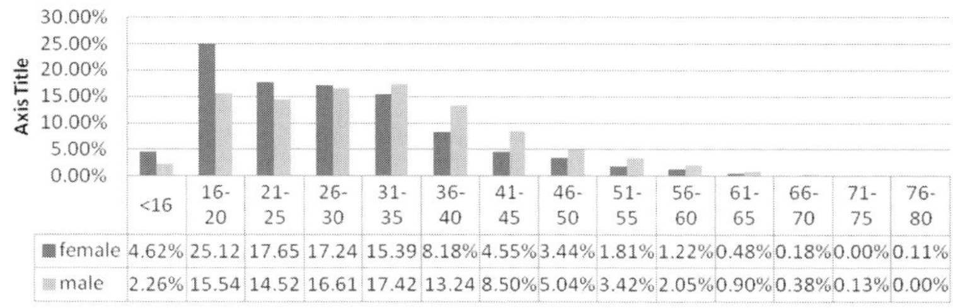

	<16	16-20	21-25	26-30	31-35	36-40	41-45	46-50	51-55	56-60	61-65	66-70	71-75	76-80
female	4.62%	25.12	17.65	17.24	15.39	8.18%	4.55%	3.44%	1.81%	1.22%	0.48%	0.18%	0.00%	0.11%
male	2.26%	15.54	14.52	16.61	17.42	13.24	8.50%	5.04%	3.42%	2.05%	0.90%	0.38%	0.13%	0.00%

FIGURE 11.4 PREGNANT variant *up the duff*, percentage of all female and all male responses, by age group

later. This female-to-male switchover is appreciably more marked with *bun in the oven* (Figure 11.3) and *up the duff* (Figure 11.4), each of which exhibit female dominance in support up to the age of 25, when male dominance begins to take over. For both of these variants, though, support holds up into early middle age somewhat more than it does for *pregnant*, although for all three variants early support is stronger than that exhibited later. The exception to the pattern of the most popular variants declining in use from early adulthood onwards is that shown for *expecting* (Figure 11.2). Here we see a variant for which support builds to the later twenties and is then maintained at a quite level intensity thereafter. Male and female support is strong throughout, level in the 31–35 and 41–45 cohorts, and has just two very obvious spikes, one for females aged 26–30 and another for males aged 51–55.

In light of abiding cultural stereotypes, of course, many might think the *OED* style labelling of *expecting* as merely 'formal' and *bun in the oven* and *up the duff* as 'slang' to be overly bland, when at a popular level at least such labels as 'delicate' for the first and 'coarse' for the last two could seem more suitable, with corresponding female and male associations implied. On the evidence here, however, it is clearly wise for lexicographers not to overstep the mark. The boundaries of linguistic selection are far from clear-cut. Men are clearly users of 'informal' *expecting*, and women, especially though not only in the earlier age groups, appear very ready to embrace 'slang' *bun in the oven* and *up the duff* as enthusiastically as do men. Nor is this to be thought a particularly modern phenomenon: twenty years ago De Klerk (1992) recognized a growing literature on the ready use of even taboo speech by women: the sex (or gender) boundaries are complex and ill-defined.

From this evidence it is clear that it would be unwise to rely exclusively on overall scores that indicate linguistic preferences by sex when forming judgements as to sex-linked support for stylistically-marked variants. The story told by Table 11.1 is certainly illuminating, and might serve for some purposes, but if we choose an alternative, more nuanced, breakdown of data, as in Figures 11.1–4, we uncover subtler shades to the male–female picture. (See Ahearn (2012: 187–213) for a rehearsal of gender-sex linguistic research issues and much else of relevance, including a summary of Hyde's Gender Similarities Hypothesis which speaks to the data treated here.) None of this is to be regarded as speaking to an *ultimate* truth, however. Our independent variables are all human constructs, culture-bound at best, whimsical at worst. Were five-year age cohorts to be replaced in Figures 11.1–4 by some other age separations, for example, we might expect a different picture and other insights to emerge.

Geographical distribution

The idea that there are distinct dialects, which can be identified as belonging to particular groups of speakers and associated with physical territories to be delineated on a map, is a most attractive one. After all, natives of the British Isles, as of other countries, are generally able to identify at least very approximately the place of origin of a speaker by their pronunciations, even if this is only based in the British case on those broadest differences characteristic of England, Scotland, Wales, and Ireland. And, if these differences diverge in some marked particulars, placement can in some cases be quite definite. The same goes too for some items of vocabulary and grammar, although it is by accent that people tend to be most reliably and closely located, and it is phonological features which are almost invariably seen by members of the general public as the most helpful clues to 'dialect spotting'.

Amongst English linguists there have been remarkably few British efforts to map dialect boundaries and so to delineate particular nameable dialects. Early attempts were those of the nineteenth-century pioneers of dialectology, Louis Lucien Bonaparte (1877) and Alexander Ellis (1889), both of whose work was phonology-based, in Ellis's case the result of a phenomenal effort to record and classify an immense amount of data and to synthesize it geographically. (It is noticeable that Joseph Wright, coming only slightly after Ellis but concentrating on lexis, did not try the same geographical exercise in the *EDD*.) The attempt at formal large-scale dialect classification then remained in abeyance until it surfaced in the much-cited England-focused work of Trudgill (1999), which also uses phonological distinctions in order to demarcate boundaries: the popularity of this slim volume says much for the appetite that there is for the clear-cut designation of dialect areas.

The hiatus between mid-Victorian times and the very late twentieth century in the demarcation and consequent counting of dialects does not of course indicate any lack of dialect scholarship, either at the level of the scholarly monograph or, more particularly, as regards large-scale surveying which might inform understanding of the distribution of linguistic features over wide geographical areas. Indeed, surveys of varying length and complexity were carried out for all constituent parts of the United Kingdom around the middle of the twentieth century (Orton *et al.* 1961–1972 [SED]; Mather and Speitel 1975–1986 [LSS]; Parry 1999 [SAWD]; Barry 1981 [TRS]). Each involved some level of mapping, that for England resulting in two substantial atlases (Orton and Wright 1974; Orton *et al.* 1978) and that for Scotland presenting its entire findings in three map-focused volumes (Mather and Speitel 1975–1986). It is significant, however, that the cartography associated with these in-depth fieldwork-based investigations has not typically attempted to aggregate findings in such a way as to permit the charting of boundaries between different varieties of English. Rather, once finely-graded data had been collected and at some level made available for scrutiny, the route selected was invariably that of presenting representative items for close study. Aggregating data and ignoring exceptions, which is necessary if whole areas are to be separated one from another, was avoided in maps, in favour of the presentation of detail. To remark only on the SED-inspired and -derived isoglossic mapping in Orton and Wright (1974), Orton *et al.* (1978), and Parry (1999), and the symbol maps of Kolb *et al.* (1979), we see not the aggregating of features in an effort to identify shared borders but atomistic, single-feature maps. Only in the occasional isogloss-bundling maps such as that for the 'Humber-Ribble line' in Wakelin (1977: 103) do we see an attempt to display several features together, and the bundling method cannot go far before the spaghetti of lines becomes impenetrable. Elsewhere (Upton 2012), following on from work with Davis and Houck (Davis *et al.* 1997), I have echoed Kretzschmar's (2002: 91) eloquent questioning of the concept of dialect boundaries in which he invokes the support of Gaston Paris, and have used SED-derived materials to illustrate an argument for the English Midlands as an essentially unstructured transition zone between all-too-readily claimed, but actually quite amorphous, Northern and Southern blocs. This *transitional* nature of the area where one feature abuts another is to be considered fundamental to a proper understanding of the isogloss, which is unique to the data collected for one feature at one time from one speaker or group, an approximation whose only reality is in inviting speculation and further study.

Dialectometry has changed the rules of the dialect-mapping game. Its application in the UK to computerized SED data, as seen in the various material appended to Viereck and Ramisch (1997), shows what can now be done to aggregate large amounts of data previously thought to be best handled atomistically rather than being aggregated. Even with the application of dialectometry, though, the goal is not to descry discrete areas where dialectal varieties are to be found. Rather, connections and disconnections become more apparent than is made possible by comparing individual maps, subtle distributional pictures emerging in consequence. Now, with the availability through *Voices* of electronically-held large-scale lexical data, and the consequent statistical clustering of variants which it enables, we have an opportunity further to probe justifications for identifying dialectal geographical distributions. Alongside data-tagging for age and gender is that for geographical location, this being identified through postcode data, both the broader postcode area information relating to 'post towns' and more finely tuned postcode district information. Analyses now underway (Holliday, Wieling, this volume; and companion website www.routledge.com/cw/upton) predictably indicate regional patterning of lexis, with selection from the various clustering models available showing something of what might be done dialectometrically with the raw *Voices* lexical data. These data are also made available on the book website to permit further use.

Demonstrating the fuzziness of boundaries, and illuminating the problem of the concept 'dialect area', is the short sequence of maps from Holliday's collection, Figures 11.5–8. (Ward's Algorithm is used here: see the work of both Holliday and Wieling for alternative clustering methods and their differing attendant outputs.) This relatively simple sequence of cluster-analysis maps shows a shifting pattern, as delineated areas alter depending on the detail with which clustering is selected. (Sensitivity is available from between five and twenty-four clusters: for simplicity here five, six, eight, and ten clusters are shown.)

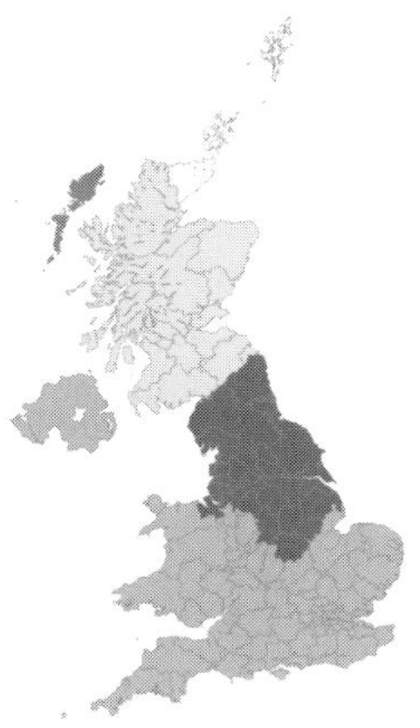

FIGURE 11.5 Five-cluster map of *Voices* lexis

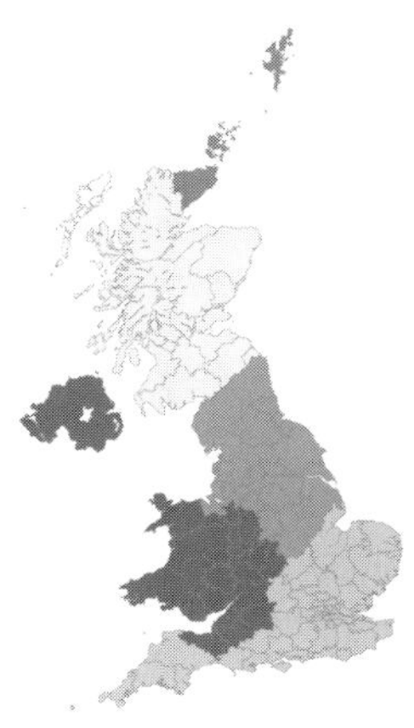

FIGURE 11.6 Six-cluster map of *Voices* lexis

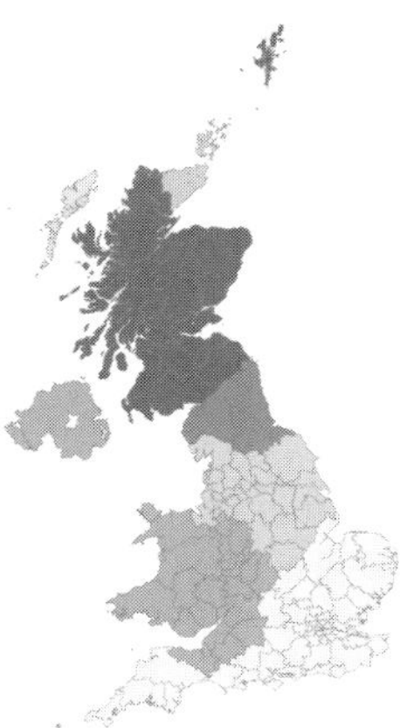

FIGURE 11.7 Eight-cluster map of *Voices* lexis

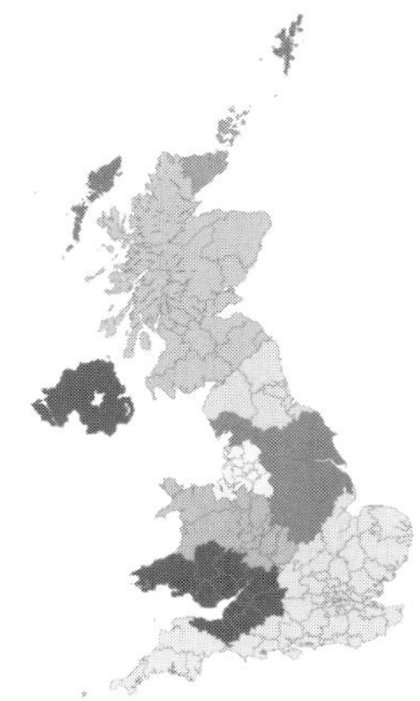

FIGURE 11.8 Ten-cluster map of *Voices* lexis

Figure 11.5, in which five clusters only are mapped, shows immediately that there is a north–south difference in lexical use in England and Wales, a fact which will surprise no-one given the proverbial 'north–south divide' which is so often commented upon by specialist and non-specialist alike. The northern sector dips further south in the east than in the west, testimony it seems to the northern, and Norse, influence historically reaching further south on that side of England. Remarkable is the inclusion of the whole of Wales, except for a tiny area southwest of the Wirral, and also Northern Ireland (Eire was not surveyed for *Voices*), with the south/South Midland area. Most of mainland Scotland shows as distinct from England and Wales, with the Western Isles, and

Orkney and Shetland together with the north-eastern mainland, each distinct again. The pattern made apparent here accords with much that we understand of the history and consequent allegiances of the UK population, including the greater separation of Scotland than Wales from England, the cultural separation of northern from southern England, and the Norse settlement and comparative physical isolation of island Scotland and its nearer northernmost mainland from the rest of the country. Just one surprising matter emerges: in spite of the close cultural and political link that undoubtedly exists between Northern Ireland and southwest Scotland, this does not show in the *Voices* data.

Lest there should be any temptation to rely on this straightforward delineation of 'dialect areas', however, Figure 11.6, for six clusters rather than five, shows that just one incremental change in the level of sensitivity in clustering changes the picture in an important detail. Northern England remains unchanged from its shape in Figure 11.5. But Wales and Northern Ireland are aligned now with the West Midlands of England and with the nearer part of the English Southwest, revealing long-entrenched links between England and Wales across the Welsh Marches and the Bristol Channel and, more obscurely but nonetheless well documented, Welsh–Irish connections dating back at least to the maintenance of medieval Norman control of Ireland through the Principality. Increasing the number of clusters to eight in Figure 11.7 separates Shetland from Orkney and northeast Scotland, suggesting a remoteness of the most northerly British islands from those nearer the mainland and the mainland itself. It also makes clear a 'Northumbrian' region that has some marked distinction from the rest of the 'North' of England, the latter allying with the North and East Midlands while the former shows historical Northumbria in a somewhat recessive form.

Figure 11.8 increases the clustering by just two more, to ten clusters. Yet at this level of separation we can see further important subtleties appear. A northwest Midland area emerges in the region of the Mersey and its hinterland, in what was formerly shown as a 'lower North': with this distinction we see an east–west split in the centre of England, highlighting a separation whose existence is often submerged in discussion of the 'north–south divide' but which is seen to be still more significant, for example, in the dialectometric analyses of SED data by Goebl and Schiltz (1997). The area stretching from the West Midlands and the northern part of the West Country into Wales separates too. The West Midlands now aligns with the northern half of Wales; the West Country is aligned with southern Wales, particularising further the cross-Bristol-Channel links referred to above.

Were further and more detailed cluster maps considered, these would show additional subtleties, each speaking to known facts of linguistic identity and in some cases, as with the West Midland–northern Wales detail, pointing to further matters deserving of note.

There are undoubted linguistic insights to be shown by such cluster maps and other kinds of dialectometric representations of large-scale data, these speaking to issues of past history and present identity. But as Wieling (this volume) points out, choice of clustering method determines results achieved and, as shown here, questions asked of even one method lead to different stories emerging. Once one moves from the delineation of a few most obvious distinctions to probing for finer detail, fragmentation of the geographical picture rapidly begins. It is as helpful to put this in reverse. If one starts with a quite complex picture and sheds distinctions to concentrate increasingly on what is held in common by speakers over wide areas, one creates a clear, broad-brush picture which might be thought sufficient for many purposes (in this case pointing up separations of insular Scotland, most of mainland Scotland, northern and north Midland England, and southern and south Midland England with Wales and Northern Ireland). But whichever way one moves, from the particular to the more general or vice versa, any boundaries are permeable and are created for the moment only, shifting both according to the data used and the purpose to which it is put.

Wieling's difference maps and reference-point maps (this volume, Figures 12.2 and 12.3) point to something of the separations apparent from Figures 11.5–8, but most especially illustrate that there are no complete breaks in dialectal continuity. In Figure 12.2 (left), heavier lines, which indicate most similarity in lexical usage between *Voices* informants from the various postcode areas, do coalesce, especially across the south of England and in the south-western part of the North. There are links from England into South Wales especially. The link demonstrated between Scotland and England, indicated by lines that are relatively faint, is quite weak, speaking to that separation seen in the previous maps. But they are not entirely discontinuous, there being sufficient linking to indicate cross-border lexical usage of some substance. Although this is not apparent on the small-scale map shown here, all areas are connected into a grid to a greater or lesser degree: there are no areas which are discrete from others nearby, no breaks in a pattern of links which might indicate discontinuity in the network structure. Though very different in form, the maps at Figure 12.3, in which comparable support for *Voices* lexical items is viewed from particular postcode areas, reinforce the point of the shading out of similarity rather than of abrupt cut-off.

A hive of activity

There is much to be done to explore the complex regional interconnections in speech that are being brought to light by dialectometric treatment of the *Voices* lexis. Already, at an early stage of analysis, clustering of large-scale data is apparent, some of it confirming what we have come to understand from more traditional and generally atomistic mapping of individual items, and some raising questions for further original investigation. It has long been recognized that there are structures in regional variation: much earlier dialectology sought to identify it, the better to understand the historical development of languages at the philological level; modern sociolinguistic focus, often no less diachronic in ultimate purpose, studies order in regional distributions in their juxtaposition with other independent variables, the better to understand mechanisms of ongoing linguistic change. The enterprise of dialect geography founders, however, when study of spatial variation is reduced to 'dialect counting', comforting though it might be to put a number to an ultimately unstructured phenomenon. We are used within England to talk at a popular level of 'the Northumberland dialect', or more generally perhaps 'the Northumbrian dialect', or even more widely 'Northern dialect'. In the UK as a whole there might be mention of 'Welsh', 'Scottish', or Northern Irish' English. But these are of course helpful fictions. County and national boundaries, like isoglosses, *contain* nothing. Lines on a map, and their respective labels, might help to direct our focus onto what, from time to time, is the object of our interest, a linguistic form that has particular local resonance, say, or a localized identity for which linguistic manifestations are sought. The more evidence one amasses, however, the more complex the picture becomes and the fuzzier the distinctions are seen to be, until the answer to the person – often a journalist seeking an interesting story with an easy answer – asking how many dialects there are is: 'How many do you want?'.

As with mapping, so with orthography, style-labelling, and denotative and connotative meaning: data available in the mass raise serious questions to challenge any too-ready assumptions we might be inclined to make. Easy talk of a literate society is given the lie by the production of many linguistically-committed citizens even when they are faced with the spelling of Standard English words, and their lack of attention to well-recognized processes of English spelling when confronted with the need to write down non-standard lexis is plain. Yet this matter obliges us to confront our understanding of what comprises 'literacy', and the extent to which, if at all, it involves the orthographic. Certainly, this does not seem to be something which is high on the agenda even of a body which, in the UK, is dedicated to advising on literacy as an aspect of the nation's life. And the same lack of the absolute can be seen to apply to the style labels and even to the meanings which we attach to lexis. Official pronouncements on such matters are, of course, valuable and necessary. They are at the heart of a proper ordering of a language, essential for instruction, a point of reference on which all can rely at need. But it would be seriously to overstate to claim a consensus on such matters as regards people's everyday speech: *Voices* data indicate considerable variability in usage, with undoubted structure to be probed but an inherent fuzziness speaking to the idiolectal beyond.

The essayist and social commentator Adam Gopnik (2012), in an extended metaphor likening human thought and the pursuit of understanding to the activity of bees, has said 'the beehive of the human mind may have order at its core, but it has lots of loose and buzzy action around its entrances and exits'. He goes on: 'The sticky honey of uncertainty, the buzz around the beehive's entrance – these are the signs of minds at work'. We see this uncertainty in the linguistic realm, and we should not be disconcerted to encounter it. The concept of orderly or structured heterogeneity (Weinreich *et al.* 1968: 99–100), on which sociolinguistics is founded, has proved to be of constant and well-founded value in making sense of linguistic differences that were once dismissed as being in free variation but which, through careful quantified analysis, are shown to have social order and meaning. The concept serves us well in our dialect enquiries, reminding us never lazily to accept the most obvious interpretations but rather to probe for reason for, and meaning in, variation. However, we should not allow 'orderly heterogeneity' to become a mantra. Identifying 'cohorts' (Chambers 2009: 13) into which to place speakers is a worthy pursuit, these being a necessary condition for the processing of those speakers as representatives. Yet the physical and social bounds of these cohorts are forever human constructs which are not tidily conformed to by the speakers themselves. Geographical locations are simply politically or administratively distinguished. Age occurs on a cline, with no in-built divisions other than those imposed by convention or by the intuition or even the whim of the researcher. While sex is biologically determined, gender is a social matter allowing of cultural interpretations. Class is a 'proxy variable' (Milroy 1987: 101) doing duty for a number of independent variables, these variously relied upon by different researchers.

Uncertainty over the boundaries of cohorts and categories should never be an excuse for avoiding rigorous examination of how connections can be made: the present and developing methods of sociolinguistics are invaluable in pushing back the boundaries of knowledge of the mechanisms of language change which have long been the target of dialectologists. But we should be prepared when our data are ultimately found to be open to conflicting analyses and interpretations, and should not strive artificially to impose boundaries when this happens. Rather, we should welcome Gopnik's 'sticky honey of uncertainty' as the tasty fare it is. Speaker communities are made up of individuals, each of whom has an idiolect; we know well that those idiolects are variable as regards their realization, depending on a complex of social and situational stimuli; the social groups they inhabit in their communities are shifting; those communities have no fixed physical bounds; our tools for quantitative and qualitative analysis are various, and liable to produce diverse and conflicting results. It is therefore inevitable that there will be a lot of loose ends, a lot of buzzing, which should engage rather than unsettle us.

References

Ahearn, L.M. (2012) *Living Language: an introduction to linguistic anthropology*, Malden, MA and Oxford: Wiley Blackwell.

Aitchison, J. (2003) *Words in the Mind: an introduction to the mental lexicon*, 3rd edn, Oxford: Blackwell.

Asprey, E., Burbano-Elizondo, L. and Wallace, K. (2006) 'The survey of regional English and its methodology: conception, refinement and implementation', in A.M. Hornero, M.J. Luzón and S. Murillo (eds) *Corpus Linguistics: applications for the study of English*, Linguistics Insights, Studies in Language and Communication. Volume 25, Bern: Peter Lang.

Barry, M.V. (ed.) (1981) *Aspects of English Dialects in Ireland Vol.1: papers arising from the tape-recorded survey of Hiberno-English Speech*, Belfast: Institute of Irish Studies, Queen's University of Belfast.

Bonaparte, L.L. (1877) *On the Dialects of Eleven Southern and South-Western Counties, With a New Classification of the English Dialects*, London: for the English Dialect Society, Trübner and Co.

Chambers, J.K. (2009) *Sociolinguistic Theory*, revised edition, Chichester: Wiley-Blackwell.

Davis, L.M., Houck, C.L. and Upton, C. (1997) 'The question of dialect boundaries: the SED and the American Atlases', in A.R. Thomas (ed.), *Issues and Methods in Dialectology*, Bangor: University of Wales Bangor.

De Klerk, V. (1992) 'How taboo are taboo words for girls?', *Language in Society* 21, 277–289.

Ellis, A.J. (1889) *On Early English Pronunciation V: the existing phonology of English dialects compared with that of West Saxon speech*, London: Trübner and Co.

Elmes, S. (2005) *Talking for Britain: a journey through the nation's dialects*, London: Penguin Books.

Goebl, H. and Schiltz, G. (1997) 'A dialectometric compilation of CLAE1 and CLAE2: isogolosses and dialect integration', in W. Viereck and H. Ramisch, *The Computer Developed Linguistic Atlas of England*, Tübingen: Max Niemeyer Verlag.

Gopnik, A. (2012) *A Point of View: on bees and beings*. Online. Available HTTP: <www.bbc.co.uk/news/magazine-18279345> (accessed 23-6-12).

Kerswill, P., Llamas, C. and Upton, C. (1999) 'The first SuRE moves: early steps towards a large dialect project', in C. Upton and K. Wales (eds) *Dialectal Variation in English: proceedings of the Harold Orton centenary conference 1998*, Leeds Studies in English 30, Leeds: University of Leeds.

Kolb, E., Glauser, B., Elmer, W. and Stamm, R. (1979) *Atlas of English Sounds*, Bern: Francke Verlag.

Kretzschmar, W.A. (2002) 'Dialectology and the history of the English Language', in D. Minkova and R. Stockwell (eds), *Studies in the History of the English Language*, Berlin: Mouton de Gruyter.

Llamas, C. (1999) 'A new methodology: data elicitation for social and regional language variation studies', *Leeds Working Papers in Linguistics*, 7, 95–119.

Markus, M. (2010) 'Introduction to Part II: The structure of Joseph Wright's *English Dialect Dictionary*', in M. Markus, C. Upton and R. Heuberger (eds), *Joseph Wright's English Dialect Dictionary and Beyond*, Frankfurt am Main: Peter Lang, 77–89.

Markus, M. and Heuberger, R. (2007) 'The architecture of Joseph Wright's *English Dialect Dictionary*: preparing the computerised version', *International Journal of Lexicography*, 20 (4): 355–368.

Mather, J.Y. and Speitel, H.H. (1975–1986) *The Linguistic Atlas of Scotland*, 3 volumes, London: Croom Helm.

Milroy, L. (1987) *Observing and Analysing Natural Language: a critical account of sociolinguistic method*, Oxford: Basil Blackwell.

Onysko, A., Markus, M. and Heuberger, R. (2009) 'Joseph Wright's *English Dialect Dictionary* in electronic form: a critical discussion of its parameters and query routines', in A. Renouf and A. Kehoe (eds), *Corpus Linguistics: refinements and reassessments*, Amsterdam and New York: Rodopi.

Orton, H. and Dieth, E. (1962) *Survey of English Dialects (A): introduction*, Leeds: E.J. Arnold.

Orton, H. and Wright, N. (1974) *A Word Geography of England*, London: Seminar Press.

Orton H., Sanderson, S. and Widdowson, J. (eds) (1978) *A Linguistic Atlas of England*, London: Croom Helm.

Orton, H., Halliday, W., Barry, M., Tilling, P. and Wakelin, M. (eds) (1962–1971) *Survey of English Dialects (B): the basic material*, 4 volumes, Leeds: E.J. Arnold.

Parry, D. (ed.) (1999) *A Grammar and Glossary of the Conservative Anglo-Welsh Dialects of Rural Wales*, NATCECT Occasional Publications No. 8, Sheffield: National Centre for English Cultural Tradition.

Penhallurick, R. (2009) 'Dialect dictionaries', in A.P. Cowie (ed.), *The Oxford History of Lexicography Volume II: specialized dictionaries*, Oxford: Oxford University Press.

Penhallurick, R. (2010) 'The dialect dictionary: what is it good for?', in B. Heselwood and C. Upton (eds), *Proceedings of Methods XIII: papers from the thirteenth international conference on methods in dialectology, 2008*, Frankfurt am Main: Peter Lang.

Praxmarer, C. (2010) 'Dialect relations in the English Dialect Dictionary', in B. Heselwood and C. Upton (eds), *Proceedings of Methods XIII: papers from the thirteenth international conference on methods in dialectology, 2008*, Frankfurt am Main: Peter Lang.

Schneider, E., Kortmann, B., Burridge, K., Mesthrie, R. and Upton, C. (eds) (2004) *A Handbook of Varieties of English*, Volume 2, Berlin: Mouton de Gruyter.

Strang, B. (1968) *Modern English Structure*, 2nd edn, London: Edward Arnold.

Trudgill, P. (1999) *The Dialects of England*, 2nd edn, Oxford: Wiley-Blackwell.

Upton, C. (2012) 'The importance of being Janus: Midland speakers and the "North–South Divide"', in M. Markus, Y. Iyeiri, R. Heuberger and E. Chamson (eds), *Middle and Modern English Corpus Linguistics: a multi-dimensional approach*, Amsterdam: Benjamins.

Upton, C., Parry, D. and Widdowson, J.D.A. (1994) *Survey of English Dialects: the dictionary and grammar*, London: Routledge.

Viereck, W. and Ramisch, H. (1997) *The Computer-Developed Linguistic Atlas of England* Volume 2, Tübingen: Niemeyer.

Wakelin, M.F. (1977) *English Dialects: an introduction*, revised edition, London: The Athlone Press.

Weinreich, U., Labov, W. and Herzog, M. (1968) 'Empirical foundations for a theory of language change', in W. Lehmann and Y. Malkiel (eds), *Directions for Historical Linguistics*, Austin: University of Texas Press.

Wright, J. (ed.) (1898–1905) *The English Dialect Dictionary*, 6 volumes, Oxford: Henry Frowde.

12

VOICES DIALECTOMETRY AT THE UNIVERSITY OF SHEFFIELD

John Holliday

Introduction

The *Mapping the BBC Voices* website at the University of Sheffield[1] (http://cisrg.shef.ac.uk/voices) presents the results of a recent study aimed at identifying the relationship between language and geography (Holliday *et al.* 2013). Based on the wealth of data collected by the BBC *Voices* project, the study attempts to identify regions of the UK which share common linguistic characteristics. The identification of this relationship is performed using a methodology known as cluster analysis (Sneath and Sokal 1973; Everitt *et al.* 2001), described below. On the website, the results of a wide range of clustering techniques can be viewed and compared.

The main result of this clustering methodology is a partitioning of the country into discrete linguistic regions separated by defined boundaries. Although such defined boundaries do not exist, with the transition from region to region being more gradual (Upton and Widdowson 2006: 9), it has been necessary to agglomerate the geographical information available in the *Voices* data to defined geographical regions, in this case United Kingdom postcode areas (PCAs). In addition to viewing the resulting linguistic regions, it is possible for users of the website to enter their own lexical characteristics using an online form. Using these data, it is possible to generate a map which illustrates the geolinguistic profile of the user. The map indicates, for each of the regions identified in the clustering stage, the probability that the user's language matches that of the region.

Data format

The data used in the study were the 38 lexical concepts collected through the Spidergram (Elmes, this volume), as well as grammatical and phonology data compiled from the analysis of 300 voice recordings taken by local BBC radio reporters (Robinson *et al.*, this volume).

Lexical data

The data for the 38 Language Lab concepts were analysed by the *Whose Voices?* project at Leeds University. During the analysis, analogous terms were grouped together and represented as one lexical item. The data were aggregated by PCA and the top ten lexical items were identified and represented as a percentage of the total for all top ten items in each PCA. (In two cases, a tie in the tenth position meant that the top eleven items were used.) Using all 38 concepts produces a set of 382 variants (percentage values). This is, effectively, a non-binary vector which can be used to characterize each PCA in terms of its lexical makeup. Table 12.1 illustrates the format of these variants in which the first ten variants are illustrated for seven of the PCAs. In this table, for example, of those people from Worcester (PCA WR) whose submissions were found in the top ten lexical items for the concept 'hot', 48.57 per cent used a term analogous with the lexical item 'boiling'.

Phonological and grammatical data

The 300 radio recordings were analysed by the British Library in order to identify grammatical and phonological features. A set of 126 grammatical features and 191 phonological features were used in the analysis, and the existence of each of these features in each recording was noted. The use of the *singular object us*, as in 'give us a go', is an example of a grammatical feature, whereas phonological features relate to linguistic sounds such as the vowel sound in 'ant' and 'grant'. A binary vector was used to represent the features for each recording, with each bit representing the existence of the respective feature. If the feature was observed at least once in the respective recording, then this was indicated by a one, otherwise the respective bit was set to zero. Table 12.2 illustrates seven of the recordings and the binary variants representing the first seven phonological features. The terms 'KIT', 'DRESS' and 'TRAP' refer to lexical sets, whilst 'RP' refers to vowel realization and 'lex.cond.' refers to lexically-conditioned variant. For a full description of the terminology, the reader is referred to the definitions of Wells (1982). The table indicates, for example, that, for recording C11902605, RP instances of KIT, DRESS and TRAP were observed.

Cluster analysis

Cluster analysis is a methodology which aims to classify a set of objects into groups such that those objects in the same group, or cluster, are more similar to each other than to those in other clusters. The methodology has been applied in many areas, ranging from document collections (van Rijsbergen 1979) to Scotch whiskies (Lapointe and Legendre 1994). In order to cluster a set of objects, it is

TABLE 12.1 Percentages of support for top ten variants across seven postcode areas

PCA	*Boiling*	*Roasting*	*Hot*	*Sweltering*	*Baking*	*Sweating*	*Warm*	*Scorching*	*Toasty*	*Melting*
WR	48.57	6.67	8.57	4.76	10.48	8.57	6.67	1.90	1.90	1.90
WS	47.19	21.35	10.11	5.62	4.49	3.37	4.49	1.12	2.25	0.00
WV	54.55	13.64	9.09	4.55	3.41	5.68	9.09	0.00	0.00	0.00
XD	100.00	0.00	0.00	0.00	0.00	0.00	0.00	0.00	0.00	0.00
Y	55.56	11.11	11.11	0.00	11.11	0.00	11.11	0.00	0.00	0.00
YO	49.47	15.96	12.77	5.85	2.13	1.60	6.38	3.19	1.60	1.60
ZE	33.33	16.67	33.33	0.00	0.00	0.00	16.67	0.00	0.00	0.00

TABLE 12.2 Incidence of phonological variants in a sample of *Voices* sound recording

Recording Code	*KIT*			*DRESS*			*TRAP*	
	RP	*Other*	*Lex.cond.*	*RP*	*Other*	*Lex. cond*	*RP*	*Other*
C11903204	1	1	1	1	0	1	1	0
C11901203	1	0	0	1	0	0	1	0
C11901204	1	0	1	1	0	0	1	0
C11901205	1	0	0	1	0	0	1	0
C11902602	1	0	0	1	0	0	1	0
C11902604	1	0	0	1	0	0	1	0
C11902605	1	0	0	1	0	0	1	0

necessary to use an appropriate clustering algorithm, and to identify a method for determining the level of similarity between the objects.

Similarity

Many methods exist for quantifying the degree of similarity between two objects (Deza and Deza 2009), with the choice of method depending on the nature of the data available. Here, we compare the similarity between one PCA and another, with the PCAs being characterized by sets of either binary or non-binary variants, as shown in Tables 12.1 and 12.2. The degree of similarity between two such sets of variants can be quantified using similarity metrics. Generally, these metrics produce a range of values with the lowest value (usually zero) indicating that there is no correspondence between the two variant sets, and the highest value (usually 1) indicating identical variant sets. Here, we have used a selection of metrics which are: the squared Euclidean distance, the Pearson correlation coefficient and the cosine coefficient, as shown in Table 12.3. Note that the first of these is in fact a distance (or dissimilarity) coefficient; this is still applicable, however, as a complementary approach is used in the clustering algorithm.

A clustering algorithm would usually start by generating all pair-wise similarity values between every object and every other object to produce an M by M similarity matrix, where M is the number of objects (PCAs in this study).

Clustering methods

The clustering algorithm is now applied to the similarity matrix to group together those objects which are most similar. Many clustering algorithms exist, and can be categorized into two main types: hierarchical and non-hierarchical.

TABLE 12.3 Similarity coefficients, in which, when comparing two objects q and p, q_i represents the i-th variant for the object q, p_i represents the i-the variant for the object p, and n is the number of variants

Squared Euclidean distance	$\sum_{i=1}^{n}(q_i - p_i)^2$
Pearson correlation coefficient	$\dfrac{\sum_{i=1}^{n}(q_i-\bar{q})(p_i-\bar{p})}{\sqrt{\sum_{i=1}^{n}(q_i-\bar{q})^2(p_i-\bar{p})^2}}$
Cosine coefficient	$\dfrac{\sum_{i=1}^{n}q_i \cdot p_i}{\sqrt{\sum_{i=1}^{n}(q_i)^2 \cdot \sum_{i=1}^{n}(p_i)^2}}$

Hierarchical clustering

Hierarchical methods can be either agglomerative or divisive. In agglomerative hierarchical clustering, each object begins the process as the only member of its own cluster. If there are *M* objects, the process then starts with *M* clusters. The two most similar objects then combine to form a cluster, producing *M*-1 clusters. This process is repeated until all objects are finally members of a single cluster. (In divisive clustering, all objects start in one cluster and the clusters are systematically divided until all clusters are separated out into the individual objects. Divisive clustering has not been investigated here.) The similarity values, calculated using the coefficients described above, represent the degree of similarity between pairs of objects. During the agglomeration process, however, it becomes necessary to identify the most similar clusters, which may contain more than one object. There are, therefore, several alternative approaches for combining clusters, resulting in alternative clustering algorithms. These include:

- *Single linkage*, in which the distance (here distance is the complement of similarity) between two clusters is given by the minimum distance between any of the objects in the first cluster and any of the objects in the second cluster;
- *Complete linkage,* in which the distance between two clusters is given by the maximum distance between any of the objects in the first cluster and any of the objects in the second cluster;
- *Average linkage between clusters (or UPGMA)*, in which the distance between two clusters is the average of all pair-wise distances between objects in the first cluster and objects in the second cluster;
- *Average linkage within cluster*, in which the distance between two clusters is the average of all pair-wise distances between all objects in both clusters (including pairs of objects in the same cluster);
- *Centroid method*, in which, for each variant, the mean value across all cluster members is taken. Comparisons are then based on this cluster mean, using a weighting based on cluster size;
- *Median method,* which is similar to the Centroid method, but does not use a weighting scheme;
- *Ward's minimum variance method* (Ward 1963), which seeks to minimize the variance of variants when clusters are combined. Two clusters are therefore combined when the effect on this variance is reduced.

The first six of these agglomerative clustering methods are illustrated in Figure 12.1. Where possible, all three similarity coefficients have been used for comparative purposes. However, for Ward's method, the Centroid method and the Median method, squared Euclidean distance is the only applicable coefficient. Since these methods are hierarchical, starting with *M* clusters and ending with a single cluster, it is possible to select the number of desired clusters at any point in the cluster hierarchy. In this study, we use data from 121 PCAs in the UK, and report our findings for between two and 30 clusters.

Non-hierarchical clustering

In order to complement the seven hierarchical methods described above, a non-hierarchical clustering method has also been implemented. The method chosen here is the *k*-means algorithm, a form of *relocation* clustering algorithm. In *k*-means clustering, the number of clusters (*k*) is pre-defined by the user. The algorithm starts with the selection of *k* objects, or cluster centres. These may be selected randomly or by some systematic method, with the aim of identifying a maximally dissimilar set of cluster centres. All other objects are classified into

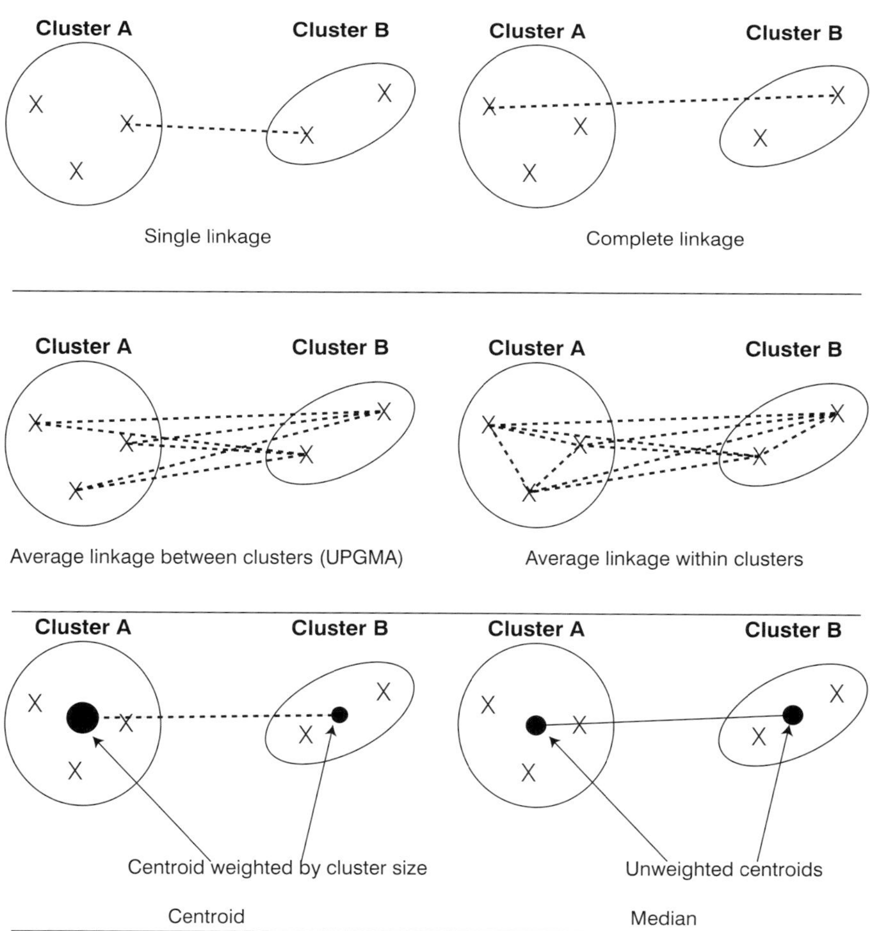

FIGURE 12.1 Alternative agglomeration methods in hierarchical clustering

the cluster of their nearest (i.e. most similar) cluster centre. Once all objects have been assigned to the cluster of their nearest cluster centre, the mean of each cluster is calculated based on the members of that cluster. The nearest object to this cluster mean is identified and this becomes the new cluster centre. All other objects are reclassified to their new cluster centre, and the process repeats until there is no change or until a user-defined number of iterations has completed. Since non-hierarchical methods output the results for the number of clusters desired (k), it is necessary to re-run the algorithm with different values for k; again; we have chosen values from 2 to 30.

Consensus clustering

For each cluster level, the clustering methods described above produce quite different results, so it would be useful to assimilate these results to a single, definitive solution. This is possible using consensus clustering, the operation of which is based on the results from the eight standard clustering methods described above (seven hierarchical and one non-hierarchical). In the standard methods, each element in the similarity matrix indicates the similarity between the two variant sets for the respective objects. In consensus clustering, each element of the similarity matrix denotes the number of clusters in which the two elements co-exist. In order that methods which use multiple similarity coefficients are not over represented, only the squared Euclidean analysis for each hierarchical method has been used in the consensus clustering stage. If two PCAs are found in the same cluster in four of the eight clustering methods, for example, then the respective similarity matrix element is set to 0.5. This similarity is then used as the basis for clustering.

Lexical maps

On the Sheffield *Mapping the BBC Voices* website, lexical maps are presented in two sections. Firstly, the raw data are presented by postcode area or by postcode district (PCD). Secondly, the clustering results are presented in three formats. In all of these displays, two maps are presented side-by-side for comparative purposes.

The Raw Data maps illustrate the top ten items for each concept. It is possible to select a concept and two lexical items. The maps use grey-scaling to represent either the proportion of submissions in the top ten (PCA) or the number of submissions (PCD). It will be seen that some PCD items have no data recorded.

In the Clustering Maps section, maps can be compared at three different levels:

- Compare Cluster Levels allows the user to select a clustering algorithm and similarity measure, and compare the results for different numbers of clusters.

- Compare Cluster Algorithms allows comparison between two combinations of algorithm and measure for a user-defined number of clusters.
- Compare Cluster Measure allows comparison between two different similarity measures for a given algorithm and number of clusters. This is only possible for algorithms for which more than one measure has been applied.

Phonological and grammatical maps

Clustering results for phonology and grammar data have been created for the Ward's clustering algorithm only. As such, comparison of cluster levels is the only option available. Since the *Voices* recordings were taken at single locations, rather than aggregated to PCA, the recording locations have been represented using Thiessen (or Voronoi) polygons (Voronoi 1908). Thiessen polygons are created by constructing boundaries at an equal distance from two neighbouring locations such that all points within a single polygon are always closest to their respective location.

Regional identification

Once the linguistic regions have been identified, using the clustering methods described above, it is possible to identify the linguistic characteristics of each region and match these to individuals. An online form has been created on which users of the website may enter their own lexical terms for the 38 *Voices* concepts. From this set of terms, and the characteristics of each linguistic region, it is possible to compare the user's terminology against each region to find the best match. The matching strategy used here is a machine learning methodology known as Bayesian classification.

Bayesian modelling is a probability-based methodology which seeks to identify those features of an object which distinguish it as being a member of a domain or otherwise. In this work, the domain is a single linguistic region and the features are the set of lexical items which characterize that region. Each feature is quantified by its ability to separate objects into those inside the domain and those outside. By using all 382 features, it is then possible to build a model which characterizes a region. This is repeated for each region to produce a model for each of our linguistic regions. The data from the user's online form are then passed through all of the regional models. Each model calculates the probability that the user data match those of the respective region. The result of this operation is a set of probabilities, one for each region, that the user's lexical terminology matches that of the region. These probabilities can then be mapped and presented as a user's geolinguistic profile.

The maps which result from this treatment illustrate, for each linguistic region, the probability that the user's terminology matches that of the region. The probability is presented graphically using grey-scale and is, in effect, a

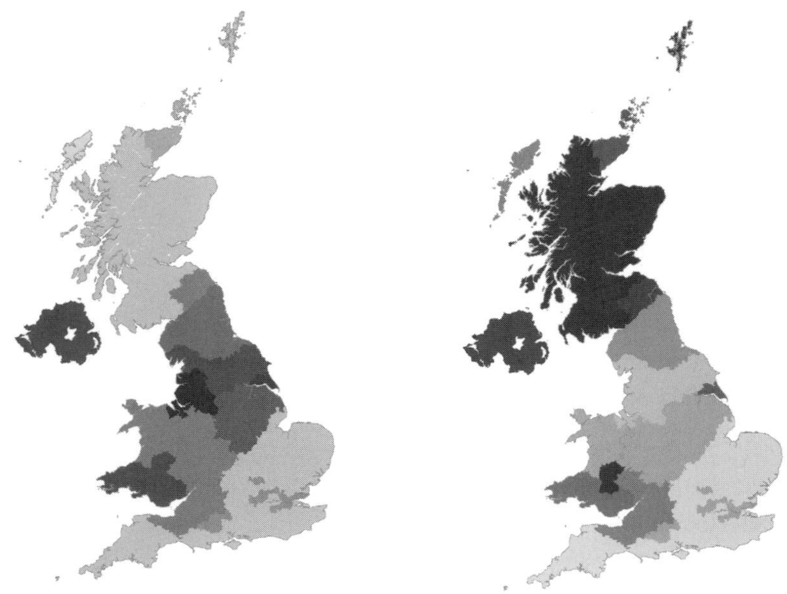

FIGURE 12.2 Profile map, subject from the Wirral

FIGURE 12.3 Profile map, subject from Clydebank

profile of the user's linguistic geography. Note that the generation of these maps is not an automated process. Figures 12.2 and 12.3 illustrate two such profile maps, the first from a test subject from the Wirral, the second from a subject from Clydebank, in which the darker shading indicates a higher probability that the subject's data matches the respective region.

Future enhancements

It is expected that increasing functionality will ultimately be included in the *Mapping the BBC Voices* website. The site includes a help page to explain its use, together with a theoretical page to explain the underlying concepts. Future enhancements will be explained in full in these pages.

Notes

1 This work is based on mapping data provided through EDINA UKBORDERS with the support of the ESRC and JISC, and uses boundary material which is copyright of the Crown and the ED-LINE Consortium.

Software and data

ArcGIS – for generation of choropleth maps: ESRI *The GIS Software Leader – Mapping Software and Data*. Available HTTP: http://www.esri.com.

CLUTO – for consensus clustering: Data Clustering Software – Karypis Lab. Available HTTP: http://glaros.dtc.umn.edu/gkhome/views/cluto.

MapServer – for web delivery of the choropleth maps: Mapserver *Open Source Web Mapping*. Available HTTP: mapserver.org.

Pipeline Pilot – for Bayesian classification: Accelrys *Scientific Informatics Software for Life Sciences, Materials R&D*. Available HTTP: http://www.accelrys.com.

SPSS – for all standard clustering applications: IBM *SPSS software*. Available HTTP: http://www-01.ibm.com/software/analytics/spss/.

References

Deza, M.M. and Deza, E. (2009) *Encyclopedia of distances*. Berlin: Springer-Verlag.

Everitt, B.S., Landau, S. and Leese, M. (2001) *Cluster analysis.* 4th edn. London: Edward Arnold.

Holliday, J., Upton, C., Thompson, A., Robinson, J., Herring, J., Gilbert, H. and Norman, P. (2013) 'Geographical analysis of the vernacular', *Journal of Information Science* 39(1), 28–37.

Lapointe, F.-J. and Legendre, P. (1994) 'A classification of pure malt Scotch whiskies', *Journal of Applied Statistics* 43(1): 237–257.

Sneath, P.H. and Sokal, R.R. (1973) *Numerical taxonomy*. San Fransisco, CA: WH Freeman.

Upton, C. and Widdowson, J.D.A. (2006) *An atlas of English dialects.* 2nd edn. Oxford: Oxford University Press.

Van Rijsbergen, C.J. (1979) *Information retrieval*. London: Butterworth.

Voronoi, G. (1908) 'Nouvelles applications des paramètres continus à la théorie des forms quadratiques', *Journal für die Reine und Angewandte Mathematik* 133: 97–178.

Ward, J.H. (1963) 'Hierarchical grouping to optimize an objective function', *Journal of the American Statistical Association* 58: 236–244.

Wells, J.C. (1982) *Accents of English.* 3 volumes. Cambridge: Cambridge University Press.

13

VOICES DIALECTOMETRY AT THE UNIVERSITY OF GRONINGEN

Martijn Wieling

In order to allow experimentation with the data of the *Voices* project, a website has been developed at the University of Groningen where dialectological analyses using the *Voices* data can be readily conducted. This website is a tailored version of the online dialect analysis application *Gabmap,* developed by the University of Groningen, and is available at http://www.gabmap.nl/voices.

Five datasets (i.e. projects) are available on the website for consultation and download: (1) the complete dataset which includes the results of men and women and older and younger people; (2) a subset including only the responses of women; (3) a subset including only the responses of men; (4) a subset including only the responses of people younger than 30; and (5) a subset including only the responses of people older than 30. For each dataset to be of manageable size, data are grouped by postcode area and include only the ten most popular variants per variable. The relative frequency of each variant is stored for each postcode area.

Within each project there are six analyses possible. The purpose of this chapter is to explain how these analyses work (on the basis of the complete dataset). In addition to the information presented here, the website includes a tutorial to help you run the various analyses.

Value maps

Value maps can be used to explore the raw data as they assign a shade of grey to every postcode area on the basis of the relative frequency of occurrence of a certain variant in the postcode area. Higher relative frequencies are assigned a darker shade of grey. Table 13.1 shows the relative frequencies for a subset of ten postcode areas for the top ten variants of the variable YOUNG TRENDY PERSON. The numbers in each row sum to 1, as variants not in the top ten are

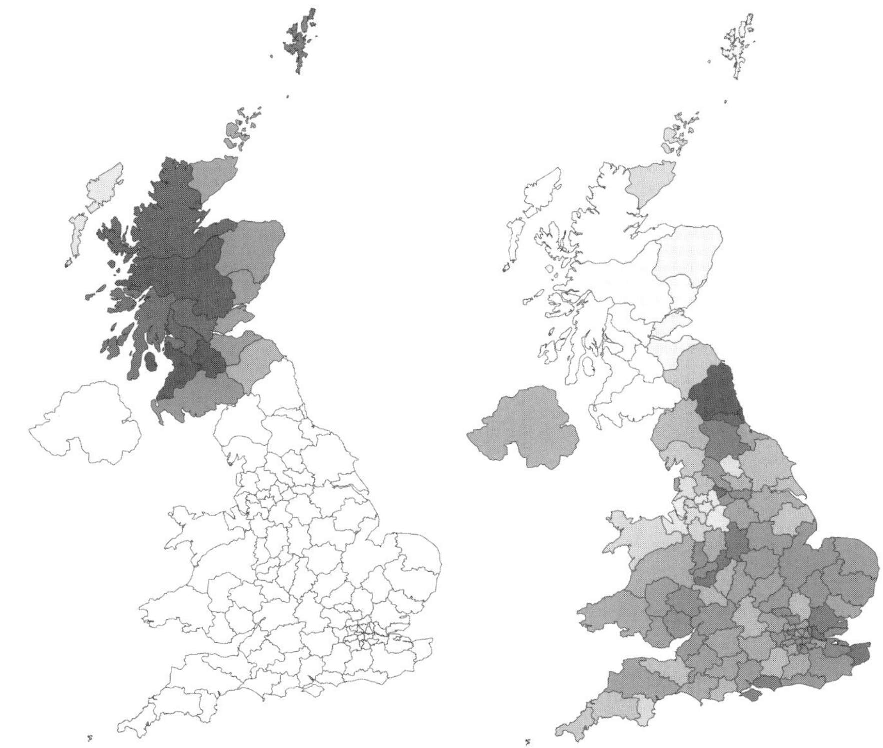

FIGURE 13.1 Value maps of two variants of the variable YOUNG TRENDY PERSON: *ned* (left) and *chav* (right). A darker shade indicates a greater relative frequency of use

excluded from the calculations. It is clear from the table that people in Aberdeen have a preference for the variant *ned* as the corresponding value is 0.624. In contrast, the other places listed (except for Bolton) are seen to prefer *chav*, as it has the highest value in each row.

Figure 13.1 shows the value maps on the basis of *ned* and *chav*, which clearly show a separation between Scotland and the rest of the United Kingdom.

Difference maps

It is also possible to determine how much two sites (i.e. postcode areas) differ in total. This can be done by averaging the differences between the relative frequencies for each variant. For example, the difference between Aberdeen and St. Albans for variant *chav* is 0.386 (0.633 – 0.247; see Table 13.1). After calculating the differences for all other variants (for all variables) and averaging these, the aggregate linguistic difference between the two sites is obtained. In similar fashion, the linguistic difference between every pair of sites (e.g. Aberdeen

TABLE 13.1 Sample of the dataset for the variable YOUNG TRENDY PERSON. Numbers represent the relative frequencies of each variant in the various postcode areas

	Chav	*Townie*	*Scally*	*Ned*	*Pikey*	*Tart*	*Kev*	*Slapper*	*Trendy*	*Teenager*
AB - Aberdeen	0.247	0.011	0.032	0.624	0.011	0.022	0.000	0.043	0.000	0.011
AL - St. Albans	0.633	0.122	0.041	0.020	0.041	0.020	0.020	0.020	0.000	0.082
B - Birmingham	0.502	0.107	0.077	0.015	0.021	0.009	0.223	0.009	0.024	0.015
BA – Bath	0.588	0.175	0.026	0.018	0.044	0.070	0.026	0.000	0.026	0.026
BB - Blackburn	0.476	0.342	0.134	0.012	0.000	0.012	0.000	0.024	0.000	0.000
BD - Bradford	0.614	0.168	0.119	0.010	0.030	0.030	0.000	0.010	0.000	0.020
BH - Bournemouth	0.509	0.208	0.009	0.009	0.170	0.009	0.019	0.019	0.028	0.019
BL - Bolton	0.309	0.136	0.444	0.012	0.025	0.025	0.000	0.012	0.037	0.000
BN - Brighton	0.609	0.135	0.032	0.026	0.122	0.039	0.000	0.026	0.000	0.013
BR - Bromley	0.607	0.036	0.018	0.000	0.321	0.000	0.000	0.000	0.000	0.018

TABLE 13.2 Aggregate linguistic differences between a sample of four postcode areas

	AB – Aberdeen	*AL – St. Albans*	*B – Birmingham*	*BA – Bath*
AB – Aberdeen	0	0.05994	0.05719	0.05856
AL – St. Albans	0.05994	0	0.03758	0.03363
B – Birmingham	0.05719	0.03758	0	0.03244
BA – Bath	0.05856	0.03363	0.03244	0

and St. Albans, Aberdeen and Birmingham, St. Albans and Birmingham) can be calculated. Table 13.2 shows the resulting aggregate linguistic differences for a sample of four postcode areas. Note that the table on the basis of all 121 postcode areas would consist of 121 rows and 121 columns.

A difference map visualizes these differences by drawing a (greyscale) line between pairs of sites. The darker the connecting lines, the more similar the postcode areas (i.e. the lower the aggregate linguistic difference). Figure 13.2 (left) visualizes the differences between neighbouring postcode areas only, while Figure 13.2 (right) visualizes the differences between all pairs of postcode

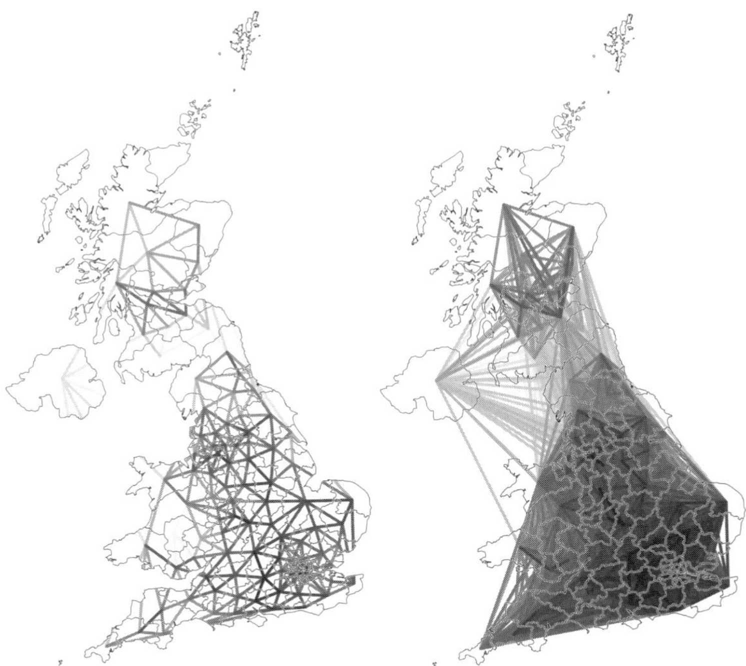

FIGURE 13.2. Difference maps. The left map connects neighbouring postcode areas, while the right map connects all pairs of postcode areas. Darker lines connect more similar sites

areas. We can clearly identify the separation of the Scottish sites from the more strongly linked sites in England.

Reference point maps

An alternative to the difference map is the reference point map, which visualizes the aggregate linguistic difference between a single reference site and all other sites. A shade of grey is assigned to each site based on its aggregate linguistic difference from the reference site. Sites which are more similar (i.e. which have a lower aggregate linguistic difference) to the reference site have a darker shade of grey than those which are less similar. This approach allows one to assess how different sites are when taking the perspective of the reference site. Figure 13.3 left and right shows the reference point maps from 'PH – Perth' and 'LS – Leeds' respectively, these sites being indicated by a star. The sites linguistically most similar to Perth are located close to Perth, and are generally located in Scotland. Similarly, the sites most similar to Leeds are generally located close to Leeds.

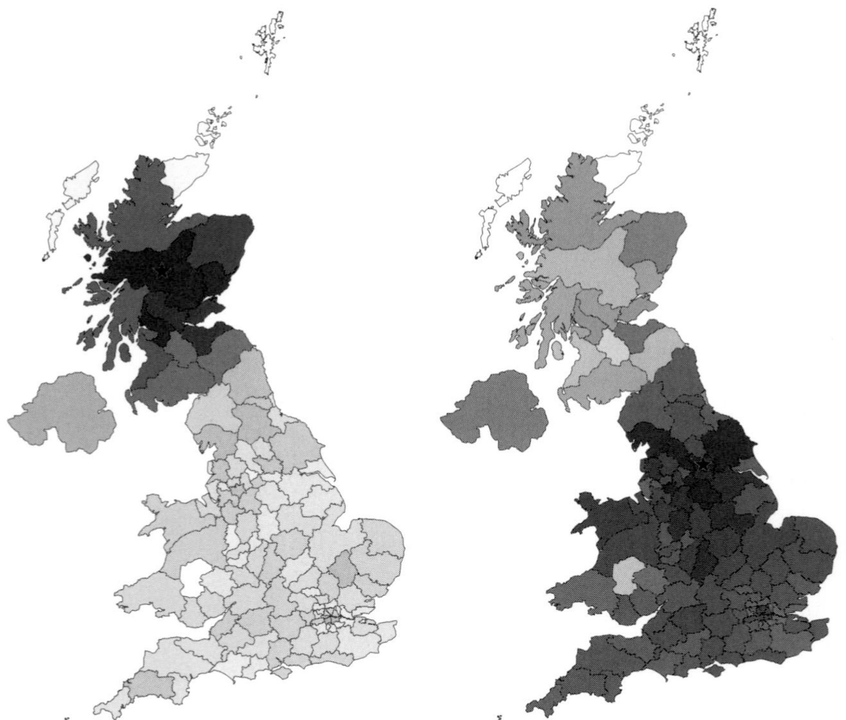

FIGURE 13.3 Reference point maps. The left map shows the visualization when using 'PH – Perth' as the reference point, while the right map has 'LS – Leeds' as the reference point

TABLE 13.3 Subset of MDS results on the basis of the complete aggregate linguistic difference table

	Dimension 1	*Dimension 2*	*Dimension 3*
AB - Aberdeen	0.616	0.592	0.725
AL - St. Albans	0.161	0.780	0.721
B - Birmingham	0.110	0.545	0.690
BA – Bath	0.149	0.765	0.722

MDS maps

While we are able to visualize the complete set of aggregate linguistic differences (see Table 13.2) using difference maps, these maps can be hard to interpret due to the overlapping of lines. A better approach to visualize the differences between all postcode areas is by applying multidimensional scaling (MDS).

Multidimensional scaling takes advantage of the fact that the aggregate differences in the original table are not independent. For example, in Table 13.2 we see that the difference between Bath and St. Albans is relatively small. Consequently, the difference between Bath and other sites will be similar to the difference between St. Albans and those sites. Indeed, we can observe that the difference between Aberdeen and both Bath and St. Albans is very similar. Based on these dependencies, multidimensional scaling converts the original difference table to a new, reduced table with the same number of rows, but only a few (e.g., three) columns or dimensions. When the values in these columns are similar, this indicates that the sites are similar. Table 13.3 shows the first three dimensions of the MDS result for the same four postcode areas as shown in Table 13.2. Clearly, Bath and St. Albans are highly similar.

The first dimension (i.e. column) of the reduced table is the most important, as it captures most of the variation of the original difference table. Adding more dimensions increases the fit between the original difference table and the new table, but three dimensions are generally enough to provide an excellent fit (i.e. more than 80 per cent of the variation of the original difference table is represented by the new table).

Having just three dimensions (i.e. columns) also enables easy visualization. Colour being available, when mapping the first column to red, the second column to the green, and the third column to blue, the values in the three columns can be combined to a single colour. For example, if one site has a 1 in the first and second columns and a zero in the third column, the colour of this site would be set to yellow (red mixed with green). In similar vein, every site can be assigned its own colour. The interpretation of the resulting map is then straightforward: sites which are similar in the relative frequency of their variants will have a similar colour, while the colour will be very different when sites have very different relative frequencies.

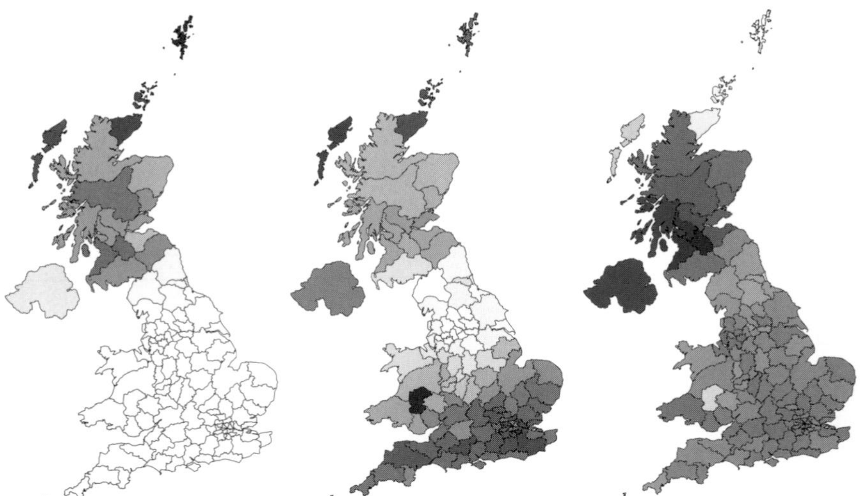

FIGURE 13.4 Visualization of the first (left), second (centre) and third (right) MDS dimensions from Table 13.3. Similar shades of grey indicate similar sites

Lacking colour here we do not show the combined map (which is included in the online tutorial), but three separate maps in Figure 13.4, one for each dimension. While the first dimension clearly contrasts Scotland from Wales and England (Northern Ireland lies in between), the second dimension separates the central part of the United Kingdom from the rest. The third MDS dimension clearly separates 'KW – Kirkwall', 'ZE – Lerwick', 'HS – Outer Hebrides', and 'LD – Llandrindod Wells' from the remaining sites. The first dimension explains 74 per cent of the variation of the original difference table. Adding the second dimension increases this number to 79 per cent, while also adding the third dimension increases it to 85 per cent. In conclusion, just three dimensions are able to capture the information present in the original difference table (of 121 columns) to a great extent, in turn enabling straightforward visualization.

Cluster maps and dendrograms

While the MDS approach is suggestive of where dialect borders might lie, it does not distinguish clear dialect groups. Using a clustering approach yields a pre-specified number of dialect areas. There are various clustering approaches, each using a different method to determine a group of related sites. We distinguish three approaches. Each iteratively merges the two nearest sites on the basis of their aggregate linguistic difference, but they differ in how they determine the difference between a group of merged sites and the other (groups of) sites:

1 'Complete Link' sets the difference between a group of newly merged sites and another group of sites, to the maximum of all differences between pairs of sites in one group and pairs of sites in the other group.
2 'Group Average', also known as unweighted pair-group method using arithmetic averages (UPGMA), sets the difference between a group of newly merged sites and another group of sites to the average of all differences between pairs of sites in one group and pairs of sites in the other group.
3 'Ward's Method' iteratively merges sites in a way that minimizes the variance in each group. This method tends to create clusters of similar size.

Figure 13.5 shows the clustering results of the three algorithms when clustering in three groups. It is clear that no algorithm yields the same result. Note that the shades of grey are arbitrary and do not convey a measure of similarity: they simply distinguish three different groups.

As mentioned earlier, all three clustering approaches are based on the iterative merger of sites. This iterative procedure is visualized using a dendrogram in which the farther to the right two groups are connected, the more different they are. For example, Figure 13.6 shows the dendrogram corresponding to Figure 13.5 (right).

It is clear that different clustering methods yield different clustering results, a drawback being that it is unclear which method is 'right'. Another disadvantage of clustering is that it is very unstable. If there are small errors in the data (and this is generally quite likely), clustering results might vary significantly when these errors are corrected. A further disadvantage of clustering is that

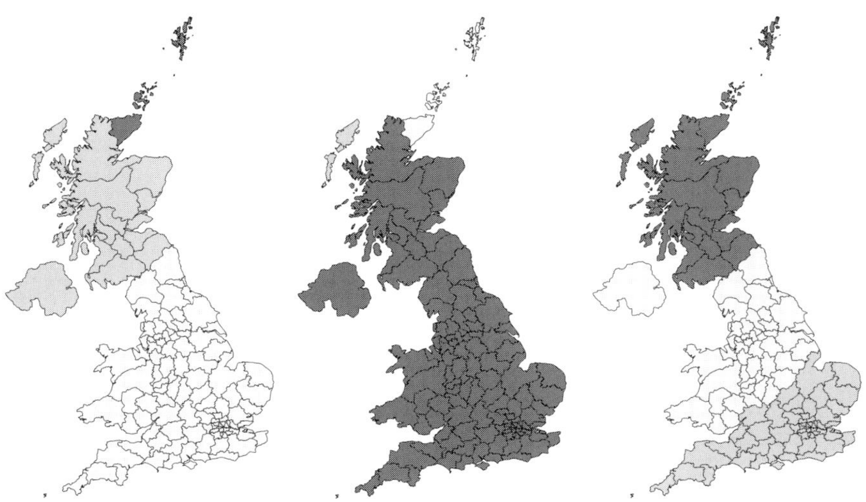

FIGURE 13.5 Clustering in three groups on the basis of 'Complete Link' (left), 'Group Average' (centre) and 'Ward's Method' (right)

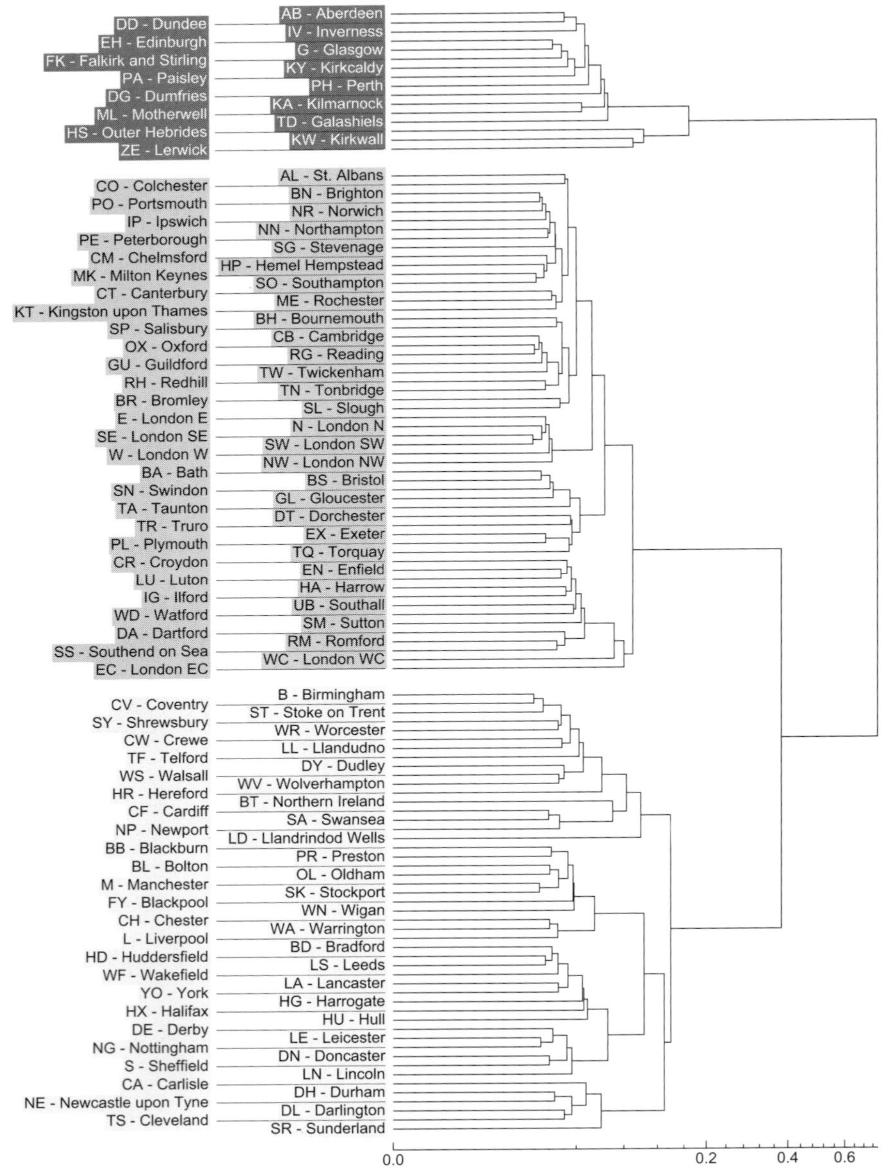

FIGURE 13.6 Dendrogram on the basis of 'Ward's Method'. The corresponding map distinguishing three groups is shown in Figure 13.5 (right)

the number of desired clusters needs to be specified in advance, and clustering will always yield that number of clusters, even though there may be fewer significant clusters in the data. For example, imagine a draughts board in the initial setting (black on one side and white on the other). It is clear that there are only two clusters of pieces (black and white), but not more. Any clustering algorithm, however, will yield more than two clusters when a higher number of required clusters is specified. Of course, determining what the real clusters are when the data are much more complex (as in our case) is not trivial. In the following section, we describe a robust approach aimed at alleviating most of the problems associated with standard clustering.

Probabilistic dendrograms

'Noisy' (or 'fuzzy') clustering is a robust clustering method. Instead of using the single difference table, this generates 100 new difference tables by adding noise. That is, small random values are added to or subtracted from some of the values in the original difference table. Consequently, each difference table differs slightly from the original difference table, and also from the other 99 tables. Each table is then used to obtain a separate clustering. Using the resulting 100 clustering results, we may count how frequently a group of sites is clustered together. A robust cluster will be characterized by sites which cluster together very frequently (e.g., in more than 90 cases), while less robust clusters will not group as frequently. To make the procedure even more robust, we can repeat the approach using different clustering approaches to obtain several hundred clustering results.

We may visualize the results of noisy clustering by using a dendrogram as before. In this case numbers are added which denote the percentage of times the sites (located to the left of the vertical bar) were grouped together. In contrast to the standard dendrogram, clusters detected in fewer than 50 percent of all cases are not shown, to allow a focus on more robust clusters. Figure 13.7 shows a part of the probabilistic dendrogram on the basis of the complete dataset (the complete dendrogram can be found in the online tutorial).

The results show the top-most cluster (representing most of the Scottish sites) to be very robust, as the contained sites group in all cases (i.e. the number next to this cluster equals 100). Similarly, 'KW – Kirkwall', 'ZE – Lerwick' and 'HS – Outer Hebrides' (the bottom-most cluster) also grouped together in 100 per cent of cases.

Finally, most of the remaining sites also group together every time. Within this large cluster, several small groups of sites clustered together. Examples include 'B – Birmingham', 'CV – Coventry' and 'ST – Stoke on Trent' (grouped in all cases), and also 'DH – Durham', 'NE – Newcastle upon Tyne', 'DL – Darlington', 'TS – Cleveland', 'CA – Carlisle' and 'HU – Hull' (grouped in 93 per cent of the cases).

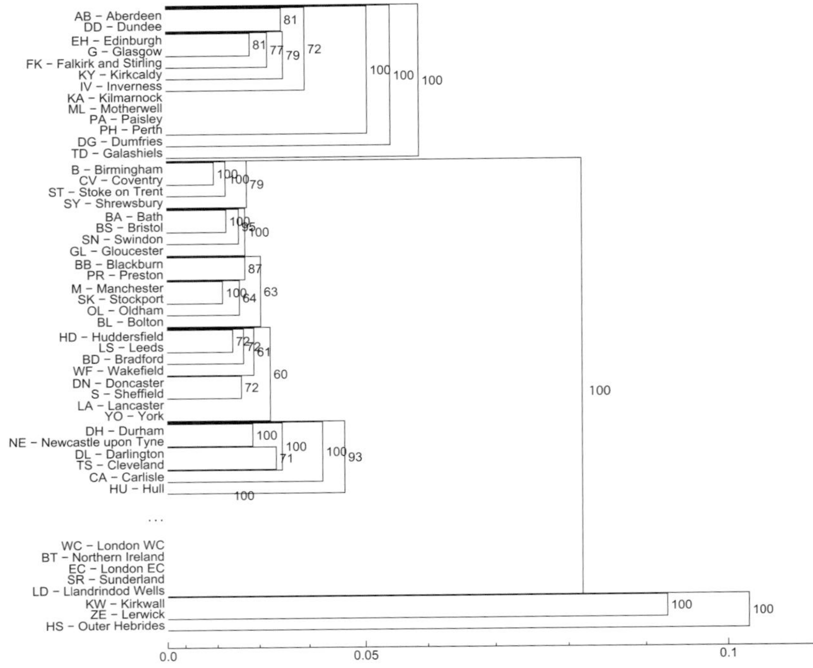

FIGURE 13.7 Part of a probabilistic dendrogram. Higher numbers indicate more robust clusters. Clusters obtained in fewer than 50% of all cases are not shown. The complete dendrogram can be found in the online tutorial.at http://www.gabmap.nl/voices

Conclusion

Most of the methods described above can be adequately used to obtain a comprehensive view of the regional patterns in linguistic variation. Standard clustering, however, is not wholly suitable for this purpose unless different algorithms are simultaneously compared and the number of predefined clusters is not overly large (to prevent reporting clusters which might not be robust at all). Noisy clustering is a considerable improvement over standard clustering, as it succeeds well in identifying robust clusters and is able to combine the results of many clustering algorithms simultaneously to increase objectivity. The other methods are also useful. A line map yields an objective view of the differences, but can be cluttered, thus limiting interpretability. Reference point maps also offer an objective view, but only from a predetermined reference site, so not offering the complete picture.

We might regard MDS maps as most suitable for the obtaining of a comprehensive view of the regional patterns in linguistic variation. MDS maps do not presuppose a distinct number of groups, but nevertheless detect distinct groups if there are any (see for example, Figure 13.4 (left)). More importantly, however, MDS maps allow one to observe the ever-present continuum of regional variation.

INDEX

Page references in *italic* represent Figures and Tables. These are also listed in full after the Contents.